Concerning Creativity

SUNY Series in Religious Studies
Harold Coward, Editor

CONCERNING CREATIVITY

A Comparison of
Chu Hsi, Whitehead, and Neville

John H. Berthrong

State University of New York Press

Production by Ruth Fisher
Marketing by Nancy Farrell

Published by
State University of New York Press, Albany

© 1998 State University of New York

For information, address the State University of New York Press,
State University Plaza, Albany, NY 12246

Library of Congress Cataloging-in-Publication Data

Berthrong, John H., 1946–
    Concerning creativity: a comparison of Chu Hsi, Whitehead, and
Neville / John H. Berthrong.
        p. cm. — (SUNY series in religious studies)
    Includes bibliographical references and index.
    ISBN 0-7914-3943-7 (alk. paper). — ISBN 0-7914-3944-5 (pbk. :
alk. paper)
    1. Whitehead, Alfred North, 1861–1947—Contributions in philosophy
of creativity.   2. Chu, Hsi, 1130–1200—Contributions in philosophy
of creativity.   3. Neville, Robert C.—Contributions in philosophy
of creativity.   4. Creative ability.   5. Philosophy, Comparative.
6. Process philosophy.   7. Neo-Confucianism.   I. Title.   II. Title:
Comparison of Chu Hsi, Whitehead, and Neville   III. Series.
B1674.W354B47   1998
100—dc21   98-22840
                                                              CIP

10   9   8   7   6   5   4   3   2   1

CONTENTS

PREFACE

The origin of this essay in comparative thought can be traced to a long conversation in Hong Kong in 1988 that I had with Robert Neville and Langdon Gilkey. We were all attending the First International Confucian–Christian Dialogue Conference, and our talk turned to the fact that Whitehead's process thought has always appeared as a viable, appealing, and even suggestive possibility for the emerging conversation between Confucianism and Western philosophy and theology.[1] However, both Neville and Gilkey were dissatisfied with the way in which Whitehead's thought was used in this intercultural exchange. Their dissatisfaction stemmed not only from the amply documented fact that neither Neville nor Gilkey are persuaded by the general philosophic claims of process though in theology, metaphysics, and ontology; the specific problem, as Gilkey and Neville understand it, is that the process movement focuses too much attention on the technical or exegetical details of *Process and Reality* and not enough on some of the equally useful and insightful material in *Adventures of Ideas* and *Modes of Thought* pertaining to history, technology, social thought, and culture.

My memory of this conversation with Gilkey and Neville lingered a long time in my philosophic subconscious. Beyond the suggestive point of the relative neglect of *Adventures of Ideas* and *Modes of Thought* for comparative and constructive intercultural exchange, there was something else that nagged me about the talk that evening. Both Gilkey and Neville know Whitehead as well as any other scholars. Their dissatisfaction with the use of Whitehead's thought in the arena of comparative philosophy spoke volumes about how process thought has been applied to the growing subfield in both philosophy and theology. I believe that Gilkey and Neville deserve an answer to their question and complaint about the underutilization of *Adventures of Ideas* and *Modes of Thought* for a process approach to comparative thought. The more I pondered their lament, the more it concealed a suggestion about how to move forward in comparative philosophy and theology without abandoning process thought as being somehow inadequate for the task of intercultural communication.

To narrow the experiment in comparative thought to a more manageable scope, I decided to focus the discussion on the concept of creativity—the notion of the creative advance into novelty—as a crucial technical issue for Whitehead and Chu Hsi.[2] As I will demonstrate, this makes sense if Chu Hsi (1130–1200), the greatest of the Southern Sung Neo-Confucians, is added to the mix as an example of an earlier East Asian form of process thought.[3] From the perspective of many Asian intellectuals, the emphasis on process or creativity is one of the most appealing features of Whitehead's thought in comparison with Confucianism, Taoism, and Buddhism. Whitehead's affirmation of the relational and processive nature of reality struck a responsive cord in many Chinese, Korean, and Japanese colleagues. Of course, this does not mean that all modern Confucians necessarily agree that Whitehead is the best or only Western resource for constructing a bridge to the East. But almost everyone concedes that process thought, because of its emphasis on creativity within a relational or organic worldview as a form of creative synthesis, was definitely a leading candidate for such philosophic reconstruction. On the process side of the ledger, creativity is so central to the whole enterprise that it is a logical candidate for such an experiment in comparative philosophic reconstruction. Further, Neville had written a challenge to process philosophy in 1980 that focused on the topic of creativity. Gilkey's and Neville's dual challenge provoked a response.

With this dialogue on comparative thought in mind, the study began as an analysis of the notion of creativity in Whitehead, Chu Hsi, and Neville, but rapidly evolved into a cross-cultural examination of Western process thought and the Neo-Confucian Way as expressed by Chu Hsi and his followers. It combines not only material from different cultures and times but also elements of hermeneutic, historical, philosophic, and theological analysis and critique. This is necessary because I believe that comparative thought demands at least these academic disciplines and probably other skills as well. Any comparativist must be an intellectual and a social historian, a literary critic, a philosopher, and even a theologian when dealing with the religious dimensions of various worldviews. Whatever else they may be, the great philosophic texts of Chu Hsi and Whitehead are not simple documents.

The specific presenting problem of the essay, as the psychologists say, is the philosophic question of the nature and origin of Whitehead's exposition of creativity and its critique by Robert Neville. My answer to Neville's question is as multivalent as are the questions he raises as he tries to interpret what creativity means in process though and other major texts—including the East Asian Neo-Confucian synthesis of Chu Hsi. The inclusion of Chu Hsi and *li-hsüeh*/school of principle ensures that the argument moves beyond the confines of a purely Western approach to the question of creativity within Whitehead's process school. My attempt to answer Neville's questions, first designed to press process philosophers to give a better account of creativity within Whitehead's mature thought, exfoliated and became the occasion to experiment with using Chinese Neo-Confucian material to render one plausible response to Neville's question. By response I do not mean an attempt to solve the question of creativity as a philosophic problem or to provide a unique or perfect answer to Neville's complaint. However, the Chinese materials do allow for a more textured rejoinder to what is a classic Western metaphysical theme than is sometimes the case. It struck me forcefully that Chu Hsi, working out of a completely different intellectual milieu, had something to contribute to the debate.

To more comprehensibly introduce Chu Hsi in terms of his own cultural milieu, I have inserted a short introduction in chapter 4 outlining the development of Chu's Sung dynasty Neo-Confucian synthesis, after chapter 3 and prior to my major discussion of Chu in chapter 5. I have been assured that not too many Western readers will be overly familiar with Chu Hsi, his massive contribution to the growth of the movement called Neo-Confucianism, or the general outlines of the development of the Confucian Tao as an intellectual movement. In another study, I have summarized the history of Confucianism.[4] Suffice it to say that there has been a revolution in the study of the diverse East Asian Confucian traditions in China, Korea, and Japan over the last three decades. Ideally it would help to present this information earlier, but that would have distorted the flow of the general argument. For those who know something about the history of classical Confucianism and its later Neo-Confucian phase, such a simple introduction is superfluous. However, those who feel at sea in twelfth-century Sung China may want to read this introductory section before tackling the first three chapters. The introduction to Neo-Confucianism provides a background and foreground to the question of creativity.

Nor is the study merely a narrative of one partial response to Neville's critique of Whitehead's theory of creativity, although I anticipate that this is one outcome of the project. Nonetheless, such cross cultural narrative intellectual history is necessary to promote communication between and among traditions that have grown to maturity in mutual isolation and incomprehension. Chinese and Western thought are paradigmatic examples of such mutual isolation between philosophic cultures that have few linguistic or cultural links. This intellectual segregation was broken decisively only in the nineteenth century.[5] Comparative philosophy and theology must begin with a translation between philosophic positions and histories; we must become clear about whether we are talking about similar things if we are to talk and clear about what in the world such as assertion of similarity means across great cultural divides. As I will show throughout the study, Neville truly deserves an answer to his serious question about the nature of creativity from a

comparative perspective. It is important to note that Neville himself introduces Chinese philosophy into his work so that Chu Hsi is not an entirely
unanticipated guest in the conversation. Moreover, it is well known that Whitehead, although he did not know a great deal about Asian thought, was still
intrigued by what he understood to be similarities between his philosophy
and certain forms of South and East Asian thought. To give my response, I
offer a constructive philosophic and theological position of my own in the
later chapters of the study. The study hence not only describes the various
ways process thinkers might answer Neville, but also adduces one hybrid
position within process thought as an emerging global philosophic movement, a Sino-Anglo-American effort based upon both Chinese and Western
material.

The style and structure of the study has antecedents in the work of Chu
Hsi and Whitehead. Both the great Southern Sung Neo-Confucian and the
Anglo-American Whitehead were fond of attacking any philosophic problem
from different angles and of returning to a problem again and again to tease
out as many permutations as possible from the text or philosophic issue at
hand. Both were also concerned with the philosophic history of their own
cultures. For instance, it is reported that Chu was still revising his seminal
commentary on the *Great Learning* just a few days before his death. Likewise, Whitehead notes his proclivity in *Process and Reality* of returning to
the same question repeatedly and that all such explorations ultimately are
tentative because we can never reach a final or an ultimate interpretation of
reality. Both Chu and Whitehead are faithful to their processive and pluralistic visions of reality in terms of their own expository forms of discourse.
There can be, on process principles, no final, perfect resting place for critical
thought. The road is always endless, but the zest for the quest is its own
reward.

The method of comparative philosophy and theology is an example of
what Wayne Booth (1988) calls coduction. Coduction is neither deductive nor
inductive, although it must include elements of both deductive and inductive
reasoning and method. Coduction is resolutely dialogical because it presents
its reasons for public criticism and comment. For instance, comparative method
must be historical because it cannot assume the easy familiarity with material
that comes from working within one tradition. Nor can it ignore the normative elements of philosophic and theological discourse. As Booth defines it,

> Coduction will be what we do whenever we say to the world (or prepare
> ourselves to say): "Of the works of this general kind that I have experienced,
> *comparing my experience with other more or less qualified observers*, this
> seems to me among the better (or weaker) ones, or the best (or worst). Here

are my reasons." Every such statement implicitly calls for continuing conversation: "How does my coduction compare with yours?" (1988, 72–73)

I am attempting an intercultural coduction as a more adequate interpretation of Whitehead's notion of creativity, as well as the articulation of what
a responsible Whiteheadian comparative philosophy should be. I also hope to
be able to answer Neville's challenge about the coherence of a process vision
of creativity. As Booth notes, I try to present my reasons for producing a
hybrid, intercultural reading of the question of creativity as a mode of comparative process thought. Such an account also honors the Chinese philosophic penchant for correlative thinking based on metaphors, exemplars, and
prototypes.

The study is arranged in two parts, with seven chapters. The first three
chapters explain why there is a problem with the notion of creativity in
Whitehead, Chu Hsi, and Neville and why this is an important issue for
comparative process thought. Chapter 1 introduces the problem of creativity
as it is found in Whitehead and Chu Hsi. I explain why such a complicated
comparative linkage of two very different philosophic systems from the modern
West and Sung China is possible in terms of an intercultural approach to
comparative philosophy and theology. For Whitehead, the main interpretive
issues revolve around the relationships of God, the world, and creativity. For
Chu Hsi, the main issue is the relationship of principle and matter–energy.
Chapter 2 reviews briefly the development of Whitehead's notion of divine
things. I agree with the consensus of Whiteheadian scholarship, that while
there is growth in Whitehead's technical treatment of the issue, there also is
a continuity of questions and vision that links all of his major works. I place
more emphasis on *Adventures of Ideas* and *Modes of Thought* than is normal
for a systematic exposition of Whitehead because I believe that both of these
books help in framing a comparative philosophy because of their attention to
the philosophy of culture and history. Chapter 3 then introduces the technical
details of Neville's critique of the notion of creativity in Whitehead in much
greater length. It outlines Neville's distinctive contribution to the ontological
quest as part of his understanding of creativity as creation *ex nihilo*. After
chapter 3 I have inserted a short introduction in chapter 4 to the history of
Confucian and Neo-Confucian thought to better explain Chu Hsi's special
contribution to the discussion. This material is designed for those who are not
familiar with the development of East Asian thought and who seek to place
Chu in his Sung intellectual milieu.

The flow of the main comparative argument begins with chapter 5, where
the focus changes from Whitehead to Chu Hsi and his understanding of
organic creativity in terms of the larger Southern Sung Neo-Confucian synthesis

of principle and matter–energy. I explain enough about Chu Hsi and his world for the discussion to be intelligible to a Western philosophic audience. From a process point of view, it is particularly intriguing that Chu Hsi has a worldview that does not depend on God for creativity. Chapter 6 next attempts a response to Neville and offers a constructive comparative philosophy indebted to both Chu Hsi and Whitehead. It is at this point that the related concepts of form, dynamics, and unification are explicated in terms of the intercultural presentation of the issue of creativity. It is here that I also make more extensive use of the method of comparative archic analysis as developed by Walter Watson and David Dilworth as yet another way to engage in intercultural philosophic analysis.[6] In conclusion, chapter 7 rehearses a trinitarian, process, and comparative theological and philosophic answer to Neville's original complaint about Whitehead's philosophic incoherence. This is done by means of introducing the notion of a creative synthesis of Chu's comprehensive principle and Whitehead's insight into the role of creativity in a world characterized by process. I have provided an appendix on the structure of archic analysis in order to provide a more detailed exposition of this form of comparative taxonomy.

At this point it will be up to the readers to say if, in Booth's words, the essay provokes continuing conversation by means of the coductive process. Whether or not it does, it is still important that we begin the effort to create effective ways to sustain comparative philosophy and theology in the one world we all now share. To modify a famous Chinese proverb, the conversation of cultures begins with a single concept.

NOTES

1. For an account of this first meeting and a selection of papers presented, see Peter K. H. Lee, *Confucian-Christian Encounters in Historical and Contemporary Perspective* (Lewiston, N.Y.: The Edwin Mellen Press, 1991).

2. In his explanation of the Category of the Ultimate, Whitehead defines creativity as: " 'Creativity' is the principle of *novelty*. An actual occasion is a novel entity diverse from any entity in the 'many' that it unifies. Thus 'creativity' introduces novelty into the content of the many, which are the universe disjunctively. The 'creative advance' is the application of this ultimate principle of creativity to each novel situation which it originates" (*PR*, 21).

A number of scholars, most prominently with Joseph Needham in the 1950s, have argued that both Whitehead and Chu Hsi share a family resemblance in that their philosophies can be characterized as being organic, processive, and relational in nature. To argue that there is strict identity of any kind would be foolish, nonetheless there is enough similarity to warrant a comparative analysis.

3. Recently Nicholas Rescher (1996) has argued that while Whitehead is clearly the best recognized Western process thinker, Whitehead is not alone in defining the nature of process metaphysics. I am suggesting that, following Rescher's list of basic process categories, Chu Hsi should be added to the growing list of global process philosophers.

4. See John H. Berthrong, *Transformations of the Confucian Way* (Boulder, CO: Westview Press, 1998) for a general introduction to the history of Confucianism in East Asia from its inception to its modern revival. This work contains a much larger bibliography on China, Korea, and Japan for anyone interested in the further study of Confucianism.

5. Of course, we remember the remarkable work that was done by the first, second, and third generations of learned Jesuit missionaries in China during the Ming and early Ch'ing periods. Also, it is well to remember that no major Western philosopher has written more knowledgeably than Leibniz on Chinese thought until Graham and Fingarette. Unfortunately, this early beginning floundered.

6. I have provided an appendix that explains the nature of archic analysis as proposed by Watson and Dilworth. This appendix summarizes archic analysis for those readers who have not encountered this form of comparative philosophic analysis. The major application of archic analysis is in chapter 6.

ACKNOWLEDGMENTS

It is always a pleasure to acknowledge those who have either wittingly or unwittingly contributed to the writing of a book. In this case I want to thank the two teachers who instructed me in the minor mysteries of Whitehead lore, the late Professor Bernard Loomer and Professor W. Widick Schroeder. It goes without saying that neither of these men is in any way responsible for my mangling of Whitehead's ideas.

I also need to thank my Confucian colleagues for the work they have done over the last three decades in revisioning one of the grand intellectual, ethical, and social ways of humankind. In particular, I want to acknowledge Professor Tu Weiming, Professor Cheng Chung-ying, Professor Liu Shu-hsien, and Professor Julia Ching. I also have drawn great inspiration from the work of Professor Wm. Theodore de Bary, as has a whole generation of students of Confucian studies.

In my local world, of course, I must thank my friend Dean Robert C. Neville for his support and cheerful willingness to endure what our graduate students have come to call Berthrong's "Neville Refuted." We have even had the pleasure of hosting seminars with this title and still remain the best of friends. If there were ever a person who embodies the profound sense of scholarly fellowship, it is Robert Neville. Other Boston University colleagues such as Professor Joseph Fewsmith, Dr. Ron Staley, Professor Peter Berger, Professor Harry Oliver, Professor John Clayton, Professor David Eckel, and Professor Wesley Wildman have encouraged the effort. In the wider world of Boston, I want to thank colleagues Professor Francis Clooney, S.J., Professor Gordon Kaufman, Professor Peter Bol, and Ms. Virginia Straus.

There also is a group of scholars dedicated to the proposition that comparative philosophy and theology does make sense. Here I thank Professor Roger Ames, Professor David Hall, Professor Harold Coward, who is also the general editor of the series in which this essay appears, and Professor Mary Evelyn Tucker.

My editors at the State University of New York Press have, as always, been unflagging in their encouragement and correction. I also want to thank the three anonymous readers for the Press who gave me such good advice about how to make a complex topic more manageable.

Last, but certainly not least, I need to thank Evelyn and Sean, along with our three poodles, Fafner, Puccini, and Tristan (especially on their walks in the woods), all of whom have had to listen to more about cosmology, Confucianism, ontology, process, and comparative thought than any family should have to endure.

ABBREVIATIONS USED IN THE TEXT

*Alfred North Whitehead

In this study references to Alfred North Whitehead's major works will follow the standardized abbreviations as outlined in *Process Studies*. I will cite *PR* according to the corrected edition of 1978.

AI	*Adventures of Ideas* (1933)
FR	*Function of Reason* (1929)
MT	*Modes of Thought* (1938)
PR	*Process and Reality* (1978)
RM	*Religion in the Making* (1996)
S	*Symbolism, Its Meaning and Effect* (1927)
SMW	*Science in the Modern World* (1925)

*Robert Cummings Neville

BMG	*Behind the Masks of God: An Essay Toward Comparative Theology* (1991a)
CG	*Creativity and God: A Challenge to Process Theology* (1980)
ETF	*Eternity and Time's Flow* (1993)
HAM	*The Highroad Around Modernism* (1992)
TD	*The Tao and the Daimon* (1982)
TP	*A Theology Primer* (1991b)
NC	*Normative Cultures* (1995)

*Ch'en Ch'un (1159–1223)

PHTI	*The Pei-hsi Tzu-i* (1986)

1

The Problem of Creativity, God and the World

INTRODUCTION

Creativity, God, and the world—Whitehead presents and challenges us with scattered remarks about his unorthodox yet haunting trinity throughout *Process and Reality*. As the most important deposition of Whitehead's understanding of the relationship of three foundational notions of his thought, Part V of *Process and Reality* contains some of the most beautiful, evocative, and ultimately ambiguous passages Whitehead ever wrote. His formulation of the relationship of God as the ultimate divine reality, creativity[1] qua cosmic generativity, and the world has defined a prime challenge to the coherence of first principles within his mature system. Likewise, its metaphorical and poetic prose account issued an invitation to and demanded a response from orthodox and unorthodox process philosophers and theologians to make sense of his doctrine of God–creativity–world relations.

So crucial was Whitehead's focus on the processive nature of the cosmological reality defined by the complex relationships of God, world, and creativity that the name "process thought," beginning with Bernard Loomer, has been affixed to a whole school of thought deriving its inspiration from Whitehead's initial exposition. Whitehead characterized his system as a form of organicism, but to most later scholars process thought seems more apt because it highlights the most original contribution of Whitehead's work. As philosophers came to ponder the place of process thought in the development of modern Euro-American philosophy, they also began to notice similarities with philosophies from other cultural areas, most specifically East Asia. While there is something incurably Western, even English, about Whitehead, there are the salient themes of process, creativity, the curiously world-dependent nature of the divine reality, and whole-part relations that link his thought to the Buddhist, Taoist, and Confucian traditions of East Asia, a fact that Whitehead himself noted in passing (*PR*, 7)

This essay embraces Whitehead's insight concerning the importance of "process" and "creativity" as cross-cultural philosophic and theological comparative conceptual metaphors.[2] Further, it defends the thesis that, as a specific instance of such comparison, East Asian Neo-Confucianism may be examined with profit to shed light on some internally perplexing aspects of Whitehead's thought. The contrast of God, world, and creativity invites the cross-cultural comparison as different expressions of what can be increasingly considered a global tradition in the making, namely modern process thought.[3]

Yet, as we shall see, it is just at the apex of Whitehead's supreme rhetorical definition of the interconnections of creativity, God, and the world in Part V of *PR* that many critics of process thought find the wedge they need to demonstrate the lack of rigor tempering the whole Whiteheadian edifice in terms of the coherence of first principles. In short, many critics of process thought believe that Whitehead's wonderful Edwardian prose about God and creativity obscures profound problems of systemic coherence. The crux of the problem has to do with the role creativity is supposed to play in Whitehead's process thought, a role that is essential in linking the divine reality or God in theistic terms with the realistic and pluralistic world of finite creatures by means of a primordial, ceaseless, and creative advance into novelty. What is not always recognized in this heady mix, but which will be crucial for our analysis, is the irreducible comparative aspect of the contrast of God–world relations mediated and provoked by the incessant creativity of the cosmic process. Fundamental to any Whiteheadian analysis of reality, I will argue, is the recognition of comparison, contrast, and connection as a crucial aspect of system building.

As Whitehead reminds us, the supreme point of contrast and comparison for any Western religious thinker is the question of God's nature.

> To-day there is but one religious dogma in debate: What do you mean by "God"? And in this respect, to-day is like all its yesterdays. This is the fundamental religious dogma, and all other dogmas are subsidiary to it. (*RM*, 67–68)

While this statement holds true for all of the great West Asian theistic traditions, it requires a drastic and analogical translation to encompass the nontheistic traditions of South and East Asia that also lay claim to being part of a larger global process tradition. One point that I seek to make in the Neo-Confucian sections of the study is that Whitehead's formulation of the problem of creativity qua divine process also finds analogies in Chu Hsi's (1130–1200) Sung Neo-Confucian philosophic essays, letters, commentaries, and dialogues. The cultural terms of reference for Chu are dramatically different, yet some of the philosophic points are similar enough to warrant comparison and in fact signal persistent issues for any process thinker trying to work in a cross-culturally comparative manner.

The fundamental problem for disclosing creativity for Chu Hsi revolved around defining the proper role for *hsin*, the Neo-Confucian term for what is often translated as the mind–heart. The mind–heart was problematic because it was defined as the seat of consciousness, the emotions, potentially guided by normative principles, and above all else, creatively responsive to the myriad influences of the cosmos. In trying to define the creativity of the mind–heart, Chu inherited a discussion of the mind–heart common to the late T'ang and Sung matrix of Confucian discourse (Bol 1992; Metzger 1977). Whereas the later historians of Neo-Confucianism traditionally labeled Chu's school as *li-hsüeh* or the teaching of principle because Chu was so concerned about the role of normative principle in *hsin*, no Neo-Confucian worried more than Chu about the definition, nature, cultivation, and role of the mind–heart.[4] His reasons for this, as were Whitehead's, were both internal to the history of the development of Neo-Confucian discourse and particular to Chu's own engagement with the tradition. In terms of the focus of this essay, Chu needed to show how the mind–heart was able to provide the fulcrum of creativity for human beings within a cosmos itself characterized by ceaseless productivity (*sheng sheng pu-hsi*). Chu thus explained how the sages were able to harness the creative process of the cosmos while remaining finite beings. In Neo-Confucian terms, what is the relationship of the mind–heart of the Tao (*tao-hsin*) as an expression of the way the world ought to be and the human mind–heart (*jen-hsin*) as the all too mundane manifestation of human ignorance, finitude, and error?

The problem of balancing God, creativity, and the world within the Neo-Confucian wing of the process tradition is more cosmological than theological from the perspective of Western speculative discourse. Yet the Sung problem of the nature of creativity, as expressed in the Chu Hsi's Sung school of principle, is conceived in radically different intellectual and historic forms and is addressed by an analytic method and a commentary so different from the Western tradition that even commonplace Western philosophic terms such as *metaphysics, ontology*, and *cosmology* conceal and confuse as much as they reveal about Neo-Confucian ultimate concerns.

So much of the conversation about the process tradition has been carried on within the purview of the Western philosophic tradition that the intrusion of Neo-Confucian discourse seems strange, decentering, even exotic. However, at one point in *Religion in the Making*, Whitehead likened the dogmas of the church to the ark upon which it rides through tides of history (*RM*, 145–146). His counsel was that even the best boat needs to open its windows from time to time to let in some fresh air. It strikes me as being useful to open these windows as widely as possible when dealing with such complex and difficult matters as fundamental ontology and cosmological questions, especially when there is something to be gained from the exercise.

What seems so inspiring and sensible to modern relational sensibilities in Whitehead's mature philosophy and natural theology on first reflection fades into the mists of poetic incoherence as one tries to make the central pieces like God, creativity, and the world fit together. Frustration overcomes enjoyment and inspiration. The Whiteheadian vision is so appealing in terms of its cosmology, and yet somehow religiously remains incomplete because of the separation of creativity from the primordial and consequent natures of God as well as the fundamental constitution of the world. For those who have found in Whitehead a stimulus for theological reflection, the abrupt, staccato cadences of Part V of *Process and Reality* leave the reader at once stimulated, tantalized, and perplexed. This is especially true for those who have been persuaded about the fundamental philosophic and theological genius of Whitehead's ontological principle: to ask for the reason for anything is to ask about the decisions, the choices of some actual entity. For those who believe that Whitehead is correct in refusing actual, real agency to anything less than the object–events[5] or actual entities of the cosmos, it seems strange or even incoherent to have creativity somehow outside, beyond, or disconnected from the supreme actual entity, God.

There is an analogous moment in Chu Hsi's tradition too. Most Neo-Confucians gravitated to Chu's vision of reality because it seems both open and complete at the same time. Chu's creative appropriation of the work of the great Northern Sung masters, and especially his reformulation of Ch'eng I's (1033–1107) seminal definition of principle in the Neo-Confucian synthesis, struck the Sung, Yüan, Ming, and Ch'ing Confucians as inspired discourse. Generations of Chu Hsi scholars in China, Korea, and then Japan were serene in the confidence that Master Chu must have answered their questions somewhere in his voluminous writings.[6] And where an obvious answer was not forthcoming, there was a deep conviction that the answer could be generated by tinkering a bit with the machinery, so that a few minor modifications would suffice to overcome the momentary flash of doubt.

The full nature of the problem became clear when Chu Hsi and his students continued to probe the various shades of meaning that Chu applied to principle, matter–energy, and the mind–heart. While Chu himself believed that he learned the most from Ch'eng I's theory of principle, he also relied heavily on Chang Tsai's reflections on *ch'i*/matter–energy and the mind–heart. In fact, it was Chang's definition of the mind–heart as being a combination of principle and matter–energy that allowed Chu to realize fully how crucial and illuminating Ch'eng's theory of principle really was. Of course, all of Chu's discourse was aimed at helping the student cultivate the mind–heart in order to recognize the principles embedded in matter–energy. Only once this kind of self-cultivation was achieved would the student be able to fully realize the Confucian ethical program.

A typical definition of Chu Hsi's program in search of the sage's mind–heart is found in the famous short essay "The Treatise on the Completion of Mind–Heart [*Chin-hsin shuo*]."

'The completion of mind–heart is knowing nature. Knowing nature is knowing heaven.' We say that a person can complete his mind–heart when he knows his nature and this capacity to know his nature is to know heaven. Now, heaven is the spontaneity of principle and the source from which humanity is born. Nature is the essence of principle which man receives to become human. The mind–heart is the way a person controls himself and fully sets forth this principle. 'Heaven is great and boundless,' and nature receives [this boundlessness] completely. Therefore the essence of the fundamental mind–heart itself is expansive and without limitation. Only when it is fettered by the selfishness of concrete things, hemmed in by seeing and hearing pettiness, does it becomes concealed and incomplete. Man can in each event and in each thing exhaustively examine these principles until one day he will penetratingly comprehend them all without anything being left out: then he can complete the broad essence of the fundamental mind–heart. The reason for a person's nature being what it is and the reason for heaven being heaven is not beyond this and is connected to its unity. (Berthrong 1979, 107)[7]

The essay on the mind–heart formulates the agenda for the Neo-Confucian discourse on the nature of human creativity and its connection to the cosmos in relation to the cosmology of the *li-ch'i* connection.

On the other hand, there was a chorus of persistent critics of Chu Hsi's philosophy of mind–heart and principle from the beginning of Chu's career in the Southern Sung.[8] These philosophers comprise an equally famous place within the tradition, beginning with such luminaries as Hu Hung (1106–1162), Lu Hsiang-shan (1139–1193), Wang Yang-ming (1472–1529), Tai Chen (1723–1777), and ending with modern critics such as Mou Tsung-san and Tu Wei-ming, representatives of the modern New Confucian movement. The critics' collective doubts about Chu's synthesis were and are severe and persistent; they sensed that there was something profoundly wrong embedded in the very logic of Chu's analysis of the mind–heart and the broader cosmology of *li-hsüeh* discourse. These critics have pointed out that Chu's famous theory of principle appears to drive a wedge between the reality of creative life and the cultivation of the mind–heart, the ethical and social essence of the Confucian Way. For instance, Mou Tsung-san argues that however brilliant Chu was, there is deep incoherence in his rationalistic, systemic overdependence on principle qua intellectual norm that simply but elegantly misses the mark of the main philosophic thrust of the classical Chou tradition of Confucius and Mencius, as well as the Sung-Ming Confucian revival of Confucianism.

I will seek to demonstrate why it is important to open these Neo-Confucian windows on the global process tradition as part of an expanding cross-cultural conversation. While I do not hold that every Western philosophic problem profits from comparison to East Asian material, there are some cases when this is true. For instance, if recourse to Chu Hsi will help in responding to Neville's sharp criticism of the process view of creativity and God, then it would be foolish not to make use of this resource. Furthermore, I believe that process thought offers an interesting way to carry out comparative philosophy and natural theology given its characteristically broad intellectual concerns. Process thought has proved to be one of the least parochial of modern Western philosophic and theological schools.[9] Its common themes— the classical questions of metaphysics, cosmology, causation, consciousness, ethical conduct, and social order—are universal enough that, along with some forms of continental philosophy, East Asians have made use of it to find links to their own traditions. For instance, Cheng Chung-ying, more a modern Chinese partisan of Chu's thought than either Mou or Tu, makes use of Whitehead to illustrate many features of Chinese philosophic discourse, as well as to suggest where such comparison is useful for the Western tradition (1991). I ask, why should international computer designers and automobile manufacturers have all the fun framing the cross-cultural nature of the new world order?

Whitehead was obviously struggling with the problem of fundamental cosmological coherence in Part V of *Process and Reality* as he sought to weave together a religious and philosophic vision faithful to his constructive endeavor to frame a coherent, logical, applicable, and adequate interpretation of human experience, including the massive deposition of the religious history of humankind. The problem is that the three themes of creativity, God, and the world remained an incomplete puzzle; they did not fit together nearly as well as so many other parts of the vision. But we must remember that there is nothing surprising about the fact that Whitehead leaves us with the themes of creativity, God, and the world at the conclusion of *PR*. As Lewis Ford has shown in such convincing detail, this was how the unfinished, evolving logic of his own speculation unfolded in the Gifford lectures.[10] Whitehead often changed his mind or drastically revised a previous position. The real problem is that the final triad does not fit together in a way that satisfies Whitehead's own admonition that "Speculative Philosophy is the endeavour to frame a coherent, logical, necessary system of general ideas in terms of which every element of our experience can be interpreted" (*PR*, 3). As with his own description of colors in a spring forest, we are haunted by the greenness of it all, even if we cannot give perfect reasons why this should be the case.

We need to remember that one of the primary appeals of Whitehead's philosophic theology is that it offers a unified view of a process cosmos. It claims to be an expansive, inclusive, and reasonably coherent worldview. It is a vision that has a place for the world of modern human beings in terms of their religious aspirations, their scientific quest, and their ethical and social endeavors to build humane civilizations. The vision's allure is the creative unity offered by a process understanding of meaning that is multidimensional and responsive to all of the diverse areas of human experience.[11] When the purported unity of the system begins to fray at the edges, the whole appeal wears thin from the rational point of view. Or even worse, one begins to wonder if the whole wonderful vision will really sustain a major theological and philosophic movement committed to coherence, applicability, and adequacy in the late twentieth century. At the other end of the Eurasian world, such a promised range of encompassing vision was also one of the prime appeals of Chu Hsi's mature thought. Chu's synthesis allowed for the interpretation not only of the texts of the Confucian tradition but also of all of the other object–events of the world. It provided a relational, processive, and rational schema and curriculum for the task of becoming a Neo-Confucian worthy—or at least pass the civil service examinations in order to enter the literati class.

Why bother to expend so much effort on a comparison between Chu Hsi and Whitehead? Would it not be better to focus more attention on the internal resolution of the problems of coherence in Whitehead's thought? Is there anything to be gained by such a cross-cultural comparison beyond the fact that it can be done? Are the similarities anything more than a trivial case of seeming congruence between such radically different worldviews? Do the results warrant the effort? What is really at stake in a cross-cultural philosophic comparison anyway?

I will argue that while it is true that the differences between Chu and Whitehead are profound, there is something in the spirit of the process (or organic, as Whitehead liked to call it) movement that draws attention to the comparative aspect of human life. Pragmatically, the intellectual world of any modern scholar in Boston, London, Moscow, Delhi, Mexico City, Beijing, Tokyo, Tunis, or Nairobi simply has become conceptually vaster than either the world of the Enlightenment or even the post–modern West have been willing to admit. We live in a time when more people are sensing that we do live in something like a global city of ideas, cultures, artistic sensibilities, scientific communication, and enabling and disabling technologies; we are connected by the bureaucracies and technologies of commerce, travel, communication, intermarriage, immigration and, increasingly, the serious interchange of ideas. There is a self-consciousness about the dynamics of this interaction that has gained momentum and self-expression since the end of World War II.

In some cases we are no longer so sure about the rationality of the process enterprise—or any other philosophic vision. The shock of the Holocaust and other human perversities from Cambodia to Bosnia have shattered the humane glow of Whitehead's more gentle Victorian–Edwardian appeal to the function of reason. We may well be living in a world aglow with twenty-first-century decadence, a new *fin de siècle* that strives for holistic visions and yet lives out of the still individualistic mind-set of the late modern Cartesian experiment. Cyberpunk meets the Japanese corporation, giving rise to a strange kind of quasi-Zen noplace without reason, even if Western philosophy and modern English are the prime matrix of discourse. This is not the experiment in reason that Whitehead wrote about, though I suspect he would have found it somehow ironic and stimulating. Some modern philosophic movements such as deconstructionism and pragmatism suggest that we abjure holistic, foundationalist, or totalistic visions at all. Hence, some form of modest, warranted application of reason is all we can hope for.[12]

Furthermore, as Alasdair MacIntyre has demonstrated in *Three Rival Visions of Moral Enquiry* (1990), comparative and cross-cultural elements have been integral to the Western philosophic and theological tradition at many defining points. In fact, MacIntyre makes the point that when we examine St. Thomas we discover an exceptionally acute form of comparative theology, even if we do not often regard St. Thomas's achievement from this perspective. According to MacIntyre's analysis, the problem St. Thomas faced was profoundly dialogical and comparative. He was confronted by the need to compare and contrast his older Augustinian theology, the common form of thought of the learned West at that time, with the new Aristotelian texts that were just beginning to circulate at the University of Paris during his day. And, of course, behind these new texts of Aristotle were all of the various Islamic theological and philosophical commentators to put the seal on the comparative aspect of the project. MacIntyre then shows what a successful job St. Thomas did of facing and integrating the comparative challenge into the complex tapestry of his science of divine things.

One of the successful things St. Thomas did, according to MacIntyre, was to provide guidelines for what constitutes a successful comparative philosophy. MacIntyre argues that good comparative philosophy or theology must do three interrelated things. First, it must seek to describe, understand, and commend the system being compared in its best and most reasonable terms. Comparative work cannot privilege some alternative system of thought immediately; it must seek to present the system under review in terms that make sense from within the world of discourse common to the system being compared. This demands both the highest ethical standards so as not to defame the other through ignorance or evil intent and the well-honed skill of dealing with materials outside the range of any one philosophic or religious system. The good comparativist must be an honest historian of religion. W. C. Smith (1981) also has argued that we do not really understand another tradition until and unless we can describe it not only in our own terms but also in terms that are regarded as being consistent with the other tradition as understood by its own members.

The second thing that the comparative philosopher must do is illumine the main problems of any system by making use of material from within the text itself. Mere external critique is not enough. The comparativist must get far enough within another system so he or she can describe accurately what is going on in the system, even far enough within to be able to see the problematic areas of interpretation, adequacy, and coherence. Furthermore, MacIntyre also argues that the good comparative philosopher has the obligation to defend the system being compared in terms of the best possible arguments available to that tradition. The vision of the tradition must be presented in the best possible internal light as well. The tradition must be given every chance to show how it can overcome its problems with its own tools or materials. The comparativist can even suggest moves internal to the tradition that may not have been articulated by members, as long as these suggestions arise from the description and understanding of the tradition itself.

Only after having completed the first two steps can the comparativist propose a new vision, the third stage of the engagement. The new vision must express the main problems of the other tradition and show how these problems cannot be solved completely by means internal to the tradition. The comparativist then suggests what needs to be done to rectify such problems. Often the modifications and suggestions have an equal impact on the scholar as well as on the target text. Comparative philosophy and theology are a dialogical enterprise if ever there is one. This is precisely what is happening on a global scale, as thinkers shuttle to conferences, publish papers, debate worldviews, and learn about new civilizations. David Lodge, the wonderfully perceptive and acerbic novelist of the academic world, is correct in saying that we live in a small world.

In many respects, this is the careful kind of comparative analysis that Neville has provided for the notion of God in process thought. He has described, understood, and commended many of the elements of process thought; but he then moves on to suggest what its problems are and how they cannot be solved by means internal to the system. Neville argues that simply reshaping Whitehead's reflections on God in Part V of *PR* will not solve the problem. For his part, MacIntyre is clear that any solutions offered by comparative thought must arise from the dialogue itself and be matched to the truthbearing aspects of the traditions in dialogue. Both sides must recognize each other, understand each other, and be transformed in the encounter. The new comparative philosophy or theology hence becomes a multiperspectival methodology for new analysis and synthesis, even though one party may be more transformed than the other in the encounter.

There is no suggestion in this three-stage comparative methodology that either tradition will disappear from the scene. Quite to the contrary, MacIntyre hopes that such careful work will allow for and encourage real dialogue between different philosophic and theological positions. It is expected that intelligent persons engaged in the dialogue will be given over to renewed reflection and even modification of their previous positions. As the Muslims remind us, reason is God's finger on the earth, and we ignore reasoned dialogue at our own peril. Because religion and philosophy often lie at the basis of all cultures, such comparative work will assist in civil discourse regarding the means and ends of humane life. This much we can claim for comparative thought in a pluralistic age.

To be realistic, none of this will come to pass without political will and the civil willingness to try to understand other people. But if there is a willingness for dialogue, then some form of comparative methodology is necessary to complete the task. Borrowing the wisdom of the Buddhist tradition, one can argue that comparative philosophy is an *upaya*, or a skillful means, for the search for truth and civilized behavior. Just because there are some glaring examples of the failure of dialogue—Bosnia, the Middle East, part of the former Soviet Union, Northern Ireland—does not absolve more fortunate cultures from engaging in dialogue. The intellectual interchange now going on peacefully between the North Atlantic world and East Asia may prove to be a good example of a more positive approach to intercivilizational exchange.

I claim that both Chu's and Whitehead's philosophies are relational, organic, and processive in nature. It strikes me that organic and relational philosophies are inherently dialogical in nature; their emphasis on communication between object–events is a logic of dialogue. They cannot afford to exclude anything that is relevant to the elaboration of their worldviews. If intercultural intellectual communication is now part of the modern reality, then anyone working out of the paradigm of process thought has an obligation to engage in comparative discourse. Even if the comparisons do not turn out to be fruitful, at least we will know the reasons why this is the case. On the other hand, if the comparison leads to new insights, then we will have been faithful to a fundamental pattern, a rhythm of the process tradition, as well as having contributed to a truly global and modern civil discourse aimed at better philosophic and religious communication and transformation. Hence, some kind of modest comparative effort appears to be in order.

In terms of the Whiteheadian version of process thought, the seeming incoherence at such a foundational level of the system is a profound challenge, because Whitehead really does offer a vision of coherence in the midst of a Western intellectual landscape dominated by philosophies of incoherence, rupture, deconstruction, and difference or value-free analytic neutrality. The grand reductionistic, fashionable, and easy response is that Whitehead was just plain wrong about unity and coherence, as is the case for so many other Western metaphysicians before him. The dream of the presence of unity—organic, creative, processive, or otherwise—is just another illusion in the faulty logic of a discredited logocentric universe. What we really need to seek is a pluriverse of interpretations, a recognition that the best we can do is create edifying discourses that will keep us warm and cozy in a cold and complex world.[13]

This reductionism in either deconstructionist or analytic mode is truly a profound challenge. Some scholars argue that the best we can hope to do is avoid the modern intellectual version of the Balkans, to retreat to quasi-civil solitudes wherein we do not try to reach other peoples and cultures from within our own worlds of discourse. Even with this model we must still talk together for the purposes of international law, order, economics, technology, and peace, despite our disagreements with each other. However profound I believe this modern deconstructionist or analytic challenge is, it is not really the main problem to be addressed in this essay—for the simple reason that to address these alternative philosophic visions would unreasonably expand what is already a lengthy study.

The second challenge to Whiteheadian process thought is even potentially greater because it comes from within the tradition itself as a form of self-critical inquiry. It is the question of internal coherence. Is there something so flawed in Whitehead's developing philosophy that makes him unable to escape the basic charge of fundamental incoherence concerning his essential insights into the nature of the divine reality? In some ways this is an even more devastating challenge to process thought than that of the post–modernist philosophers. One can argue with deconstructionists and neopragmatists such as Rorty about the adequacy of the process vision as being just one more version of foundationalism, but the more pressing issue is the query about its internal coherence. For this reason we must also seek to answer the coherence question of Neville's critiques of Whitehead's notion of God, based on his exegesis of Whitehead's own best defense of the system.[14] Only if both the external and internal challenges can be met can we continue to defend process philosophy and natural theology as being viable members of the intellectual dialogue of the modern world.[15]

Although after writing Part V of *PR*, Whitehead never systematically returned in his later works to an exhaustive treatment of the topic of God's multifaceted nature, it is clear that the question of the relationship of God and the world continued to tease his speculative imagination. In this regard, I believe that it behooves process philosophers and theologians to revisit *Adventures of Ideas* and *Modes of Thought* in order to respond to philosophically astute critics of Whitehead such as Neville. Moreover, this is not merely an externally motivated apologetic move. If I am correct, there are solid internal reasons why we should explore the later Whitehead to better understand God, creativity, and the divine world relations. Nor should such an invitation be surprising at this point in the history of the process movement. One of the main philosophic and theological crises of process thought has to do with the apparent incoherence of the separation of God and creativity in *PR*.[16]

Many other Whiteheadians have gone this way before, the most exemplary being Charles Hartshorne, William Christian, John Cobb Jr., Lewis Ford, Robert C. Neville, and Jorge Luis Nobo.[17] For instance, Cobb tried to rescue the Whiteheadian vision of the divine reality from the charge of incoherence in his influential *A Christian Natural Theology* (1965).[18] As for Hartshorne, one can make a strong case that most of his constructive exposition of philosophic theology is directed toward making sense of Part V of *PR* as neoclassical discourse. No one has made more of an effort to clarify one possible coherent solution to the mysteries of Part V than Hartshorne, although his solution is no mere scholastic tightening of Whitehead's own position. While Hartshorne is deeply appreciative of Whitehead's position, he has tried to make it clear that he does not believe that his own constructive work is a slavish imitation of his teacher. Hartshorne pays Whitehead the highest intellectual compliment in taking Whitehead seriously enough to try to correct what he regards as an error in Whitehead's vision of process thought.[19] Much the same thing can be said about Neville's critique of process thought.

Other major defenses of the coherence of Whitehead's vision of God have been mounted by Lewis Ford and Jorge Luis Nobo. Along with the key contemporary study of the development of Whitehead's thought, *The Emergence of Whitehead's Metaphysics: 1925–1929*, Ford has also written *The Lure of God: A Biblical Background for Process Theism* to illustrate the usefulness of Whitehead's notion of God for constructive theological reflection.

Combined with Nobo's *Whitehead's Metaphysics of Extension and Solidarity*, Ford has carried out the most careful textual work on the development of Whitehead's system and the question of the complex nature of God. Both Ford and Nobo have been interested in defending the coherence of Whitehead's notion of God. Nevertheless, it is fair to say that both Ford and Nobo focus their research on Whitehead's position in *PR* as the basis of their reconstructive efforts. Neither Ford nor Nobo have made extensive use of themes suggested by *AI* or *MT* in trying to deal with critics such as Neville[20]—much less make use of material drawn from South or East Asian philosophic traditions.

Nonetheless, the problem of the relationship of creativity, God, and the world is a persistent theological and philosophic issue. As we shall see in chapter 3, this is the key question of the most internally astute critic of Whitehead's theology, Robert C. Neville. One of the main aims of this essay is to answer Neville's trenchant attack on this crucial theological issue in process theology. I believe that no one from the process camp has really responded adequately or in sufficient length to Neville's 1980 challenge to the coherence of Whitehead's notion of God.[21] It strikes me that unless this can be done, process philosophy and theology is not in a very good position to face its more distant external critics such as the deconstructionists, post–modernists, and neopragmatists.

My main thesis is that one reason for the lack of a satisfactory response to Neville is that no one can adequately answer Neville by merely repeating Whitehead's 1929 unmodified position. A flawed, incomplete, or incoherent position is just that, and someone as insightful as Neville will demonstrate the errors of the position with gusto to defend his own speculative Platonic, even Peircian, re-reading of the Western tradition. Whitehead once remarked that Hume's critique of traditional Christian theology was devastating if those traditional positions Hume outlined were the only voices in the dialogue. What Whitehead meant was that accepting Hume's version of theological discourse leaves no way to escape the logic of Hume's attack. The same can be said concerning Neville's critique of Whitehead's explanation of the relationship of God and creativity in its unmodified version based on Part V of *PR*.[22]

Twist and turn as they might, Neville has process philosophers and theologians on the run as long as they remain faithful to the Whiteheadian tradition as it is expounded on the basis of *PR*. But we need to remember that Whitehead wrote quite a bit after 1929, most specifically *Adventures of Ideas* and *Modes of Thought*. If we read these later works as indicators of a possible revisioning of the 1929 position in terms of further reflection, then we can modify the 1929 position rather than abandon it to Neville's critical attack. I believe that Neville carries out a successful flanking attack on Whitehead, but that Whitehead's position can be strengthened on the basis of material found in *AI* and *MT*—as well as the introduction of cross-cultural material drawn from the East Asian philosophic tradition of Neo-Confucianism, which is in concord with this material.

I am not the first scholar to notice that there is a problem of God–creativity–world relations in *PR* or that Whitehead returned to these questions in both *AI* and *MT*. The problem that has complicated any appeal to material in *AI* and *MT* is that neither of these books is as philosophically technical nor systematic as *PR*. In a philosophic sense, one must always build upon *PR*, even if one recognizes that there are points of detail that need to be improved—even major points such as the relationship of God and creativity. In terms of the scholasticism of process thought, *AI* and *MT* are, it often seems to me, treated as something like nontechnical addenda to the serious detailed philosophic work of *PR*. They are interpreted as interesting studies of intellectual and philosophic history of ideas, but rarely is there an attempt to make use of them to modify or correct anything fundamental in *PR*. I believe this is a grave mistake if Whiteheadian scholars are going to debate successfully with astute critics such as Neville on the question of the divine reality. I will demonstrate that Whitehead makes enough suggestive hints in *AI* and *MT* to warrant an attempted reconstruction of the structure of the relationship of creativity, God, and the world as it bears on philosophic cosmology and theology, especially when this re-reading is combined with material drawn from Chu Hsi's Neo-Confucian philosophy. Such a reconstruction will provide one reasonable answer to Neville and other critics of process thought in terms of its coherence and adequacy.

It is at this point that I will also introduce Chu Hsi as another contributor to the modern global movement of process thought. Although Chu was dealing with a completely different culture of philosophic discourse, some of his insights and problems shed light on the question of God, creativity, and the world—or the relationship of the Tao, human nature, and the mind–heart to express the problem within Sung Neo-Confucian categories. If the Neo-Confucian materials serve to nudge the Whiteheadian debate along, they will have served one of the great purposes of comparative philosophy, namely the mutual enrichment of the conversation.

I believe that Whitehead knew he had a problem with his notions of God and creativity at the end of Part V of *PR*. However obliquely, Whitehead returns to these themes in both *AI* and *MT*, but not with the scope or precision, or even intent, of *PR*. This is the reason that much of Whiteheadian scholarship correctly ends its creative advance into process philosophy and theology with reflections based exclusively on *PR*. I will also argue that this problem is one of the reasons that causes independent thinkers such as

Hartshorne and Neville to move away from purely Whiteheadian solutions to the problem of the relationship of creativity, God, and the world. For instance, Hartshorne seeks to solve these problems through his redefinition of God as a society and not as an individual object–event in Whiteheadian terms. For his part, Neville strives to move beyond the whole Whiteheadian metaphysical and cosmological discussion toward a radical ontology of creation *ex nihilo*, designed in part to solve this Whiteheadian dilemma concerning the God–world relationship.

But this may be giving up too soon on an internally adequate and a coherent orthodox Whiteheadian answer to these questions. There are ways to defend the Whiteheadian vision on serious Whiteheadian grounds if we take *AI* and *MT* more seriously. I am mindful of David Hall's and Roger Ames's warning, found in a footnote in their book on Confucian discourse, that studies such as mine can be read as a form of eager scholasticism that much too quickly tries to force Whitehead's philosophy back into the safe confines of traditional Western metaphysics. Hall and Ames argue that Whitehead became a victim of his disciples, who used his process thought to find the One True System. According to Hall and Ames, much of the power of Whitehead's work came from his poetic style and metaphors. At least part of my argument is that a comparative study of Whitehead shows that seeking to remove incoherence from part of his system does not mean we must abandon process for a reaffirmation of some kind of "ultimacy of fact," as Hall and Ames allege.[23]

For instance, the Canadian theologian Laurence Wilmot has sketched just such a defense on the basis of his reading of the relevant theological sections of *AI*, buttressed further by reflections on selected Christian patristic texts. Wilmot's essay has not received much positive attention because of some very serious defects in its textual, hermeneutic, and general interpretation of Whitehead.[24] Nonetheless, it is a suggestive interpretation that, if purged of its shortcomings, provides a way to answer Neville's charge of a fundamental incoherence in Whitehead's notion of God by means of a creative use of themes drawn from *AI* and *MT*.

In all honesty, I must point out that for most competent Whiteheadian scholars these extensive flaws in Wilmot's analysis obviate any positive value for his suggested theological reconstruction. I have sympathy both for what Wilmot attempted and for his critics, who have pointed out where he went wrong. Yet Wilmot's basic instinct is helpful in indicating at least one way out of the problem on strictly Whiteheadian grounds, based on material taken from *AI* and *MT*. As Whitehead once noted, it is sometimes more important for a thesis to be interesting than strictly logically ordered. However, it is best if it is both interesting and true for it to count as a viable reconstruction.

The key to Wilmot's revisionist position is Whitehead's claim in *AI* about the development of the Western philosophic tradition after Plato. "These Christian theologians (Whitehead takes these to be the schools of Alexandria and Antioch) have the distinction of being the only thinkers who in a fundamental metaphysical doctrine improved upon Plato" (*AI*, 214–15). Anyone who knows Whitehead's veneration of Plato should take immediate note of this confession. Whatever this improvement is, it deserves careful attention. While Whitehead does not spell out in detail precisely what he means, Wilmot observes that Whitehead explicitly believes that the early patristic theologians offer some kind of solution to the problem of the relationship of God and the world that will make sense of the claims of Part V of *PR*. Wilmot makes a strong case, based on impeccable Whiteheadian grounds, for the creative use of *AI* in order to work on the problem of God, creativity, and the world. That Wilmot is rash in his attempt to show that Whitehead was an orthodox trinitarian Christian should not be taken to prove the completely different thesis that Whitehead in *AI* never offers improved reflections on God, creativity, and the world.

It is no easy task to show what Whitehead was doing systematically in *AI* in terms of the notions of God, creativity, and the world and how this triad is linked to early Christian theology. Although Whitehead admired the creativity of these early Christian theologians, his admiration knew limits. Whitehead argued that the problem of God–world relations arose in Western religious thought, specifically in Plato and Aristotle, long before it became a highly charged theological problem for the early Christian theologians. The focal point for the Christian was how to resolve the unity and internal diversity of God's nature as expressed in the doctrine of the Holy Trinity. Historically, the solution of the problem demanded a doctrine of the person of Christ because of the Arian challenge to the orthodox Christian affirmation of the mysterious yet complete unity of God and Christ. Whitehead holds that these theologians were correct in that "They decided for the direct immanence of God in the one person of Christ. They also decided for some sort of direct immanence of God in the World generally" (*AI*, 216). This, according to Whitehead, is the basis for their advance on Plato. "It is in this respect that they made a metaphysical discovery" (*AI*, 216).

But once having made their metaphysical discovery, the theologians failed to advance toward what Whitehead calls general metaphysics. The reason for this was "another unfortunate presupposition. The nature of God was exempted from all the metaphysical categories which applied to the individual things in this temporal world" (*AI*, 216). In most respects, Whitehead's philosophic quest can be viewed as a return to this early patristic breakthrough without exempting God from the analysis. For whatever reason, the Christian theologians, and most theologians ever since, suffered from what Whitehead calls a failure of nerve in metaphysical vision.

> They made no effort to conceive the World in terms of the metaphysical categories by means of which they interpreted God, and they made no effort to conceive God in terms of the metaphysical categories which they applied to the world. (*AI*, 217)

From a Whiteheadian perspective, this was unfortunate. But it does not mean that modern philosophers of religion and philosophic theologians cannot return to this initial breakthrough and try to create a more adequate notion of God–world relations. This is basically what Wilmot tries to do, however flawed the execution of the project may have been.

Whitehead in *AI* goes on to point out that the problem with this gulf between the metaphysics of divinity and the temporal world leads to an inability to figure out what is going on in terms of God's relationship to the world. He argues that unless we develop a more adequate doctrine of a divine world relationship, we must resort to silence on the issue or deploy the long bow of mysticism because we cannot know anything about the divine on the basis of the mundane (*AI*, 217). Even as an Englishman with a natural veneration for the long bow, Whitehead does not believe that this solution will work outside of purely Christian circles. Some kind of reasonable discourse on divine things is not only possible but necessary for religious and philosophic reconstruction.

To locate this revised notion of God within process thought, in chapter 2 we will explore briefly the development of Whitehead's notion of God. What distinguishes my commentary from other standard scholarly accounts is that it will focus attention on those aspects of the Whiteheadian corpus that allow for a revised process philosophic and theological position on the question of God–world relations, a position also to be enriched by recourse to an examination of Chu Hsi's Neo-Confucian process thought. In chapter 3 we will then address whether Neville's doctrine of creation *ex nihilo* is a brilliant example of an arrow shot from the long bow of mysticism into the silence of the other side of what we call God. Is Neville's provocative rendition of Platonic or Neo-Platonic mysticism all that can be said of God, the world, or creativity? In chapters 4 and 5 we will introduce Chu Hsi as a dialogue partner on the issue of God, creativity, and the world.

We must now return briefly to Wilmot's reconstruction (1979). He looks at the theologians of Alexandria and Antioch to discover what Whitehead was exploring in terms of God–world relations if and when we take material from *AI* and *MT* in order to understand a possible revision in Whitehead's thought.

Wilmot then proceeds to frame his own argument in terms of what he takes to be a Whiteheadian response to the metaphysics of Plotinus, an important figure in the development of Platonic theology in late classical antiquity. Wilmot takes Whitehead at his word and looks very carefully at the writing of a representative theologian of the period, Athanasius, to see what this advance in metaphysics might be. And of course Wilmot concludes that this advance, by the necessity of the logic of the theological argument, takes us directly into the heart of the Christological controversies of the fourth century. In his enthusiasm for the argument, Wilmot makes the claim that the "problems facing Athanasius and Whitehead are identical" (1979, 143). It is just this kind of excessive rhetoric that causes many sober Whiteheadians to discount Wilmot's work.

Furthermore, Wilmot ends his book by trying to argue that Whitehead was an orthodox trinitarian Christian. This is simply too much for many scholars to credit because of what we know about Whitehead's negative opinion of the Church and his relationship to it. It may be the case that Whitehead was impressed with some of the early Christian theologians, but to try to bring Whitehead himself safely back into the embrace of the Church strains credulity, given Whitehead's caustic opinions about the Church of his day. All one has to do to make the point here is to re-read Lucien Price's 1954 *Dialogues of Alfred North Whitehead* to get the point. Whitehead may indeed have had a high opinion of the insights of Jesus of Nazareth and some early Christian thinkers, but this does not mean that we can infer something about his own faith stance vis-à-vis the existing Christian churches. Nonetheless, this does not mean that Wilmot is not on to something that can help resolve the problem of God–world relations in process philosophy and theology.

What Wilmot points toward is one possible response to internal critics such as Neville who have made a telling point about the lack of coherence caused by the diremption of God and creativity within *PR*. Some kind of speculation on trinitarian theory may indeed be helpful in resolving this dilemma in a manner different from Hartshorne's revision of Whitehead's categories or Neville's rejection of process cosmology as a metaphysics without ontology. At this point it is important to keep in mind that although Neville rejects Whitehead's metaphysics, he still relies on Whitehead's cosmology when he comes to frame his own creative cosmological exposition, as first expressed in *The Cosmology of Freedom*.

In Chu Hsi's case, it is more difficult to locate any particular famous passage on the role of principle and matter–energy that becomes the focus of debate in quite the same way Part V of *PR* does for Whitehead. However, the first six chapters or sections of Chu's recorded conversations or dialogues with students and friends also provide ample material for exploring the Sung analog to the problem of the separation of God and creativity as first principles in Whitehead. The Neo-Confucian problem has to do with the analysis of the relationship of principle (*li*) and matter–energy (*ch'i*) in Chu's mature thought. The first six sections of the conversations (*yü-lei*) and the anthologies based on them, have set the standard for the pan-East Asian discussion of this quarrelsome issue right down to today.

However, even if the textual location of the debate is diffuse, the heat generated by Chu Hsi's discussion of the relationship of principle and matter–energy is intense.[25] Chu's analysis of principle-*ch'i* relations provided a great deal of material for conversation with his own students and friends. In fact, Ch'en Ch'un (1159–1223), as we shall see, devotes a great deal of his philosophic energies to trying to get straight just what the master taught about this topic. All later Neo-Confucian philosophers took a stand on the relationship of principle and matter–energy. While none of the schools wanted to be labeled dualists in terms of their analysis, there was a persistent suspicion that Chu's theory did seem to tend toward a quasi-dualist reading of reality. While this potential dualism was extremely different from the kind of dualisms familiar to the post–Enlightenment West, it was still a problem for the Neo-Confucian tradition. On the one hand, Chu himself denied that we can interpret principle and matter–energy as being cosmologically separable dualistic principles. But on the other hand, if this were the case, then what was the true relationship of principle and matter–energy if not some kind of dualism? Surely the mere fact that there are different and important distinctions to be made indicates that Chu was talking about at least two different things—or modes, manifestations, levels of analysis, and so on.

Is there something in all process philosophies that abhors a fundamental, ontological dualism and yet always embraces a dualistic analysis of reality?[26] Does the admission of dualism somehow detract from the cogency of the argument? This often appears to be the common assumption when we review the Neo-Confucian debates. Chu Hsi's most trenchant critics sought to find a more unified position than they discovered in Chu's analysis. In some cases they were clearly monistic in intent. For instance, some of the very acute Ch'ing dynasty Evidential Research scholars, such as Tai Chen, affirmed that matter–energy was the prime and only basic category of analysis. They recognized principle but only as a pattern within matter–energy. To suggest, as they often took Chu to be doing, that principle and matter–energy have some kind of cosmological parity was a category mistake of the highest order for someone like Tai Chen. Chu's defenders countered that the critics had misunderstood the essential argument for parity that lies at the heart of Chu's mature thought. But in both cases, the critics and the supporters defended the need for an essential unity of first principles—principle and matter–energy—even if they were not comfortable with Chu's philosophy of principle.

Many other favorite topics of Neo-Confucian discourse were spin-offs of the principle–matter–energy debate. Much of the direction of later East Asian Neo-Confucian speculation depended on whether the philosopher in question chose to defend or attack Chu. Until one could provide a coherent reading of the question of principle and matter–energy, it was, for instance, almost impossible from within the Neo-Confucian worldview to give meaning to the notion of the mind–heart, human nature, human feelings, the nature of morality, and all of the other issues so near and dear to the Confucian Way. And if Chu were wrong about his approach to such a fundamental question, what credence could be given to all of his other commentaries and insights into the Way of the Sages? In a link to the Whiteheadian tradition, we note that Neville has written extensively on the Neo-Confucian tradition, often seeking the support and illumination of contrast from this East Asian tradition as he develops his own critical project.

A REVISED WHITEHEADIAN METASYSTEM

One clue about how to proceed is to review briefly some key passages from *AI* as they pertain to this issue. As it has been amply demonstrated by Lewis Ford in *The Emergence of Whitehead's Metaphysics: 1925–1929*, Whitehead was quite capable of changing his mind as he worked through a problem. Ford has done a masterful job of demonstrating how Whitehead arrived at his final conclusions in *PR* without sometimes even bothering to remove earlier drafts expressing different positions from the newer layers of the text. As it is well known, Whitehead wrote quickly and did not take much care in the final editorial preparation of his books. *PR* is a perfect example of this rather lax process (*PR*, v–x).

More germane to our problem, however, is that Whitehead does return to basic speculative issues in *AI* and *MT*. In terms of Sung Neo-Confucian discourse, Chu thought systematically but never wrote a study of physics like Aristotle, so it does not make a great deal of sense to instantly link his speculative reflections on the nature of things to a characteristic Western ordering of the sciences. Chu's more characteristic way of systematic reflection is similar to what Hall and Ames (1995) describe as analogical or correlative discourse or what Lakoff (1987) construes as reliance on metaphor or prototype. In both Whitehead's and Chu's case, there is an attempt to explain the world in ways that are not immediate copies of ontology or cosmology as pure theoretical or abstract disciplines. In Paul Feyerabend's radical formulation (1988), both Whitehead and Chu are more historical than abstract thinkers.

Furthermore, Whitehead is not always as clear as we would like in defining what he takes his own system to be. For instance, is it metaphysics, ontology, or cosmology, or some mixture of all three? I find it instructive that he called it a philosophy of organism whereas it has become known as process philosophy in the scholarly literature. At various places Whitehead does label the system a cosmology and metaphysics. It has also been called an ontology. While, at least in Western philosophy, cosmology, ontology, and metaphysics are often closely allied disciplines, I do not want to prejudice our examination by deciding which term is appropriate in all cases in dealing with Whitehead's thought. My hesitation results from internal and external considerations.

Internally, we need to be careful about just what Whitehead is doing. For instance, I have always considered it important that he labels *PR* an essay on cosmology. Externally, as modern academic philosophy and theology haltingly become global in their appropriation of the history of human thought, we may want to employ some non-Western modes of analysis in our interpretation of Whitehead in order to better understand certain facets of his thought. The introduction of Chinese Neo-Confucian material is helpful in both an analysis of the problem of relationship of creativity, God, and the world and in framing a terminology to describe the situation. For instance, following the studies of Confucius and the Chinese tradition by David Hall and Roger Ames (1987, 1995), we shall discover that it is fruitful to make use of their category of *ars contextualis* as one definition of global process thought when contrasted with the classical Western division of metaphysics into ontology and cosmology. While it is true that Whitehead wrote within the Western tradition of metaphysical interpretation, we need to expand our vision to include other forms of process or organic thought to cope successfully with Neville's challenge.

The sensibility and vocabulary of the Western philosophic tradition needs some new tools in its encounter with other cultural systems. The difference between the imperial and metric systems of measure comes to mind—while you can use the tools across cultures, sometimes the fit is not very precise. It was recognized by Whitehead and others that his thought has some suggestive similarities with certain forms of Indian and Chinese speculation (*PR*, 7). In a parallel fashion, Hall and Ames have argued that we cannot, without a great deal of prior clarification, simply apply the notions of ontology and cosmology to early Chinese thought.[27] They have invented the term *ars contextualis* to describe the relational and processive aspects of Confucius's thought that have so fascinated students of the Chinese sage. For this and other reasons, I have decided to use the neutral term *speculative discourse*, or philosophy, to describe such disparate thinkers as Whitehead and the great Southern Sung Neo-Confucian Chu Hsi, one of the greatest of the Chinese organic thinkers. This affinity will be explained in much greater detail in later sections of the study (especially chapters 4 and 5).

In an earlier independent study, Hall (1982b) also called this emerging process paradigm a philosophy of creative synthesis. In *The Uncertain Phoenix*, Hall indicated that he believes it is time for Western speculative thinkers to become open to alternative paradigms from the East. His favorite form of Chinese philosophy is Taoism, along with Ch'an Buddhism. In Chinese Taoism, Hall finds a form of philosophic speculation radically more pluralistic, process oriented, and productive of creative synthesis than any of the reigning Western paradigms.[28] In many respects I agree with Hall's suggestive reading of the two great early Chinese Taoist texts, the *Tao Te Ching* and the *Chuang Tzu*. They are as wonderfully anarchic as Hall suggests them to be.[29] But we need to remember that they are only one strain of early Chinese thought. One thing I want to do in this study is introduce the Neo-Confucians, specifically Chu Hsi, as a contrast between Hall's anarchic Taoist chaos and Neville's determinate creation *ex nihilo*. Someone needs to defend the Confucian love of humane principle.

Whitehead is still trying to get things right in *AI* that were left untidy in *PR*, although with a different format entirely. I confess that I find *AI* the most Confucian of Whitehead's work in that he makes great use of historical and cultural narrative to underline his philosophic points.[30] One of the things he is struggling with is another way to describe the ultimate categoreal notions necessary to frame any speculative vision of reality. In his chapter on "Adventure" in *AI*, Whitehead adumbrates what he calls the three metaphysical principles necessary for any broad and rich description of reality. It is important to note that whenever Whitehead uses such language, however poetic, presystematic, or vague, he is signaling that he is expressing what he takes to be something of real philosophic importance. Besides, as the Confucians noticed long ago, there is nothing wrong with using history to make a point within organic/process-oriented traditions. It is useful to rehearse these three principles here, prior to their more careful elaboration in later chapters.

Whitehead begins, as any student of *PR* would expect, by stating that "One principle is that the very real essence of real actuality—that is, of the completely real—is *process*" (*AI*, 354). Whitehead believes that he can cite the later Plato here in terms of rejecting the notion of a static self or universe. Whitehead argues that Plato's later thought revolves around seven key notions, namely, the ideas, the physical elements, the psyche, eros, harmony, the mathematical relations, and the receptacle. Regardless of how you choose to weave together these seven key notions, Whitehead submits that you will be driven, especially by the notion of eros, to an understanding of reality based on process and relationship. There is food for thought in Whitehead's framing of this first principle when we notice that he begins with process and actuality and not the notion of creativity. There is a strong emphasis on something akin to Hall's category of creative synthesis.[31] This will be a key point in our answer to Neville and other critics of Whiteheadian thought.

The second metaphysical principle returns Whitehead to a favorite emphasis on the ontological principle, as it was called in *PR*. "It is the doctrine that every occasion of actuality is in its own nature finite" (*AI*, 356). Whitehead wants to dissuade one and all that finitude is somehow imperfect, negative, or evil. He goes on to argue that the constitution of any actuality is the result of its harmonization of its possible choices. This also is a key feature of Neville's cosmology, and he clearly acknowledges his debt to Whitehead at this point. In terms of our Neo-Confucian contrast, we will discover that Chu Hsi agrees completely with Whitehead on the role of harmonization in the creation of finite creatures. It also is this kind of doctrine, and its correlates in *PR*, that has proved so disturbing to the theological community, because it implies that God is finite in some fashion. We must remember that Whitehead's notion of God in *PR* is that of an actual entity, even if a very special kind of divine entity.

The third category in the *AI* list is the principle of individuality, and it concerns Whitehead's doctrine of harmony or creative synthesis as the cosmological basis of any object–event whatsoever.

> At the base of experience there is a welter of feeling, derived from individual realities or directed towards them. Thus for strength of experience we require to discriminate the component factors, each as an individual 'It' with its own significance. (*AI*, 361).

We will here again discover that the notion of harmony also is very important for Neville and is perhaps the best explication available for trying to understand what Whitehead was getting at through the conjunction of individuality and harmony. Likewise, we will discover that the idea of harmony is extremely important to Chu Hsi and his school.

A key question will be, does this kind of restatement of basic metaphysical principles represent a way forward or merely a verbal repositioning of previously held positions on Whitehead's part? I suggest that even if these three metasystemic principles expressed in *AI* are not spelled out within anything like the extended exposition found in *PR*, we can employ them to reexamine the problem of the relationship of God, creativity, and the world. However, this argument anticipates Neville's challenge to the whole process tradition discussed in chapter 3.

In terms of global or comparative aspects of this essay, I offer the following formulation of the three basic reformed process speculative principles (to be fully discussed in chapter 6). I have, for reasons of comparative interest in the Chinese *li-hsüeh*, or learning of principle, as defined by Chu Hsi, chosen to call these the triad of form, dynamics, and unification.[32] These three terms are less specific, vaguer than Whitehead's own terminology because they have been abstracted from the technical discourse of Sung Neo-Confucian thought as well as from Western process philosophy and theology. The proximate Western theological source is Tillich's systematic theology. I have chosen them because they are useful for the task of comparing the Neo-Confucian thinkers and Whitehead, precisely because of their bicultural origins.

As I will show in detail in chapters 4 and 5, this comparison of Whitehead and Chu Hsi has been commonplace in the study of Chinese philosophy ever since Joseph Needham first made the contrast in the 1950s. I have no greater desire than Needham to push the comparison too far. I offer the comparative element as a limited check on the excessively Eurocentric focus of even such an irenic thinker as Whitehead and the Western process school. In Whitehead's defense, he was always interested in all human thought; in this intercivilization interest he was certainly an example to be emulated. We will return to the question of terminology and its role in comparative thought in later chapters of this study. I hope to demonstrate, especially in chapters 4 and 5, how reflection on similar problems in Chu Hsi can assist us in formulating an adequate and applicable response to the critics of process thought on the question of creativity.

Beyond the broad philosophic similarities, which are fascinating in their own right, of Chu Hsi and Whitehead, we must note that Chu Hsi also had a structural problem similar to the one faced by Whitehead caused by the separation of God and creativity. As noted before, this problem was thematized in the history of Neo-Confucian thought as Chu Hsi's potentially dualistic interpretation of the connection of *li* and *ch'i*. The first thing we need to remember is that Neo-Confucian dualism, if there is such a thing, in no way resembles the dualism of Western or Indian traditions. As we shall see, it has its own special characteristics. The nub of the problem is the relationship of principle (*li*) and matter–energy (*ch'i*). Chu Hsi's critics, just like Whitehead's, suggested that if principle and matter–energy were really separate in some kind of fundamental way, then this indicated a profound incoherence in Chu's thought. In terms of Neo-Confucian discourse, the incoherence of the potential dualism of principle and matter–energy was as grave as Whitehead's purported separation of God's primordial nature and creativity.

Chu Hsi spent a great deal of time responding to his students and critics about the proper way to understand the relationship of principle and matter–energy. This also has continued to be a major theoretical problem in the development of the East Asian Neo-Confucian tradition. Later Korean and Japanese scholars joined the debate about whether or not principle and matter–energy were synergistically interconnected or whether they were, in some profound fashion, separate. The notion of some kind of ultimate separation of first principles even in intellectual analysis was denied by Chu Hsi himself and his later defenders.[33] Yet it was a problem that would continue to engage the attention of the best scholars of the tradition right down to the modern period. For instance, the great modern Confucian Mou Tsung-san continued to write on the topic, albeit from a comparative global philosophic perspective vastly different from Chu Hsi's own world of Sung Neo-Confucian intellectual culture.

While a resolution of the Neo-Confucian debate on the relationship of principle and matter–energy is not the main thrust of this essay, reflection on the specifics of the Neo-Confucian problem will be one by-product of the investigation. If the use of Neo-Confucian intellectual history sheds light on a Western debate, perhaps the Western material also can assist the reformulation of the intra-Confucian dialogue about principle and matter–energy. If Chu and Whitehead were really both speculative philosophers of process, then it is plausible that they will have some of the same structural problems and challenges within their systems. Of course, and it should go without being repeated, there are immense differences in the thought of Chu and Whitehead.

It is interesting to note that Chu Hsi's most analytic student, Ch'en Ch'un, also performed a role for his teacher analogous to that of Hartshorne, Cobb, Ford, and Nobo for Whitehead. While Chu was a clear writer, known for his ability to explicate complicated matters in a comprehensible fashion, his thought was compact enough that it needed interpretation and expansion. Ch'en sought to do this when he wrote his famous philosophic glossary of key Confucian terms. One of Ch'en's aims was to show the ultimate coherence of his master's system. The defense of the Chu Hsi system by Ch'en shows that there are always problems of coherence and adequacy for process thought in its Chinese as well as its modern Western mode. Not the least of these problems is the potential for the incoherence of first principles, namely the notion of God for Whitehead and principle for Chu Hsi. Hence, there is a comparison to be made not only of the systems but also of the defense of these systems and the problems common to both.

However, clearness of exposition, even coherence of first principles, is not everything for thinkers like Chu Hsi and Whitehead. There has to be some point to the decisions of the creatures of the world. One is almost tempted to add a fourth element to the triad of form, dynamics, and unification. Chu would have called this *chih-shan* or ultimate goodness or *ho*, harmony, the peace that passes beyond all expectation. At the end of *AI*, Whitehead wrote, "This is the secret of the union of Zest with Peace—That suffering attains its end in a Harmony of Harmonies. . . . In this way the World receives its persuasion towards such perfections as are possible for its diverse individual occasions" (*AI*, 381). Talking about the ultimate aims for a civilized life, Confucius, in Simon Leys's new translation, said, ". . . At fifty I knew the Will of Heaven. At sixty, my ear was attuned. At seventy, I follow all the desires of my heart without breaking any rule" (Leys 1997, 6). Each of these harmonies, each of these followings of desire becomes so personal, so individual that it is impossible to define them at all. They are the perfected metaphors of our lives.

Because we live in a pluralistic world, we might as well make use of this material for philosophic and theological reflection. This is not an easy task for a number of reasons. The first has to do with the generic problems of comparative thought. Anyone who has tried to compare a Buddhist thinker and Western intellectual knows how hard the task is; cross-cultural comparison is definitely an example of Aristotle's *phronesis* rather than a purely deductive science. Wayne Booth has coined the term *coduction* to speak of this special art, in his case, in terms of literary criticism (1988, 70–77). This is a kind of study situated between deduction and induction, in that coduction demands careful attention to George Herbert Mead's world of sociality. Mead admired Whitehead's process thought and believed its doctrines of relativity and pluralism were mirrored in the creation of the human self, a self Mead called social because it could never arise except in a social setting.[34]

This does not mean that comparison is irrational, rather, the difficulty lies more in the complexity of what is to be compared, as well as in the problem that so few scholars are cross-cultural or multilinguistic in outlook and training. Systems of ideas are generated within their own cultural matrices, and we cannot assume that comparison is an easy task. Second, cultural construction means making certain choices about the range of options open to philosophic and theological imagination. Historically, these choices have been expressed by the living out of the cultural norms of these specific intellectual constructs, however nebulous, such as Western European post–enlightenment culture, Islamic civilization, the Buddhist dharma, or the Confucian Tao. Most great thinkers have remained faithful to the genius of their respective intellectual cultures, even when it is obvious that these cultures are amalgams of diverse intercivilizational resources.

It remains to be seen if anyone can actually construct a new global civilization that is self-consciously pluralistic in form.[35] There is a great deal of merited resistance to the notion that cultures can be constructed in the same way a person can wander around a modern Western supermarket. Nonetheless, just as we find tofu and kimche in North American supermarkets, so too we must come to grips with the impact of new philosophic and religious ideas—as the Western tradition has always done when confronted with new philosophic texts. We also must remember that some of the most characteristic edifices of Western European intellectual history were generated from their own contact with a wider pluralistic world. St. Thomas Aquinas, as MacIntyre and others have conclusively shown, thought and wrote out of a comparative matrix of diverse cultures, including his inherited late Greco–Roman Augustinian theology, the impact of the Islamic challenge, and the arrival of Aristotle's thought as mediated by the Islamic world. This was a heady mixture, surely as challenging and diverse as the comparison of Chu Hsi and Whitehead. No one will deny that St. Thomas was successful in responding to the challenge of his day through the synthesis of all of the best knowledge available to him. To do less today would be to admit an intellectual timidity not worthy of the best of the Western European heritage.

But before we engage in the responsive and comparative aspects of the essay, we now need to re-examine the development of Whitehead's reflections on the divine reality. This will set the context for the problem and its possible resolution. This is important to do in order to lift up those elements of Whitehead's reflections on the nature of God, creativity, and the world that might be useful in answering such astute critics as Neville before presenting our reformed and comparative process speculative philosophy.

NOTES

1. Lewis Ford notes that the very term *creativity* is a Whiteheadian neologism. The origin of the term is traced to *RM*, first published in 1926. While there may have been at least one stray use of "creativity" before Whitehead, it does appear to be the case that it was Whitehead who introduced the term into common usage. See Ford, "Creativity in a Future Key" (1987, p. 179).

2. My understanding of the role of metaphor in categoreal schemas has been shaped by the collaborative work of George Lakoff and Mark Johnson (Lakoff and Johnson 1980; Lakoff 1987, Johnson 1987, 1993). Metaphors are more friendly to process than they are to fixed, rigid substances and utterly logical sets of defining propositions.

3. For instance, the modern Confucian intellectual Cheng Chung-ying has written extensively on the relationship of key Neo-Confucian concepts and Whitehead

(1991). There seems to be a natural affinity among the various manifestations of global process thought that demands and encourages comparative interpretation. Nicholas Rescher (1996) argues that although Whitehead is the best known modern Western process philosopher, he certainly is not the only Western thinker to appreciate the role of process in speculative discourse. In fact, Rescher makes a plea that we see process thought as a major form of thought, even in the West.

4. For instance, Ch'ien Mu, in his magisterial study of the development and structure of Chu Hsi's thought, has shown that Chu was passionately concerned, even obsessed, with the role of mind within his philosophy (1971).

5. The term *object–event* or *object–events* is drawn from a process reading of Chu Hsi. Chu was interested in the analysis of all events and objects, the actual entities of his mature philosophic system.

6. Chu Hsi's writings are truly vast, much on the scale of St. Aquinas, but even more extensive. Chu wrote essays, commentaries, poetry, letters—all in profusion. One of the reasons for this scholarly creativity was the fact that he passed the imperial examinations when he was only eighteen. The average age of a scholar passing the last imperial examination was about thirty-five. So when most scholars of his day were still busy preparing for the examinations that would allow them access to the national civil service—a calling central to the Sung Confucian worldview—Chu was able to pursue scholarly inclinations for about two extra decades.

As students of Chu Hsi's life have pointed out, he was interested primarily in the Sung Confucian scholarly pursuits. When he was called to formal public service, he did well but always sought to resign active government service in order to return to the study and teaching of the Way.

7. In this section of my dissertation, I exegete a number of passages on the mind–heart. See John Berthrong, "Glosses on Reality: Chu Hsi as Interpreted by Ch'en Ch'un" (Ph.D. dissertation, University of Chicago, 1979, pp. 102–09).

8. For the best discussion of this matter see Hoyt Cleveland Tillman, *Confucian Discourse and Chu Hsi's Ascendancy* (Honolulu: University of Hawaii Press, 1992).

9. There are a number of reasons for this appeal. One is that process thought is not overly committed to the common linguistic usage of the Western tradition. This does not mean that modern linguistic or analytic philosophy cannot be applied to comparative studies; it only means that it may be biased toward particular linguistic models common in the English-speaking world. However, this is a complicated empirical question that need not detain us here. I am sure that analytic philosophers will dismiss much of Chinese Neo-Confucianism as muddled mysticism or worse, confused thinking and the generation of new category mistakes.

10. Lewis Ford (1984) has amply demonstrated that Whitehead was constantly revising his work as he wrote. The textual history of Whitehead's canon is as complicated as that of any major Western philosopher. What is clear is that Whitehead was perfectly willing to modify his previous position or even change it dramatically as he

continued to reflect on the outlines of his philosophy. The question of the development of the notion of the divine reality is a perfect illustration of this developmental process.

11. There may be other, less rationalistic reasons for the appeal of Whitehead's relational and organic vision. If Camille Paglia (1991) is to be believed—another matter entirely—then there is something to be said for organic philosophies that try to encompass the rich vitality of life. While Whitehead was hardly decadent in Paglia's sense of modern sensibility, is there something romantic about Whitehead that lures us to a vision beyond the merely technically rational? Doesn't Whitehead promise more than the typical Monday-morning-first-cup-of-consciousness that is so typical of modern academic philosophy? Does organic philosophy always promise or allow for the darker sides of creative nature to spring forth or at least be acknowledged and remembered?

12. Oddly enough, some defenders of relativism have a much more robust belief in the ability to defend the use of reason than do other modern cultural critics. Margolis, for instance, mounts an impressive defense of the sophistic tradition of relativism that has a very pronounced place for reason and disputation.

13. The modern pluralistic literary critic Wayne Booth demonstrates that such a complex vision of different readings of diverse forms of artistic excellence does not need to abandon the search for ethical critique (1988). Pluralism does not mean that we have to give up the hope for a civilization of excellence.

14. It is characteristic of Robert Neville to include significant reflections on process thought when he writes about modernity. *The High Road Around Modernism* (1992) is an excellent example of this tendency and contains some of his most focused critique of process thought since his 1980 study of process theology.

15. I agree with Stephen Toulmin that we are not living in a post–modern world—rather, we are in a late stage of the modern Western world that Toulmin most convincingly traces at least to the sixteenth century (1990). While Toulmin agrees that there are stages in the development of modern Western thought, he argues that we are still in this world of discourse and have not yet developed paradigmatically different styles of thought to warrant the claim that we are in some "post–modern" world. He believes this is an especially persuasive argument if we remember such irenic and pluralistic thinkers such as Montaigne. Hence I will continue to use the languages of modernity while recognizing that we are in a stage of its development quite different from the phase marked by the eighteenth, nineteenth and early twentieth century versions of it.

16. Of course, not all competent Whitehead scholars would call this separation a crisis, even though most take pains to try to explain this particular feature of Whitehead's definition of the category of the ultimate. For instance, see Christian (1959), Ford (1984), and Nobo (1986) for some detailed exegetical analysis of the issue. Wilmot, although with a very flawed methodology, makes this a central concern in his study of Whitehead's notion of God (1979).

A solid argument could also be made that Charles Hartshorne's revised neoclassical metaphysics is yet another attempt to get right Whitehead's insight into the nature of God and creativity. Cobb's influential study of a Whiteheadian natural theology likewise addresses the issue (1965).

17. The list of those who have written intelligently about this topic is much longer. I am primarily interested in those who have tried to develop their own constructive interpretations rather than those who have commented at length on the problem. Given the complexity of the Whiteheadian corpus, there is an entire commentarial tradition that tries to make sense out of what does not always seem to be coherence in Whitehead. For instance, William Christian (1959) is an excellent example of a learned commentator who deals with the notion of God's complex internal nature, as well as the God–world relationship. Another excellent commentary on *PR* that attempts to explicate the nature of God and creativity is Elizabeth M. Kraus (1979).

18. I find it interesting to note that Cobb, at the end of his interpretation of the relationship of God and creativity, stops with a reference to *PR* (Cobb 1965, 203–14). I believe that Whiteheadians can strengthen their arguments by making specific appeals to some parts of *AI* and *MT* as well as *PR*.

19. Although the rise of the modern process movement is marked by Whitehead by most scholars, Hartshorne and others have tried to demonstrate that Whitehead was not alone in attempting to bring process back into philosophic prominence in modern Western thought. For instance, James R. Gray's, *Modern Process Thought: A Brief Ideological History*, chronicles a number of other contributions of the process movement before and after Whitehead and Hartshorne.

20. Lewis Ford is the major exception to this generalization concerning responses to Neville's critique. He has taken Neville's criticism very seriously and has responded to these challenges in a number of important articles over the years that deal with a sophisticated Whiteheadian hermeneutic. For instance, his articles of 1987 and 1991, both of which deal with the question of creativity, try to show how Whitehead's thought can be modified to respond to Neville in terms of the coherence of process thought. The 1991 article on creation as creativity is especially noteworthy for offering a revision of Whitehead's theory of cosmological creativity.

21. Not long after the publication of *Creativity and God*, Hartshorne, Cobb, and Ford did write a collective response. While their responses clarified some of the issues between them and Neville, they did not attempt—and how could they have in a few short pages—to develop a major response. In the next issue of *Process Studies*, Neville thanked his critics without withdrawing his criticisms. However, it is important to note that Lewis Ford continues to respond to Neville, most recently in a 1991 journal article on alternative notions of creation.

22. Lewis Ford, also reacting to Neville's criticism, has made his own modification of Whitehead's notion of creation and God.

23. See David Hall and Roger Ames, *Anticipating China: Thinking through the Narratives of Chinese and Western Culture* (Albany: State University of New York Press, 1995, p. 293, n. 140).

24. The many problems with Wilmot's interpretation have been amply illustrated by David Griffin's (1981) extended and careful review of the book. While Griffin is correct in many of his points, he does not address the major problem with which Wilmot was trying to grapple: How to reconnect creativity and God in some coherent fashion. Perhaps there is no way to do so, but I believe that Wilmot was on to something, however flawed his presentation of the insight was.

25. In fact, the greatest debate in Korean Confucianism was the focus of a discussion about the relationship of *li-ch'i*. This was the famous "Four-Seven Debate." What makes the Korean debate so interesting is that it revolves around the question of the fundamental creativity of principle.

26. Arthur O. Lovejoy (1930) made just this sort of charge against Whitehead in his famous *The Revolt Against Dualism*. Of course, Lovejoy's book was completed before the publication of *PR, AI,* and *MT*.

27. Roger Ames (1993) has demonstrated that this kind of analysis of the assumptions of even a work such as Sun-tzu on the art of warfare share a common philosophic heritage with the other major pre-Han texts. We need to proceed with great caution in applying terms such as *metaphysics, ontology, and cosmology* to these basic classical Chinese intellectual assumptions until we have examined what we are doing philosophically. As we shall discover, it is not that the Chinese, especially the great Sung Neo-Confucian philosophers, were not interested in these issues, they just approached the questions involved from different historical angles and with different basic methodological assumptions.

The locus of Hall's and Ames' first discussion of *ars contextualis* is in their 1987 study of Confucius. It has been supplemented in their 1995 examination of the origins of Western and Confucian patterns of discourse.

28. The authors collected by Paul Kjellberg and Philip J. Ivanhoe in their study of Chuang Tzu would, no doubt, agree with Hall's hypothesis. The *Chuang Tzu* is truly a radical book, though none of the sinologists agree completely about how to define Chuang Tzu's particular brand of skepticism and relativism. Another study of Chuang Tzu, Kuang-ming Wu, *The Butterfly as Companion: Meditations on the First Three Chapters of the Chuang Tzu* (Albany: State University of New York Press, 1990), also shows what a free spirit Chuang Tzu was compared to the Confucians.

29. Chad Hansen (1992) has published *A Daoist Theory of Chinese Thought* based on his interpretation of Daoist thought as a key to understanding early Chinese intellectual history. Hansen, who truly loves the Daoists and Mohists as much as he dislikes the Confucians, has interesting insights into both Lao Tzu and Chuang-tzu. Hall and Ames (1995) make the claim that Hansen really has quite a non-Taoist theory if we accept the traditional Chinese understanding of Taoism, especially Chuang Tzu.

30. Of course, Whitehead makes use of his reading of the history of philosophy in *PR*. But in *AI* and *MT*, he expands the range of his commentary to include more social, technological, and economic history.

31. We also need to remember that Hartshorne called one of his major works *Creative Synthesis and Philosophic Method* (1970).

32. My formulation of the triad of form, dynamics, and unification originated in the matrix of my comparative study of Whitehead and Chu Hsi (and Ch'en Ch'un). The terms themselves are borrowed from the Whiteheadian sociologist W. Widick Schroeder (1976, 189 ff.). Of course, Paul Tillich contributed to Schroeder's terminology. See Paul Tillich, *Systematic Theology*, 3 vols. (Chicago: University of Chicago Press, 1951–63), 1: 174–82. Schroeder applies form, dynamics, and unification to the role of religious institutions in society. Schroeder's aim is descriptive of the sociology of religion whereas I use the triad for metasystemic analysis. I have discussed the use of this terminology and defended its appropriateness in another study. See also Berthrong (1994) for a longer discussion of the use of these terms.

33. For instance, see Irene Bloom's careful study of Lo Ch'in-shun's attempts to defend Chu Hsi against the attacks of other Ming thinkers who believed Chu did not understand the proper way to interpret the notion of the mind–heart (1987).

34. For a study of Mead's concept of the social self in relation to East Asian thought, see Odin (1996). Odin is primarily interested in the Japanese Zen tradition, but demonstrates how Mead's social self also fits quite well Neo-Confucian discourse.

35. This has been the substance of the debate that swirls around the work of Samuel Huntington and his thesis of the clash of civilizations. Huntington believes that there are truly separate civilizations and that there is no chance that one super, inclusive civilization is likely to appear in the immediate future. Therefore, the task of the diverse civilizations is to learn how to live together with some common civility. For the extended discussion of his thesis, see Huntington (1996).

2

The Development of God

The title of this chapter acknowledges a fruitful, complex, and perhaps even an illuminating ambiguity in the unfolding of Whitehead's narrative of God's relations with the world, an ambiguity transmitted as a fundamental problem for all Western philosophic theologies derived from his process philosophy.[1] Does the ambiguity reside in God *a se*? Or does the ambiguity reside in the developmental stages of Whitehead's own pilgrimage toward envisaging the divine reality? Or was Whitehead simply wrong on this point? Or does it signal a need for further refinement? Of course, whether or not this is viewed as fruitful ambiguity depends upon one's general interpretation of Whitehead's thought. For instance, if it really is the case that the ambiguity of exposition somehow expresses a fundamental ambiguity in God, then this view may be rejected on traditional theological grounds. Such ambiguity hardly seems to square with a notion of divinity without a shade of change. On the other hand, it also could be taken to express a modified form of the classic Calvinistic caution about the final inability of humankind to frame adequate descriptions of the divine reality.

There also is little doubt that, taken as a whole, Whitehead's notion of God is ambiguous or uneven, jagged—even if it is equally suggestive for theological discourse. The simple reason for this is that Whitehead, as Ford has demonstrated textually, was truly a philosopher in process (1984). Whitehead always appeared willing to revise and revisit his previous positions in light of further reflection and criticism. Both Whitehead and Chu were not afraid to review their work and to recast it in order to clarify or correct some previous mistakes, confusions, or oversights. That the subject matter itself might just be inherently ambiguous is always a possibility—especially so when the subject matter at hand was the divine aspect of the universe itself. Hence, I assume that Whitehead was aware of the problematic aspects of his notion of divine reality and continued to try to revise or refine his doctrine throughout his long and productive career in philosophy. As we shall see, *AI* does try to recast the discussion of divine matters technically defined in *PR*. Much the same can be asserted concerning Chu in terms of his persistent attempt to describe, for instance, the relationship of principle and matter–energy within a processive and relational world. In short, Chu was eager to describe the Tao in terms of the emerging and complex Neo-Confucian worldview.

The main burden of my present argument in this chapter is that Whitehead continued to revise his notion of God in certain sections of *AI*. Further, I posit that these Whiteheadian hints form the basis for a defense of his general philosophic theology, as well as a fertile matrix for a comparative philosophy that can engage other organic philosophic schools from different cultural traditions. The revised Whitehead schema I will elaborate is modified slightly from the picture we have based on Part V of *PR* in order to be receptive, at least in part, to larger global issues of comparative thought.

Furthermore, I need to be extra careful with this stage of the argument and not make too much of the hints that I believe I discern in *AI*. It is clear that Whitehead did not attempt a major revision of his natural theological, as recorded in *PR*, in *AI* or *MT*. Nonetheless, he does circle around the vexing themes of the divine nature, adding lapidary comments that warrant expansion by future generations. The Neo-Confucians would also certainly approve of this commentarial approach to the topic. I often have the sense that Whitehead must have known that he was providing a potential philosophic cottage industry because of the speed with which he wrote. He was right.

THE ENVISAGMENT OF GOD: *SCIENCE IN THE MODERN WORLD* TO *PROCESS AND REALITY*

The history of the unfolding of Whitehead's notion of God is a complicated subject.[2] The purpose of this chapter is not to review the whole history of the scholarly interpretation of the development of Whitehead's notion of God; however, the arguments for a revised Whiteheadian notion of God will not make a great deal of sense until we have an adequate outline of the basic material that needs to be modified. For instance, one cannot understand the strength of Neville's challenge to process theology unless there is a review of the ways Whitehead grappled with and transformed his notion of God from the preliminary explicit expositions of *SMW* and the reflections on the ultimate nature of divine concern found in *MT* at the end of his career.

While there is a great deal of debate about just what Whitehead meant by God, there is a growing consensus about the general pattern of the development of his reflections on the divine reality. For instance, as Ford (1984) has shown, the notion of God as a key formal element in Whitehead's maturing metaphysics emerges decisively in chapter XI of *SMW*. The second phase of the development takes place in *RM*; the third phase, and most influential stage, is the elaboration of the divine reality in terms of the primordial and consequent natures of God discussed in *PR*. I will argue that there is, at least in outline, a fourth stage to be found, however implicitly, in *AI* and *MT*. A great deal of my argument depends upon my demonstration that the fourth stage of *AI* and *MT* builds upon and attends to some of the problems occurring in the first three phases. It is this fourth stage that allows for a rich comparative philosophy and theology, especially a comparison to the East Asian Neo-Confucian tradition represented by Chu Hsi.

It is important to remember that the concept of God becomes important for Whitehead not as a religious issue or faith crisis but as a problem in philosophic speculation. His first appeal is to Aristotle, whom he believes is the last disinterested metaphysician in the Western tradition (*SMW*, 173). After Aristotle, Whitehead claims that ethical and religious motives enter into speculation about the nature of the divine reality that preclude a dispassionate philosophic investigation of divine matters. As we shall see, the religious turn is not a wholly negative development for Western intellectuals. Whitehead himself notes in *SMW* that without some kind of religious speculation, it is hardly likely that Western metaphysics would ever have moved much beyond Aristotle in this regard.

Whitehead's analysis of the Western proclivity for mixing philosophy and natural theology is in pointed contrast to the Confucian experience in East Asia. For instance, there have been endless arguments ever since the arrival of the Jesuits and other early modern Christian missionaries in China about whether or not one can find theism in the Chinese classics. The Jesuits developed a theory that the Shang notion of Shang Ti and the later related Chou idea of T'ien as High Heaven are resolutely theistic.[3] Hence some Jesuits demonstrated, at least to their own satisfaction, that early Chinese thought was theistic.[4] The problem for the early Christian missionary history of Chinese thought then was to explain how things had gone so wrong after such positive beginnings in the Shang and Chou dynasties. For the Jesuits, the wrong turn was supremely self-evident in the Sung renaissance with scholars like Chu Hsi and his Northern Sung masters. The standard Jesuit line was that Chu Hsi was an out and out materialist, a representative of a perverse naturalist school that had lost contact with the God of the early Confucian classics. It was one of the duties of the Jesuit mission to reintroduce the Chinese literati to their authentic religious and theistic past. Most Chinese Neo-Confucians politely declined the Jesuit offer to combine philosophy and natural theology.[5]

What frustrated the early Jesuits, often remarkably able scholars of the Chinese tradition, was the refusal of the literati to see the importance of the Jesuit rediscovery of the proper reading of the primal Confucian religious past. There are few more wonderful examples of ships passing in the night of conceptual and intellectual taste than the early Jesuit–Confucian encounters. At best, the Chinese simply ignored the Jesuit gambit for the impeccable cultural reason that most of the development of Confucian discourse simply took another direction.[6] David Hall and Roger Ames, in trying to focus our attention on this difference in cultural sensibilities, have even devised a separate name, *ars contextualis*, to label the characteristic Chinese fundamental intellectual preoccupations (1987, 1995).[7] The long and the short of it was that God was simply not on the agenda of the typical Neo-Confucian.[8]

Returning to Whitehead, most scholars argue that the short chapter on God in *SMW* was his first major attempt to restate the metaphysical nature of the divine reality based on his post–Enlightenment understanding of science and cosmology. In the philosophic sense of natural theology, Whitehead tries to update Aristotle on the basis of contemporary science and cosmology. Such a revisioning suggests to Whitehead the notion of God as the principle of limitation. Whitehead argues that if we accept the reality of the actual entities, then

> ... we must provide a ground for limitation which stands among the attributes of the substantial activity. . . . In this argument the point to notice is, that what is metaphysically indeterminate has nevertheless to be categorically determinate. (*SMW*, 178)

Although the image of God in *SMW* is not as robust or active a concept of God as will emerge in Whitehead's later writings, it does not contravene the main points of Whitehead's more mature doctrine. First, Whitehead's God always provides certain limitations to the potential and actual creativity of the cosmos at any given point by means of the divine envisagement of appropriate initial aims for the concrescing creatures—to borrow the more complex language of *PR*. Second, God is indeed a most active if austere agent throughout Whitehead's mature philosophic development in the United States. This is one of the main points of contention with Neville, as we shall see in chapter 3. On the other hand, the early doctrine of limitation also is an important strength for those who take Whitehead to be headed in the right direction in terms of the definition of God's nature and role in creation.

In chapter XII of *SMW*, Whitehead engages in a discussion of the nature of religion and science. In terms of religion, it is plea for religion to realize that even its most cherished expressions and dogmas change over time. "Its principles may be eternal, but the expression of those principles requires continual development" (*SMW*, 189). At the end of the chapter he expresses his conviction about what the real worship of God requires. "The worship of

God is not a rule of safety—it is an adventure of the spirit, a flight after the unattainable. The death of religion comes with the repression of the high hope of adventure" (*SMW*, 192). Whitehead will return to this supreme adventure in *AI*, as we shall see.

It is interesting to note that Whitehead also offers one of his epigrammatic, terse definitions of religion in *SMW*. "Religion is the reaction of human nature to its search for God" (*SMW*, 191). With appropriate modification, this is probably as good a one-sentence definition of religion as one can expect from a Whiteheadian perspective. Unfortunately it is not the single definition often remembered and celebrated in critiques of the process tradition; that distinction goes to the Whiteheadian observation that religion is what we do with our solitariness. This second definition of religion as the solitary is consistently misinterpreted as a suggestion on Whitehead's part that religion is something singular, isolated, and individual. Even a cursory reading of *RM* should illumine the fact that the pure solipsistic nature of an isolated religious quest is not what Whitehead meant by religion, even though he did recognize the personal nature of religion. Whitehead knew that religion is a profoundly collective activity.

The search for God as the divine reality is, if given a broad enough definition of God, within the purview of Chu Hsi's Neo-Confucianism. For Chu, the search for reality ultimately leads to the profound transformation of the human mind–heart, the real and actual conformation of human nature to the divine nature (if we understand the Neo-Confucian interpretation of the primordial Mind of Tao as a Confucian analog to the Western divine reality— which I admit is a grand conceptual leap of faith). Having learned more about various South and East Asian religions since Whitehead wrote, we will want to translate the West Asian and European theistic term *God* into something more like ultimate reality, or even more austerely if we really take our Buddhist colleagues seriously, as the way things really are insofar as they can be known by the human intellect. Recently John Hick (1989) has argued that this search for the divine reality is a search for the soteriological turn from ignorance, blindness, or self-centeredness to reality-centeredness. The theological quest, at its best, assists the soteriological transformation and is not just an intellectual quest for proper terminology per se.

In terms of the evidence for the divine reality, in no sense does Whitehead privilege one tradition over another. He is a pluralist in the sociology of religion as well as in cosmology.

> A diversification among human communities is essential for the provision of the incentive and material for the Odyssey of the human spirit. Other nations of different habits are not enemies: they are godsends. Men require of their

neighbours something sufficiently akin to be understood, something sufficiently different to provoke attention, and something great enough to command admiration. (*SMW*, 207)

This is, in terms of David Tracy's (1981) outline of the structure of the audiences for modern theology, a fundamental theology in that it does not warrant the specific theology, canon, or scripture of one tradition over another. Rather, it is unspecific (or vague as Neville puts it, following Peirce in this thematization of such hypotheses) in terms of the method, sources, and content of the search for God by means of the revealed theology, tradition, and experience of any one tradition. However, in our search for the divine reality, what we find represented in living persons as embedded, organic members of a tradition is much richer in specificities due to the fact that each and every one of us is a member of a special religious culture, even if that culture is itself multiform in tradition, method of interpretation, praxis, and content.

Even in *SMW* Whitehead provides some clues about what he thinks a mature modern religious consciousness should be.

> Religion is the vision of something which stands beyond, behind, and within, the passing flux of immediate things; something which is real, and yet waiting to be realised; something which is a remote possibility, and yet the greatest present facts; something that gives meaning to all that passes, and yet eludes apprehension; something whose possession is the final good, and yet is beyond all reach; something which is the ultimate ideal, and the hopeless quest. (*SMW*, 191–92)

What is fascinating is how often Whitehead resorts to such paired contrasts—the realized and what needs to be realized, what is within and beyond, and so on—when he speaks of the divine reality. There is always, just as in Part V of *PR*, the balance of complex and dynamic interaction of the world and God, the notion of what is and what is not and yet what can be the source of hope in the midst of despair. Whitehead's own search for this something beyond the raw data of purely concrete empirical comprehension continues in all of his later writings.

Whitehead returned to the question of God's nature in *Religion in the Making*. Here too he is seeking to

> ... direct attention to the foundation of religion on our apprehension of those permanent elements by reason of which there is a stable order in the world, permanent elements apart from which there could be no changing world. (*RM*, preface ii)

And again, although this is not the way he puts the issue in *PR* and *AI*, there is nothing in this notion of the religious quest that contravenes his further search for a specification of the divine reality. Chu Hsi likewise becomes justly famous for making a similar kind of philosophic move in basing a critical part of his philosophy on Ch'eng I's notion of principle as the formal element of any object–event. Principle as the Supreme Ultimate expresses these permanent elements of the world without which there would be no order at all. This gave Chu the key he needed to meld the thought of his Northern Sung masters into his distinctive synthesis.

Major sections of *RM* are given over to Whitehead's examination of the religious history of humankind.[9] Without such a recourse to religious experience and history, Whitehead did not believe that a philosopher could move much beyond Aristotle's austere notion of divinity as the unmoved mover. In terms of the broadest sweep of human religious history, Whitehead argues that the notion of the divine reality usually takes one of three forms in the modern world. First, there is the East Asian notion "of an impersonal order to which the world conforms." Second, there is the Semitic notion "of a definite personal individual entity, whose existence is the one ultimate metaphysical fact, absolute and underivative, and who decreed and ordered the derivative existence which we, as finite creatures, call the actual world." Third, there is the pantheistic notion "of an entity to be described in the terms of the Semitic concept, except that the actual world is a phase within the complete fact which is this ultimate individual entity" (*RM*, 66–67). As we shall see, none of these forms is acceptable to Whitehead in an unmodified fashion, even though he is willing to consider the partial vision of each of these definitions of the divine reality as contributing to an enriched understanding of God. It strikes Whitehead as silly to not make use of our increased awareness of the divine reality brought about by a broader angle of vision as it would be to refuse to let modern science guide us in our understanding of cosmology.

Lewis Ford, along with every other major Whitehead scholar, is correct in noting a truly major shift in Whitehead's philosophic development in *RM*, a shift that has dramatic implications for his theory of God (1984). For one thing, Ford observes that in *RM* Whitehead conclusively embraces cosmological pluralism. Ford argues that prior to this espousal of pluralism in *RM*, Whitehead really had a more monistic cast to the structure of his thought. This kind of monistic analysis seems just a bit forced, as no one would ever mistake Whitehead for Sankara or Spinoza. What Ford means by monism is that Whitehead in *SMW* held that all of the creatures were "merely modes of the underlying substantial activity" (Ford 1984, 127). Ford understands this substantial activity to be something like Bergson's *élan vital* in the sense that all things are created as modes of this underlying reality. In terms of Watson's and Dilworth's archic analysis of global philosophic families (see appendix), Whitehead moves from an early and tentative affirmation of a substrative ontological focus to his mature essentialist focus on the pluralistic actual entities of *PR* and all of his later works.

What is clear is that in *RM* Whitehead now sketches the following picture of his system, with an expanded role for God.

1. The creativity whereby the actual world has its character of temporal passage to novelty.
2. The realm of ideal entities, or forms, which are in themselves not actual, but are such that they are exemplified in everything that is actual, according to some proportion of relevance.
3. The actual but non-temporal entity whereby the indetermination of mere creativity is transmuted into a determinate freedom. This non-temporal actual entity is what men call God—the supreme God of rationalized religion. (*RM*, 90)

Along with a clearly pluralist vision of the cosmos, Whitehead is moving toward a doctrine of God as an actual entity among the other actual entities or object–events. This is one of the distinctive features of his mature thought that separates process thought from most other strains of contemporary theology. We also need to notice that in *RM* God and creativity are considered separate modalities of the system; this is a feature of Whitehead's reflection on the divine reality that raises the question of coherence for him and his interpreters. Also, the final terminological refinements for God as thematized in *PR* as the primordial and consequent natures are not yet in place. Nonetheless, we do have most of the major actors of the drama of creation in place: creativity, God, the world, the actual entities and ideal entities (later called eternal objects).

As Ford correctly observes, the shift to pluralism has implications for Whitehead's analysis of the process by which creatures come to be concrete object–events. Most specifically, "The shift to pluralism also focussed Whitehead's attention upon the nature of an actual occasion's internal process" (Ford 1984, 129). The reason for this new concern is that Whitehead now has to demonstrate how the actual entities manifest their unique creative advance into novelty. In many ways, *PR* is an extended examination of the question of the concrescence of actual entities necessitated by a pluralistic vision of reality. Again, there are distinctive Sung Neo-Confucian analogies to Whitehead's concern in Chu Hsi's attempt to show what the role of creativity is within an organic Confucianism. For Chu, the real problem is how one can become a sage by means of the cultivation of the mind–heart/*hsin* that unifies the emotional and analytic sides of human nature. While Chu borrowed the notion of principle from Ch'eng I, his favorite interpretation of the role of the mind–heart is drawn from Chang Tsai (1020–1077). The key for Chu is Chang Tsai's doctrine that the mind–heart unites human nature (principle) with human emotion (*ch'i* or matter–energy).

As we indicate previously, Ford argues that *RM* lacks one more essential item in Whitehead's theory of divine reality: God's consequent nature. Ford's argument is highly technical and basically boils down to the claim that although we have anticipations of the notion of the consequent nature of God the distinctive articulation of this additional refinement does not actually emerge until Part V of *PR*.[10] Whereas Ford is no doubt correct in terms of the specifics of the technical vocabulary and complexity of insight, Cobb (1965) is likewise astute in arguing that language about God in *RM* prefigures the more technical discussions of God's various natures in *PR*. Both Cobb and Ford agree that the language about God in *RM* is highly proleptic when compared and contrasted to *PR*.

All Whitehead scholars agree that the third phase of Whitehead's elaboration of the notion of God comes with *PR*. Here, all of the technical elements, all of the verbal tools for explication of the divine reality, are collected if not reconciled. Most importantly, as Ford has documented, the consequent nature of God is added to the mix. As we would expect, this additional material is important for the major argument of this essay as it relates all three parts to Whitehead's analysis of God in *PR*. These three elements are the primordial, the consequent, and the superjective nature of God (*PR*, 87–88). For my constructive and comparative purposes, the consequent and superjective natures are the most interesting. Briefly, the three aspects are

> *Primordial Nature*: "The 'primordial nature' of God is the concrescence of a unity of conceptual feelings, including among their data all eternal objects" (*PR*, 87–88).
> *Consequent Nature*: "The 'consequent nature' of God is the physical prehension of God of the actualities of the evolving universe" (*PR*, 88).
> *Superjective Nature*: "The 'superjective nature' of God is the character of the pragmatic value of his specific satisfaction qualifying the transcendent creativity in the various temporal instances" (*PR*, 88).

I will not devote a great deal of time to addressing the third stage of Whitehead's speculations on the divine reality at this point in the argument. Questions about the nature and relationships of the various aspects of God as outlined in Part V of *PR* will be recurring themes for the next five chapters of the study. Besides, many competent commentators, such as Ford, Nobo, Christian, Hall, Neville, Wilmot, Kraus, and Sherburne, can be consulted for detailed exegesis of the terminological, textual, philosophic, and theological questions raised by Whitehead's discussion of God in *PR*. At this time, I merely want to flag the potential problem that the description of the superjective nature of God raises for the whole enterprise. Furthermore, I note the introduction of pragmatic aims, values, and specific satisfaction qualifying transcendent creativity in the third aspect of God's tripartite nature as superjective. I also will defer my discussion of Whitehead's further suggestions about the divine reality in *AI* and *MT* until a later section of the essay.

THE PROBLEM OF THE SEPARATION OF GOD AND CREATIVITY IN *PR* IN TERMS OF THE FUNDAMENTAL ELEMENTS OF THE SPECULATIVE SYSTEM

We must now seek to discover if we have a major problem caused by the separation of God and creativity, and if we do, how significant it really is for process philosophy and theology. My belief, following such commentators as Christian, Cobb, Ford, Nobo, Neville, and Hall, is that we do indeed have a problem with the separation of any and all of God's various natures from the primal category of creativity, as elaborated on in *PR*. However, the estimation of the kind and severity of the problem varies from interpreter to interpreter. Some, like Ford, believe that the separation of these important notions of God and creativity is not a problem but rather a strength. Hence, Ford argues that what is taken for an incoherence by critical scholars such as Neville is not really a problem at all if understood as one of the truly creative aspects of Whitehead's achievement. But if we accept for the moment that the separation question is a problem, what kind of problem is it? Does it indicate a fatal flaw in Whitehead's philosophy? Does it damage the potential use of Whitehead's philosophy for fundamental theological and philosophic reconstruction?

To answer these and other related questions, we must return to the scene of the crime, Whitehead's masterpiece of creative speculative thought, *PR*. The origin of the perceived problem begins as innocently as any fundamental problem can in Section II of "The Categoreal Scheme." It is here that Whitehead introduces his 'Category of the Ultimate,' the locus of the contentious problem of God and creativity. "The Category of the Ultimate expresses the general principle presupposed in the three more special categories" (*PR*, 21). Key to Whitehead's explanation of this category is the notion of creativity with a capital C.

'Creativity,' 'many,' 'one' are the ultimate notions involved in the meaning of the synonymous terms 'things,' 'being,' entity.' These three notions complete the Category of the Ultimate and are presupposed in all the more special categories. (*PR*, 21).

Generations of theologians, no doubt eager to make sure that God receives all of the metaphysical compliments due God's status in the Western tradition, have been quick to notice that God is not one of the primal notions found in the Category of the Ultimate. Many theologians simply lose interest at this point. Some have gone on to argue that creativity is really Whitehead's ultimate divine reality because God, along with everything else, is in the grip of creativity. They point out that, however interesting this linking of God and creativity may be in terms of natural theology, it does little to help reform Christianity in the late twentieth century in terms of systematic or praxis theology.[11] At best, it is a kind of deism that lacks any truly sustained connection with the narrative of the Christian gospel, traditions, or church theology.

Nonetheless, it was clear that Whitehead is extremely interested in the notion of creativity in this laconic exposition of the Category of the Ultimate. The initial sequence of the definition of the traits of the ultimate, creativity takes pride of place before the notion of the "many" and the "one." For instance, we find these statements about the nature and role of creativity following one after the other in this definitional exposition in Part I of *PR*.

> (a) " 'Creativity' is the universal of universals characterizing ultimate matter of fact. It is the ultimate principle by which the many, which are the universe disjunctively, become the one actual occasion, which is the universe conjunctively."
> (b) " 'Creativity' is the principle of *novelty*. An actual occasion is a novel entity diverse from any entity in the 'many' which it unifies."
> (c) "The ultimate metaphysical principle is the advance from disjunction to conjunction, creating a novel entity other than the entities given in disjunction" (*PR*, 21).

However, it is important to remember that whatever the high value Whitehead places on creativity, it was only one of the elements embedded in the Category of the Ultimate. There are other crucial aspects of his philosophy that must be kept in the penumbra if not focal range of consciousness when considering Whitehead's metasystem. For instance, following Whitehead's list in *AI*, I believe that there are at least seven key elements of Whitehead's metasystem that cannot be overlooked in trying to place any part of the whole in its proper context. These seven are: (1) The Ontological Principle, (2) the Category of the Ultimate, (3) the Principle of Relativity, (4) the Principle of Process, (5) the hope of rationalism, (6) the Final Triad and (7) God as an actual entity. Given the complexity of the development and content of Whitehead's thought, other scholars have their own favorite lists of key elements.[12] There is actually a great deal of overlap in all of these lists, with the notions of creativity, process, actuality, and relatedness being key to all of the taxonomies. Even Whitehead's short list of seven items in *AI* is functional rather than exhaustive or even systematic.

Whitehead begins his exposition of the metasystem of *PR* by indicating the resolutely realistic and pluralistic nature of his vision. " 'Actual entities'—also termed 'actual occasions'—are the final real things of which the world is made up" (*PR*, 18). The final facts, the explicanda of all that is, are basically the same cosmological units, object–events in my own terminology, in terms of the metasystem. Some object–events are surely more important than others, but all are of one kind in terms of cosmological and ontological parity in a pluralistic cosmos. In this regard, Whitehead, at least in terms of his own self-understanding, wants to link his philosophy to Descartes and John Locke; Whitehead is well within the discourse of modernity itself, even if he represents a later phase of its development.

Whitehead's technical term for his defense of a realistic pluralism is the "Ontological Principle" as the principle of actual entity/object–event as the foundation of all that is, at least in this cosmic era. "The Ontological Principle can be summarized as: no actual entity, then no reason" (*PR*, 19). Or, "In other words, final causation and atomism are interconnected principles" (*PR*, 19). I believe that there is a reason that Whitehead begins here with the actual entities rather than with notions such as process or creativity. Whitehead's mature philosophic position is finally and ultimately a realistic pluralism: there are many things— from God to the most insignificant puff of existence in the farthest reaches of space—and all are equally real according to the Ontological Principle. In this he is distinctly modern, as Neville has located process thought within the history of modern philosophy as yet another example of a modern philosophy of cosmological closure or pluralism (1992, 1993). Whitehead asserts that we cannot get behind the actual entities in search of something more fundamental to the cosmos—either this cosmos or any other for that matter. This is a key philosophic trait shared by Chu Hsi and his school in their self-definition as a realistic teaching (*shih*). An organic event pluralism is one of the features Chu believed differentiated Confucian thought from Taoism and Buddhism, traditions of nothingness (*wu*) and emptiness (*k'ung*), respectively.

This is precisely one of the nodes of contention between Whitehead and his modern Platonic critics, such as Neville. If there is a fundamental ontological difference such as radical transcendence between God and the world, much less the creatures of the world, then it is hard for the creatures to make any sense of the utterly transcendent nature of God, which is not subject to any rational principles of analysis as are all of the other creatures because it is, per definition, utterly transcendent. In fact, if utter transcendence is all that can be said (and Neville agrees with this kind of statement),[13] it is then impossible to say anything definite about God, who may be the "ground" of creation in some analogical or poetic fashion, but is not one determinate thing among the other things. As we shall see, Neville believes that the notion of God as creator demands this indeterminate understanding of the divine reality. Whitehead disagrees.

> The worst of a gulf is, that it is very difficult to know what is happening on the further side of it. That has been the fate of the God of traditional theology. It is only by drawing the long bow of mysticism that evidences for his existence can be collected from our temporal world. (*AI*, 217)

In short, what is a virtue for Whitehead, namely the creaturely nature of the divine reality, is a fault for Neville. But faithful Whiteheadians should remain skeptical about claims from knowledge gotten by the shots of an ontological long bow, even as elegant and as sophisticated as Neville's bow may be.[14] Of course, there may be other ways to find out what is on the other side of the ontological gulf according to many religious traditions. There is always personal religious experience and special revelation in private and public ways; there is the beauty of liturgy, ritual, chant, light in stained glass, prayer, and meditation. If revelation is recorded as a text, scripture, or canon this can provide knowledge about the divine reality to those who accept the revelation, even if it is stoutly maintained in the specific revelation that the divine reality is not really much like the mundane things of the mundane world. Nonetheless, Whitehead's Ontological Principle stands as a principle of radically realistic pluralism precluding any such mystical or communal appeal to special revelation on natural philosophic grounds.

Because I have already outlined the details of the second element of the short list of essentials of Whitehead's thought, the Category of the Ultimate, I will not repeat what was said there beyond remarking that this is the category in which creativity emerges as an important, even defining, element of the Whiteheadian system. But it also is important to remember that the Category of the Ultimate includes as well the notion of the many, the one, and creativity. Whitehead does not want us to forget the explicit pluralism of the Ontological Principle.

The third element is the Principle of Relativity. One of the more illuminating of Whitehead's definitions of this principle is stated as the fourth of the Categories of Explanation. "In other words, it belongs to the nature of a 'being' that it is a potential for every 'becoming.' This is the 'principle of relativity' " (*PR*, 22). This is Whitehead's way of stating the universal relatedness of all that is, all that can be dreamed of, all of whatever constitutes any possible world.

> The principle of universal relativity directly traverses Aristotle's dictum, 'A substance is not present in a subject.' On the contrary, according to this principle an actual entity *is* present in other actual entities. In fact if we allow for degrees of relevance, and for negligible relevance, we must say that every actual entity is present in every other actual entity. The philosophy of organism is mainly devoted to the task of making clear the notion of 'being present in another entity.' (*PR*, 50)

Anyone who has tried to understand Whitehead's later elaboration of the concrescence of actual entities will fully appreciate how seriously he took this principle.

Whitehead also is clear that the Principle of Relativity is not a form of radical relativism wherein anything goes and that any opinion is as logical or coherent as any other.[15] Quite the contrary, Whitehead's version of the Principle of Relativity expressed the real importance of each actual entity for the internal constitution of every other actual entity as a locus of value and not the indifference of relativism qua indifferentism. For Whitehead, things are relative in the sense of being related, but not always in the sense of mattering in a conscious or even a meaningful sense. All things matter to each other in varying degrees, from the crucial to the casual, and perfectly for the divine reality, that great lover of all the details. Here again we also see that agency qua actuality is the function of object–events. God is the supreme example of this agency, but is not the only such agent. As Hartshorne so often argues, God is the supreme example of relationality in any cosmic epoch but not the only example (1948).

The fourth item is the Principle of Process. Whitehead defines this principle as the ninth of the categories of explanation.[16]

> That *how* an actual entity *becomes* constitutes *what* that actual entity *is*; so that the two descriptions of an actual entity are not independent. Its 'being' is constituted by its 'becoming.' This is the 'principle of process' (*PR*, 23)

Later he notes that "This principle states that the *being* of a *res vera* is constituted by its 'becoming.' . . . Process is the becoming of experience" (*PR*, 166). Here again we can see the relentless realistic pluralism of Whitehead's vision. Process is important in the system, but so are the object–events that become. There is the process and the reality of actual entities co-constituting the eternal creation of new actual entities and their creative experience of value, form, and some kind of unified actuality. It is just this understanding of the creative drive of the universe that has caused the movement derived from Whitehead's mature thought to be called process philosophy and theology. But however important process is, it is salutary to remember that Whitehead himself called his philosophy a system of organism.

The fifth item is not an ultimate category or even a major principle within Whitehead's system. Nonetheless, I believe that without the fifth item we cannot understand what drove Whitehead to elaborate this system. I have chosen to call this the hope of rationalism.

> That we fail to find in experience any elements intrinsically incapable of exhibition as examples of general theory is the hope of rationalism. This hope is not a metaphysical premise. It is the faith which forms the motive for the pursuit of all sciences alike, including metaphysics. (*PR*, 42)

Such rationalism is not very popular these days in theological, philosophic, or cultural-critical circles. For instance, deconstructionism tells us, in principle, that Whiteheadian rationalism is just another bad example of the dream of presence, a search for the foundation of being that cannot be found, and in fact, should not be sought. But it is just as important to note what Whitehead does not say as what he does say. He does not argue that we can explain everything adequately; this is especially the case for metaphysical foundations. Human finitude, ignorance, and error always make it possible that we will be wrong and that there will simply be events or things or even actual entities that we cannot explain. Chaos is as real as order, at least in this cosmic epoch. Notwithstanding such ruminations, Whitehead still holds that we should, on principle, devise systems that can deal with all of our experience, drunk as well as sober, constructive and deconstructed.

While it is clear that Whitehead is not an orthodox Christian, the element of hope does speak to faith in the depths of its seeking the divine reality. If theology is the science of interpreting our experience of the divine reality, then it is an aspect of the hope of rationalism that we can say something rational about God. Whether Hartshorne is correct in his various statements about what we can really know about God, Whitehead would probably have approved of his student's willingness to explore the meaning of the divine reality in terms of the hope of rationalism. Hope is just that and nothing more. It is a not a mystical appeal to private experience or revelation. "But in itself the faith does not embody a premise from which the theory starts; it is an ideal which is seeking satisfaction. Insofar as we believe that doctrine, we are rationalists" (*PR*, 42). The hope of rationalism is one of those places where moral intuition passes over into religion.

The sixth item in the list is what I call the Final Triad of God, the World, and Creativity. I should note that this is my phrasing and not Whitehead's way of stating the issue. By calling these three elements a triad I stress the tripartite nature of his system as well as highlight a very problematic area of his thought for theology; it also allows me to signal the cross-cultural comparative element of the discussion because of its connections to *li-hsüeh*. For Chu Hsi's axiology as moral anthropology, the triad includes the mind–heart, the emotions, and human nature. I will thematize this triad as form, dynamics, and unification.

Whitehead defined the Final Triad in the following way:

> God and the World are the contrasted opposites in terms of which Creativity achieves its supreme task of transforming disjointed multiplicity, with its diversities in opposition, into concrescent unity, with its diversities in contrast. (*PR*, 348)

This is precisely the kind of statement that causes critics such as Neville to claim that Whitehead suffers from an incurable strain of arbitrariness. The reason for this arises from the following kind of self-interpretation of the Final Triad: "Both (i.e., God and the World) are in the grip of the ultimate metaphysical ground, the creative advance into novelty. Either of them, God and the World, is the instrument of novelty for the other" (*PR*, 349). As we shall see in the next chapter, Neville rightly jumps all over this kind of explanation of the Final Triad, an explanation that separates creativity from the essence of the divine nature. My proposal will be directed toward an alternative reading of the Final Triad in light of Whitehead's own further reflections on the nature of the divine reality in *AI* and *MT*.

As we have already seen, Whitehead's Final Triad also allows the introduction of materials from the Sung Neo-Confucian synthesis of Chu Hsi and his school. As I argue in chapter 5, the Chu Hsi school has a tripartite system that offers instructive analogies to Whitehead's work. In fact, I believe that both Chu Hsi and Whitehead are members of a larger relational and process family of philosophic speculation. Their differences are as important as their similarities, yet the larger structure of their work provides a wonderful harmony for the generation of new symphonic variations of world philosophy and theology.

The seventh and last item from the *AI* list, and a crucial one for my argument, is Whitehead's stated conviction that God is an actual entity.

'Actual entities'—also termed 'actual occasions'—are the final real things of which the world is made up. There is no going behind actual entities to find anything more real. They differ among themselves; God is an actual entity, and so is the most trivial puff of existence in far-off empty space. But, though there are gradations of importance, and diversities of function, yet in the principles which actuality exemplifies all are on the same level. The final facts are, all alike, actual entities; and these actual entities are drops of experience, complex and interdependent. (*PR*, 18)

Many questions have been raised about this way of stating the issue as far as the divine reality is concerned. For instance, many Christians theologians, raised on the notion of radical transcendence, believe that such a doctrine of God's nature violates revelation as well as the foundational Western sense of the divine numinous as somehow separate from the creatures of the world. Furthermore, does this kind of doctrine contravene Neville's interpretation of the role of Creativity in the Final Triad? As a working hypothesis, I will try to construe Whitehead's intent with utter religious and philosophic serious-ness when he says that God is an actual entity and will apply this insight to the philosophic reconstruction of his natural theology.

I also realize that this assertion of the ontological priority of actual en-tities (or object–events in light of the Neo-Confucian contribution) is one of the most complicated and contested questions in process thought. It is such a difficult notion that Hartshorne abandons the notion of God as an actual entity simpliciter as an incoherent notion and replaces it with his social definition of God (1948, 1967, 1970, 1972). Hartshorne believes that we should view the divine reality in terms of what Whitehead calls a "society of actual entities." Or, in Hartshorne's more technical way of stating the issue, God has the ability to surpass even God's own previous realities and hence is a social rather than solitary, unconnected atomic self. God cannot be sur-passed by another object–event but can surpass any previous state in terms of the unique process of divine creativity itself. Hence Hartshorne is extremely nervous about the definition of God as an actual entity in any simplistic fashion that would imply complete singularity or isolation as definitive for the divine reality. In fact, almost all Whiteheadian scholars, with Hartshorne and Neville being two prime examples, have problems with Whitehead's state-ment that God is an actual entity.[17]

I contend that we should not give up too quickly on the notion of God as an actual entity/object–event. Whitehead stated it often enough that he must have believed that this was the right direction for the analysis and understanding of the divine reality. It was not a casual or nontechnical state-ment. Nor was it an example of Whitehead's poetic prose. It is a sober statement of what Whitehead took to be the case about the divine reality. However, all of this preliminary affirmation does not mean that there are not any problems with the way the issue is worked out in *PR*. Merely stating that something is so does not make the case nor does it provide a reasoned defense of the position. One of the main points of this study is that, especially in terms of the separation of creativity from God's nature, the notion needs to be refined fairly radically. *AI* and *MT* must be revisited to discover one way out of the problems noticed by Hartshorne and Neville.

A PATRISTIC INTERLUDE

Many scholars have been perplexed by the nature of Whitehead's problematic assertion about the essential separation of God and creativity. Nor do I assert that my revisionist comparative schema is the only viable solution to the question; the question, by its very nature, is not susceptible to consensus even among the learned at this point, or perhaps any point. This kind of question may be the sort that the Buddhists call a question without an answer.[18] That is why people are always nervous about discussing religion, ontology, cosmology, and politics.

The resolution of the problem that I propose also has a distinctively comparative bias in terms of its theological and philosophical referents. I believe that Chu Hsi can really assist the search for a solution to the question of the place of creativity within global process thought. What I will seek to do, in terms of revisioning Whitehead's thought, is to show that one can frame a notion of God that includes creativity in such a way that it remains faithful to Whitehead's own vision, as well as to address the pressing questions of scholars like Neville who have challenged the process answer to this question of the separation of God and creativity.

As Whitehead himself noted in *AI*, some early Christian intellectuals tried to deal with this question, albeit with a restricted focus, in the extended discussion of the question of the nature of Christ. What I understand Whitehead to be suggesting in *AI* is that this was a fruitful way to proceed in the analysis of the problem, even if the early Christian thinkers did not expand the range of their discussion far enough to give a better answer to the question of creativity and God–world relations. So much is clear from Whitehead's own comments.

This theological bias toward patristic theology relates to an important influence attributed to Whitehead's own work. One of the greatest impacts of the process movement has been on theological studies for the obvious reason that Whitehead was indulging in philosophic speculations with a distinctly theological tone.[19] One could make a good case that Whitehead has created a new and modern natural theology because of his speculation on God's nature. But whatever else Whitehead's theological speculations were, they were not sectarian in a confessional or conventional Christian sense. They were not specifically Christian except for the fact that Whitehead himself was raised in a Christian environment and knew much more about the Christian intellectual tradition than any other world religion. We know that Whitehead also was very interested in other religious traditions, especially Buddhism, and that his natural theology is not just a Christian reflection, even though its matrix was Christian in terms of his own life. Whitehead's rejection of any intellectually limiting sectarian Christian affiliation or intent was carefully recorded by his friends in various private conversations.[20]

At the end of his life, no one could claim that Whitehead was an orthodox Christian, either by profession of faith or active participation in any church polity. Nonetheless, he still did write natural theology in that he speculated, perhaps more like Plato, Aristotle, and Hume than St. John, St. Paul, or St. Thomas, on the nature of the divine reality he called God. Nor could anyone who had not been steeped in Christian liturgy and piety have written Part V of *PR*.

In truth, Whitehead only left some suggestions about what he thinks this revised natural theology should look like. It is true that Whitehead indicates approval of the work done in Alexandria and Antioch, but there is enough Whiteheadian silence on these topics to make us cautious. For instance, it is not always obvious who Whitehead had in mind in his short list of those who made a philosophic advance on Plato. We know from Whitehead's conversations with his friends and students, as recorded by Lucien Price (1954), that there was a period in his life that he read a great deal of theology in Cambridge.[21] But we also should remember that he often used his theological reading to overcome insomnia, and when he could sleep again, he emphatically gave up his study of Christian theology. However, the impact of all this reading and reflection surely also stayed with Whitehead, at least as some kind of somatic background to his future speculations, even if the details became a bit fuzzy over time due to a lack of sustained interest in the subject qua Christian systematic theology.

For instance, Laurence Wilmot mistakes Whitehead's suggestion about a possible solution to the problem of the relationship of God and creativity for the much stronger claim that the early patristic fathers really did solve all of the problems involved in the proper definition of the divine reality. What Whitehead seems to have meant is that these early Christian thinkers *indicated* a direction wherein progress can be made in revisioning the nature of the divine reality. There is a great deal of difference between a plausible suggestion and an actual articulation of a coherent, logical, adequate, and applicable systematic treatment of the issue. For instance, I believe that Whitehead would demand a wider range of vision than just early Christian sources for the construction of a modern natural theology. This is clear from his discussion of the wide range of religious experience in *RM*. This need for a wide range of religious resources is one reason Whitehead called for a new reformation in *AI*—the need for a religious vision for a global and humane human flourishing. As an addition to Whitehead's interest in civilized experience, I have included a discussion of the Southern Sung Neo-Confucians, with a focus on Chu Hsi and Ch'en Ch'un (1159–1223), in order to expand the conversation beyond the boundaries of the Western European intellectual tradition.[22]

One of the key goals of this essay will be to reconstruct a plausible version of what Whitehead might have said if confronted with an articulate critique of process cosmology, such as R.C. Neville. As I will argue, I believe that we can find significant hints about how to proceed in the direction of theological and philosophic reconstruction based on *AI* and *MT*. The key question, as Whitehead recognized it would always be for theology, is what we mean by God. It is to this question as posed by Neville that we now turn in the last section of this chapter and chapter 3.

THE ANTICIPATION OF COORDINATION

Wilmot explains Whitehead's problem with the definition of God's creative agency as follows: "What becomes evident throughout this section (i.e., Part V of *PR*) is that the category of the ultimate, Creativity, is now clearly hypostatized and treated as itself a purposive agency" (1979, 66). Neville will agree with this and argues that such a move on Whitehead's part is another indication of process thought's embrace of the modern trend toward the philosophic closure of the cosmos—or the embrace of a radical cosmological pluralism without any supporting ontology. This being the case, Neville observes that Whitehead's quasi-Platonism is not enough to solve the problem. Part V of *PR* is also the place where Whitehead introduces, however briefly, the notion of the third and fourth phases of the description of the nature of God, the phases in which the kingdom of heaven becomes the love of the world. "The action of the fourth phase is the love of God for the world. It is the particular providence for particular occasions" (*PR*, 351). It is likewise here that Whitehead provides us with his famous and moving definition of God as "the fellow-sufferer who understands" (*PR*, 351).

While the move toward the hypostatization of creativity as Creativity beyond God's primordial and consequent natures saves Whitehead from some problems for the short term in Part V, it creates more of a problem for the general coherence of the system. Moreover, it is just at this point that White-head reflects again on the nature of God in *AI* in terms of the diversity internal to God's complex nature. As Whitehead writes about the Alexandrian theologians, "The accepted solution of a multiplicity in the nature of God, each component being unqualifiedly Divine, involves a doctrine of mutual immanence in the divine nature" (*AI*, 216). The key idea or cluster of ideas to register here is the emphasis on mutual immanence in the divine nature. This is certainly a direction of analysis that signals Whitehead's desire to find a place for creativity within a unified image of God as creator, sustainer, and redeemer of the cosmos, however broadly the classical Christian symbolic resources must be stretched.

Wilmot notes that this move on Whitehead's part solves at least three separate problems found lurking at the end of *PR*: (1) It helps explain the divine agency of creativity via a foundational multiplicity in the nature of God; (2) It removes "all forms of qualification and subordination, a constant feature of the Platonic triad;" and (3) It establishes that "God is God in all his manifold operations in the world" because of mutual immanence within the divine nature (1979, 174). While it is doubtful that the mere introduction of the words "mutual immanence" solves all of these problems with the stroke of a pen, it does anticipate a way forward. One revision will introduce the comparative categories of form, dynamics, and unification and their contrast with the Sung Neo-Confucianism of Chu Hsi and Ch'en Ch'un.

There are, of course, other comparative cross-cultural methodologies for trying to solve this series of interrelated problems. For instance, David Hall has tried to show how we can make use of Taoist notions of chaos to free ourselves from the present confines of Western thought to introduce the really radical meaning of creativity and process into philosophic world making (1982b). For Hall, Whitehead's attempt to redefine the divine nature is only a partial fix for a much more difficult and deep-seated problem. Hall goes on to argue that we should not have expected more from Whitehead at this point. Whitehead was trying to introduce a new way of viewing reality, or at least a new way for the Western intellect, and he was forced to put his insights into the language that would make some sense to those who did not share his new vision. I have the distinct feeling that Hall is one of those scholars who wants to excise a sectarian Christian God from Whitehead. In fact, this is basically what Hall does by his appeal to Taoist wisdom; for Chuang Tzu, there is as little use for God as there is for a moralist like Confucius. For a good Taoist, my Westernized Neo-Confucian introduction of yet another set of proposed "principles" such as form, dynamics, and unification is merely a repetition of what has gone on before in Neo-Confucian thought. At best, it is an amusing exercise in Confucian pomposity.

According to Wilmot, what Whitehead does by the appeal to the patristic literature in *AI* is to make creativity "one expression of the creative process initiated and sustained in being by a Creator whose relations with the universe and man require that he be regarded as Personal" (1979, 176). This is a typical statement for Wilmot that demonstrates both the key insight and the problems with his excessive claims for the patristic gambit. I will argue later that Wilmot is correct in indicating that we can read the later Whitehead as moving toward an understanding of the divine reality that brings creativity back into the purview of the Ontological Principle. But I do not agree that this also means that Whitehead embraces the particular Christological doctrines cited by Wilmot as definitive in *AI*.

It is just at this point that Chu Hsi's analogous struggle to interpret the multivalent qualities of principle (*li*) is helpful for the articulation of a comparative process philosophy and theology. Chu had a similar problem trying to explain the unity and diversity of principle (*li-i fen-shu*) as the formal element of his process-based system. This unitary and diverse Neo-Confucian reading of principle made principle per se is the locus of creativity in the sense that we cannot call anything creative that does not create something definite, and we cannot recognize anything at all unless and until it is differentiated from all other things—until it has some kind of form or formal principle. I take this to be at the heart of the Ontological Principle in Whitehead and Chu Hsi. Here I believe that Neville challenges and clarifies the fundamental intent of the process tradition with his notion of the discursive person with essential and conditional features.[23] Where I differ from Neville (1974) is in my suggestion that this clarification of the discursive person also applies to God as well as creatures. I firmly believe that this is Whitehead's basic intent in framing and defending the Ontological Principle as a principle of fundamental ontological parity, the notion that all reality must be referenced to some object–event.[24] It is here that I side with Whitehead and Chu against both Hall and Neville. I want to embrace neither the Taoist vision of Hall's interpretation of Lao Tzu and Chuang Tzu nor Neville's powerful and all-encompassing ontological creator *ex nihilo* of everything that is. While not accepting the Buddhist dharma, I too seek a middle path between creator and nothingness.

I also depart decisively from Wilmot's claims to re-Christianize radically Whitehead's suggestions about the divine nature in *AI* and *MT*. I want to explore another path altogether, namely the articulation of a global comparative process discourse on these issues with specific details drawn from Whitehead and Chu Hsi. When I translate between the Christian and Confucian side of my comparison, I want to be clear why I do this and to suggest that this is a move faithful to Whitehead's own belief in the efficacy of comparative philosophy. Likewise on the Confucian side, while I will not argue that Chu Hsi would have done the same thing if he were somehow able to enter the debate.[25] However, I observe a number of modern New Confucians such as Mou Tsung-san, Tu Wei-ming, Liu Shu-hsien, and Cheng Chung-ying doing this exact kind of comparative philosophy when they write about the reformation of the Confucian Way in the modern world.[26] In this regard, I approve and agree with Neville's own attempts to read the Confucian tradition in terms of its affinities with process thought as defined by the North Atlantic Whiteheadian school.

THE HOPE FOR COMPOSED HARMONIES

This brief outline of the development of Whitehead's reflections on the divine reality is not intended as a complete review of the topic of God in Whitehead's thought. As I have observed repeatedly, the discussion of the nature and development of Whitehead's notion of God is a very complex form of process scholasticism in both detail and exegesis. What I have sought to accomplish is something different from offering new light on this debate. First, I have sought to show the general outlines of the development in terms of its relationship to the more specific question of the relationship of God and creativity. I take this to be a key topic for the formulation of a reformed and comparative global process vision of the divine reality.

Second, I have sought to assemble the various notions scattered in Whitehead's mature philosophy that can be reassembled into a vision of the divine reality that includes an integral place for creativity within its wider ambit. If I am correct, such a revisioning of Whitehead and Chu Hsi should continue to stimulate further debate about the continuing relationship of process philosophy and comparative theology. The most important elements presented here are the notions of God's primordial and consequent nature, as well as the ideas of the divine eros in *AI* and concern in *MT*. Also important to the mix is Whitehead's discussion of the metaphysical appeal of whole-part relation in terms of identity, contact, and overlap. In terms of Whitehead's analysis of the consequent nature of God in *PR*, Part V, I am particularly concerned to explicate his comments about the third and fourth phases of the objectification of object–events in the divine consciousness and how this passes back into the perfected reality of the relation of God to the world. As Whitehead wrote, "But the principle of universal relativity is not to be stopped at the consequent nature of God" (*PR*, 350).

While I am not as concerned in this study with an elaborate examination of Chu Hsi's thought, I will also explore the relationship of the mind–heart and principle in a way analogous to Whitehead's discussion of God, creativity, and the world. Chu's philosophic history, Neo-Confucian philosophic methodology, and nontheistic approach provide a much needed contrast to move the Western debate off dead center. Chu's vision of the difficult search for the perfected harmony in the mind–heart of the sage suggests yet another way to deal with some of the problems Neville has pinpointed for Whitehead at the end of PR.

It is now time to introduce Neville's detailed criticism of process thought as well as to begin the comparative task of incorporating Chu Hsi's insights into the Western discussion in chapters 3, 4, 5, 6, and 7.

NOTES

1. Most Western process philosophers also do double duty as Christian theologians, however unorthodox their work is considered by their ilk. Some members of the school, such as David Hall, have abandoned the Christian theological quest even though they remain profoundly engaged in religious speculation. At one point, Donald Sherburne tantalized the process community by announcing that he would provide scholars with a revised Whiteheadian philosophy without God (1971). This promise has not yet become a major study, even though many eagerly await Sherburne's sustained argument. It still remains the case that most Whiteheadians continue to be fascinated by the religious dimensions of his work. Furthermore, Rescher (1996) has pointed out that process thought is a larger movement than its Whiteheadian subfield.

2. Some of the most serious and careful Whiteheadian exegetes have undertaken the search for the development of Whitehead's notion of God. Along with Lewis S. Ford (1984), Nobo (1986), Cobb (1965), Christian (1959), Suchocki (1992), Mays (1959), Pols (1967), Lowe (1962), Wilmot (1979), Kraus (1979), and Emmet (1932) have all tried to explain the nature as well as the development of his notion of God.

3. Robert Eno (1990) has a good summary of the early Chinese material. Suffice it to say that this is still a contentious issue. Whether or not a scholar identifies "God" in early Chinese writing often depends on her or his working definition of religion. See also Jensen (1997).

4. David E. Mungello (1985), John D. Young (1983), Jacques Gernet (1985), as well as some of the selected articles collected in Ching and Oxtoby (1992), tell the tale of Jesuit reflection, including the Chinese response, on the nature of the early Chinese religious tradition. For an overview of Chinese religion, and especially the earliest stratum of the tradition, see Julia Ching (1993).

5. For a fascinating account of an early literati convert, Wu Li (1632–1718), see Jonathan Chaves' study of this famous painter's and poet's encounter with and conversion to the Christian faith (1993). See also Young (1983), Standaert (1988), and Gernet (1985) for other accounts of early Christian–Confucian encounters.

6. Of course, the reasons for the Neo-Confucian reaction to the Jesuit interpretation are highly complex. If modern philosophic critics and philosophers such as Pepper (1942, 1966), Watson (1985), Dilworth (1989), and Booth (1988) are correct, at least part of what is going on is the fact that there is a real fundamental worldview clash occurring between the Neo-Confucians and the Jesuits. My argument is that the Neo-Confucian direction is organic, relational, and processive in nature. In Pepper's terms, Chu Hsi had a different root metaphor than Ricci or any of the other early Jesuits.

7. At the other end of the philosophic sinological scale, Chad Hansen (1992) has made a similar argument about Western inabilities to understand early Chinese thought. Hansen argues that all Chou philosophic culture after Mo Tzu is dominated by the philosophy of language, a philosophic vision seeking to direct the conduct of life by means of understanding the role and function of language. If Hansen is even partially correct, this is yet another reason why the Chinese have never been very interested in classical Western natural theology. To be interested in Western natural theology means also to be fascinated by the collateral disciplines of metaphysics, ontology, cosmology, and epistemology.

8. Standaert (1988), Gernet (1985), and Young (1983) all provide information about those Confucians who did take the theistic question seriously.

9. It is difficult to know precisely how much Whitehead knew about the diverse religious history of humankind. At least, compared to many of his colleagues, he did realize that this history included South and East Asia. While he may not have known much detail about Buddhism, Confucianism, Taoism, or Shinto, he did believe that we should know something of these traditions if we are to have an adequate dialogue about religious experience.

10. Though a technical argument, this is not a contentious issue among Whitehead scholars, all of whom accept the notion that there were developmental stages in Whitehead's examination of the notion of God. For instance, Randall C. Morris makes much the same point in his study of the political implications of process thought (1991).

11. Gordon Kaufman's (1993) new systematic theology is a good example of this kind of reaction to Whitehead's work. Kaufman, like so many other confessional Christian theologians before him, wonders if Whitehead's notion of the divine reality has much to do with the biblical God, or even the God that Kaufman finds in modern human experience.

12. For instance, Hartshorne (1973, 100–03), in a short list of the features he understands to constitute the process family of philosophies, lists twenty-five ideas and theses held by Whitehead. In terms of philosophic thought, John Cobb, Jr., and David Ray Griffin (1976, 14–29) list eight elements as the basic concepts of process thought.

13. It is always perilous to state dogmatically what a living philosopher will say—philosophers have been known to change their minds repeatedly even on key

issues. This is a plausible reading, however, of Neville's persistent defense of the notion of creation *ex nihilo*.

14. Neville often makes the point that his arguments about the nature of God's transcedence do not depend on mystical experience. They are, according to Neville, dialectical in structure.

15. However, Joseph Margolis has argued that the fear of relativism is misplaced (1991). Relativism, according to Margolis, can defend choices and opinions as better or worst, hence avoiding one of the major arguments made against relativists as intellectual anarchists. It strikes me that there is emerging a defense of relativism that is not a form of intellectual indifferentism. Anyone who cares to follow Margolis's carefully crafted argument cannot argue that all relativists are neither unconcerned about public disputation nor merely defending personal feeling. For an even more radical defense of relativism, see Feyerabend (1987; 1988). Nelson Goodman (1978; 1988 with C. Z. Elgin) also defends a relativism that avoids some of the problems identified with the tradition. Probably the most radical of modern relativists is Paul Feyerabend (1987) in *Farewell to Reason*. For other overviews of the problems and pleasures of relativism, see Rom Harré and Michael Krausz (1996), Gregor McLennan (1995), and Nicholas Rescher (1993).

16. One of the minor mysteries of Whitehead's Categories of Explanation is why there are twenty-seven of them. Perhaps some Whiteheadian Cabalist will be able to explain the numerology of the categories, but the reason for the number twenty-seven eludes me. It remains a pleasing puzzle for those inclined to try to find a reason for everything.

17. Even Ford, who defends the notion of God as an actual entity, acknowledges that it is a contested part of Whitehead's thought. I agree with Ford. Neville takes this to be a grave mistake (1980).

18. John Hick makes use of this Buddhist notion that there might simply be some ultimate questions that have no possible answer, both in terms of empirical reality and the limits of logical analysis (1989). The Buddhists also make the point that there are even some questions that might have answers, but that the effort to try to solve these tricky questions does not help the student seek liberation or salvation.

19. Many scholars love to point out that professional Western philosophers have not been nearly as interested in Whitehead as have the theologians. Frankly, given the very narrow focus of much modern North Atlantic professional philosophy, I wonder that anyone would take this to be an insightful remark. Professional Western philosophers are in a very narrow and parochial phase, though there are hints that this may even be reaching a stage of terminal boredom for the philosophers as well as for their audience. Foundational theologians, given the fact that there are Christians in many different cultures, are almost automatically comparative in their approaches. Whitehead's openness to comparative thought helps explain why he is a popular resource for modern theology.

20. Lucien Price (1954), with Whithead's approval but not editorial review, took notes of Whitehead's conversations over the years in his summer house near the Blue Hills south of Boston. It is in these accounts as recorded by Price that we can see how Whitehead was not precisely an orthodox Christian.

21. Victor Lowe also writes about these issues in his biography of Whitehead (1985–1990). It is a great shame that after Lowe's death the rest of his biography of Whitehead was not finished with the loving care that Lowe lavished on his work. For instance, there is no extended treatment of *AI* or *MT*—surely an oversight for any complete intellectual biography of Whitehead. If the biography had really been completed, we might have had more insight into Whitehead's reflections on the relationship of philosophy and religion.

22. Chu Hsi and Ch'en Ch'un also were interested in comparative thought in terms of their reaction to Chinese Buddhism. Stimulated by this contact, Chu and Ch'en developed the Neo-Confucian synthesis, at least in part, to point out the philosophic errors of the Buddhists. Members of the contemporary New Confucian movement, such as Mou Tsung-san, Tu Wei-ming, Cheng Chung-ying, and Liu Shu-hsien, also are engaging in the comparative reconstruction of the Confucian tradition. These modern Confucians have shown themselves to be just as eager to engage in a universal dialogue as Whitehead ever was. For a brief examination of modern Confucian–Christian dialogue, see Berthrong (1994).

23. The first major exposition of Neville's notion of the discursive person comes in *The Cosmology of Freedom*. It is also in this work that Neville makes the most sustained use of Whitehead in a positive sense. Neville explains this to be the case because of his appreciation of Whitehead's cosmology. Neville almost always has positive things to say about Whitehead's cosmology; nonetheless, it is Neville's belief that Whitehead does not have an adequately dialectical ontology.

24. Students of Justus Buchler, who originally developed the concept of ontological parity, will be taken aback by my characterization of Whitehead's ontological parity. What I mean to do is defend the idea that a revised version of Whitehead does fit Buchler's model of a philosophy of ontological parity. One way to do this is to show how creativity is not an ontological surd floating free from any and all cosmic agency.

25. The whole question of Chu's interest in other philosophic traditions is a complex and contentious issue. For instance, there are many scholars, albeit most of an older generation, who make the case that Neo-Confucianism is nothing but a Confucianized version of the great T'ang Buddhist schools. On the other hand, there are those who reject all notions of borrowing on Chu's part. The truth lies somewhere in the middle. While it is certain that Chu knew a great deal about Buddhism and Taoism, he did not take these materials to be essential for his synthesis. Like all educated Confucians of his age, Chu knew the literature of the Taoists and Buddhists and was surely stimulated to respond to their claims, all of which he believed were false.

26. By "exact thing" here I do not mean that all of these exemplars of the New Confucian movement are in agreement with my reconstruction of Whitehead or my interpretation of Chu Hsi. For instance, it is certainly the case that Mou and Tu are much more interested in reviving Wang Yang-ming than Chu Hsi. Cheng and Liu, on the other hand, along with de Bary in the West, have done a great deal to clarify Chu Hsi's position on these matters in terms of modern global comparative philosophy.

3

Neville's Challenge

NEVILLE ON THE PROCESS TRADITION AND GOD

Robert C. Neville has been one of the most sympathetic, insightful, and persistent critics of the process tradition in philosophy and theology. What makes his challenge illuminating as well as provocative is that his critique is based on a careful reading and deep appreciation of Whitehead's project. In fact, much of Neville's own constructive ontological, cosmological, axiological, ethical, and theological speculations can be interpreted as revisions and expansions of Whiteheadian philosophy.[1] Beginning with works such as *God the Creator* (1968) and *The Cosmology of Freedom* (1974) and continuing with *Behind the Masks of God* (1991a), *A Theology Primer* (1991b), *The Highroad Around Modernism* (1992), *Eternity and Time's Flow* (1993), and *Normative Cultures* (1995), Neville demonstrates his own philosophic creativity and his profound debt to Whitehead's process cosmology by continuing a critical reading of key Whiteheadian texts and an examination of difficult issues raised by the process tradition. Moreover, Neville has always acknowledged Whitehead's and Hartshorne's influence on his own project, although he is presently more interested in Peirce and the American pragmatic tradition as the basis of philosophic reconstruction. Nonetheless, Neville has been equally clear that he has been a critic of Whitehead's and Hartshorne's ontology and metaphysics while appreciating their cosmological vision and willingness to address questions of a natural or philosophic theology.

Neville's persistent complaint is that while Whitehead's cosmology is highly suggestive for the reconstruction of modern philosophy, neither Whiteheadian nor Hartshornian metaphysics are adequate tools for the task of sustaining the cosmology developed from their initial premises. Neville's own work has been an attempt to provide just such a support for his own version of cosmology, ontology, metaphysics, axiology, social ethics, and, most recently, natural theology. Nesting at the center of Neville's revisionist philosophy and theology is the concept of creation *ex nihilo*. Because of Neville's concern for a holistic and dialectically adequate theory of creation as the most coherent and satisfactory explanation of divine agency, it is obvious that he wants to discover whether or not Whitehead's separation of creativity and God's primordial and consequent natures in *PR* makes philosophic sense in terms of generating a modern systematic metaphysics. In all of his various responses to process theology to date, Neville has maintained that the separation of creativity and God is a mistake of the highest order. It is a mistake so grave that it precludes process thought from providing a truly adequate systematic metaphysics.

Beyond his persistent criticism of Whitehead, which is only a small part of his total project, Neville has been a highly productive scholar working in many different philosophic fields.[2] These have included general cosmology, ontology, metaphysics, spiritual formation, comparative theology and religion, social ethics, hermeneutics and interpretation theory, and studies of Asian traditions such as Buddhism, Taoism, and Confucianism. More recently, Neville's long-standing theological interests have involved him even more directly in the field of Christian natural and systematic theology.[3] For instance, in ETF, Neville conjoins a philosophic analysis of the nature of time with reflections on God's eternal creation and immortality. This fusion of speculative philosophy and natural theology is a development that should surprise no one who has followed the development of Neville's corpus from *God the Creator* to *The Highroad Around Modernism, Eternity and Time's Flow*, and *Normative Cultures*.

As previously noted, Neville has written extensively in the area of comparative religion and theology, with important studies such as *Soldier, Sage, Saint, The Tao and the Daimon, The Puritan Smile,* and *Behind the Masks of God.* Neville has begun an effort to articulate a major systematic theology, with *A Theology Primer* functioning as a preface to his more extended projected reexamination of Christian theology. In the midst of these constructive works stands his critical 1980 challenge to process philosophy, *God and Creativity.* As we have already seen, the 1980 essay goes directly to the heart of his critique of the acknowledged problem of the relationship of creativity and God in Part V of *PR.*

His profoundly appreciative and creative reading of Whitehead makes Neville a potentially devastating critic of the process tradition at least in terms of the coherence and adequacy of its systemic vision. The systemic aspects of the process tradition are crucial because it is in just this particular area that Whitehead is perceived to have made his greatest contribution to the formation of a modern natural theology. If Whitehead is mistaken or incoherent at this point, even if we are still moved by the wonderful Whiteheadian rhetoric about God, creativity, and the world, then much of the rational charm of the cosmology loses its immediate intellectual appeal. One of the real sources of the appeal of Whitehead's philosophy is its ability to fuse material from modern science, logic, art, and religion into one interpretive schema. If there are, as Neville argues, real problems with the coherence of the schema then the appeal and usefulness of the whole Whiteheadian edifice is lessened for the task of comparative philosophy and theology.

The potential havoc caused by Neville's challenge increases with the lack of a proper response by the more established members of the process movement. What is needed is a response proportional to the challenge that cogently follows Whitehead's own vision, even to the point of offering a revised comparative Whiteheadian philosophy. It is interesting to note that David Hall, who started his career as an orthodox Whiteheadian, has also generated his own version of a comparative philosophy based on his re-reading of the process tradition. While Hall is as equally interested in the Chinese tradition as Neville, he has been more fascinated with the Taoists than with the Confucians. My own inclination is to locate my revision of Whitehead between Neville and Hall—following Whitehead and the Neo-Confucians.

The true power of Neville's critique, as MacIntyre (1984) would approve, comes from the fact that he subjects the process tradition to an accurate internal reading. Neville is completely at home in the texts and ethos of the process movement because he shares much of the Whiteheadian cosmology, as well as an interest in process, creativity, and the relational nature of the divine reality. What Neville intensely dislikes is the sense of cosmological closure that qualifies both Whitehead and Chu Hsi.

As every disputer knows, it is one thing to be able to refute external criticism when it is shallow and based on a biased misreading of texts. It is even fairly easy to argue with thinkers from other camps when the basic differences in worldview are evident. In that case you can indicate the main difference in worldviews and continue the discussion with the recognition of difference.[4] Such differences demonstrate that disparate questions are being asked, different evidence counts for answers, different worldviews are being expressed, and different strategies for the culture of disputation are being followed.[5] It is much more difficult to deflect arguments when the criticism comes from within the same school and is accurate in terms of the way the internal debate has been joined on the basis of a common store of accepted wisdom. Or so it seems.

As I see it, the problem with the response to Neville's challenge to date from within the process camp is twofold. First, many members of the guild of process thinkers (and I count myself among them in terms of commitment to Whitehead's original vision) occupy themselves with trying to restate Whitehead's own position as an answer to Neville's various challenges, specifically in terms of Whitehead's own most elaborate statement of his thought, *PR*. There are some very important reasons why this tactic has been used as often as it has in the past. As David Hall observes, the power of

Whitehead's work is derived from the fact that it offers an atypical paradigm for Western speculative thought. One of the tasks of the emerging process tradition has been to check and recheck its verbal formulations to ensure that the authentic Whiteheadian voice is not deflected or edited or merely reduced to some more typical paradigm of Western thought in the interpretive act.[6]

But as we have noticed in chapter 1, this is hardly an adequate response or defense of process thought if Neville is correct in pointing to a real problem with Whitehead's own formulation of the question of the separation of God and creativity in *PR*. Just repeating variations of Whitehead's argument over and over again in different verbal formulations will do no good if there is something more than verbal confusion depending on the separation of God and creativity. My contention is that Neville deserves something more subtle in terms of an internally coherent Whiteheadian response or the process movement will have to admit that he is right and follow his constructive leadership into a post–Whiteheadian process movement.

The second main response to Neville from within the process movement has been by Hartshorne.[7] And of course Hartshorne himself has had similar internal arguments with Whitehead about the ultimate nature of the divine reality. In fact, Hartshorne and Neville are really quite alike in the aim of their philosophic projects. While both are profoundly influenced by Whitehead, they have real difficulties in remaining orthodox Whiteheadians. They incontestably pay Whitehead the ultimate philosophic compliment of taking him seriously enough to argue with him in order to try to show where he went wrong.

In Hartshorne's case, this has led to his defense of the notion of the social nature of the divine reality. Neville's characteristic analysis of divine things relies on an intricate defense of the notion of God as the creator of all that is, a modern restatement of the classic Christian doctrine of creation *ex nihilo*. If Hartshorne has become famous (or infamous) for his defense of the ontological argument, then Neville is probably going to achieve a similar reputation for his refurbishment of the doctrine of creation *ex nihilo*. In any event, it would be impossible to conceive of the work of either man, independent of the influence of Whitehead. And in both cases, Hartshorne and Neville are not very pleased with Whitehead's separation of creativity and God in Part V of *PR*.

NEVILLE ON COMPARATIVE DIVINITY

In terms of the method of archic analysis, Neville speaks with a number of authorial voices. Sometimes he writes as a Western metaphysician interested in the grand themes of the Western religio-philosophic tradition such as space, time, causation, epistemology, religious formation, social order, and personal ethics. Sometimes he writes as a comparative religionist, interested in the great South and East Asian traditions of Buddhism, Hinduism, Taoism, and Confucianism. And sometimes he writes as a systematic Christian theologian. In all of these voices, the question of the divine reality is a challenge for his constructive project. While he is personally committed to the Christian way, he believes that the task of comparative theology is inclusive of any thinker who takes the issue of divine reality seriously—at any time, place, and culture. Furthermore, Neville argues that we need not be confined just to the study of thinkers with overtly theistic persuasions. For instance, Neville has become fascinated with Sung and Ming Neo-Confucian discourse as a form of religious speculation, even though it is highly ambiguous concerning the divine referent from the classical standpoint of Western philosophic theism.[8] Such comparative interests and analyses of Chinese thinkers such as Chu Hsi and Wang Yang-ming (1472–1529) are commensurate with Whitehead's own comparative concerns and invite the use of comparative material as an integral aspect of my revisioning of the Whiteheadian tradition in comparative terminology.

For instance, in *The Tao and the Daimon* (1982), Neville writes a great deal about Buddhists, Taoists, and historically crucial Neo-Confucians such as Chu Hsi and Wang Yang-ming. In his later works, he has become ever more fascinated by the Chu Hsi school while retaining his earlier admiration for other Neo-Confucian schools of thought. Neville is not a partisan in the perennial battles between the Chinese, Korean, and Japanese Neo-Confucian followers of the School of Principle and the School of Mind. He has argued that anyone who pretends to write a contemporary theology must come to terms with the insights of a master such as Chu Hsi. Neville believes that the Neo-Confucian emphasis on learning and civil service seeking the highest standards of ethical and intellectual conduct remains a model worthy of emulation by human beings seeking a truly civil society. Neville firmly concludes that Chu Hsi's speculation on the Supreme Ultimate and other matters of ultimate concern for the *li-hsüeh* school are elements that need to be addressed in Christian speculation on the nature of the divine reality. In this regard, Neville is one of a growing number of scholars who affirm the profoundly religious dimension of the Confucian tradition.[9] Neville's interest in Neo-Confucianism invites a more focused discussion of Chu Hsi's role in the reconstruction of Whitehead's interpretation of God in chapter 5 as a response to Neville's criticism of process thought.

NEVILLE ON THE DIVINE REALITY

A brief review of Neville's understanding of the divine reality is now in order. This summary will rely on his most recent and concise statement of the God problem in *TP, BMG,* and *HAM.* Along with *ETF, TP* is also Neville's most overtly systematic theological work to date. In fact, although *TP* stands alone as a work of theological reflection, it also is an extended preface and outline of a much more detailed systematic theology to come. *ETF* is another work dealing with a number of theological as well as philosophic themes. It is more specialized than *TP* because it focuses on the nature and interpretation of time and eternity as a single problem for modern thought. *ETF* typically repeats Neville's emerging pattern of mixing speculative philosophy, comparative studies, and specific Christian theological issues. Neville is always careful to point out that his use of Christian material comes from the fact that this is his religious standpoint; however, he hopes that his thought is irenic enough that what he says about divine matters from the Christian perspective will also apply, when translated into other forms of discourse, to the other religions of the world. Neville is hardly sectarian in his aspirations or in the range of his material.

BMG deals with many of the same problems, but from the perspective of the history of religion or comparative theology, including discussions of various Buddhist and East Asian traditions. *HAM* is not a theological treatise at all, but as with all of Neville's recent works, it does address questions of religion and modern culture as expressions of the nature of the modernist turn in philosophic culture. *HAM* also includes Neville's most recent extended discussions of the process tradition. *HAM* is Neville's answer to many so-called post–modern thinkers who argue that it is now impossible to do metaphysics at all. Needless to say, Neville remains a staunch defender of the metaphysical urge within the modernist movement and its role for enlightened religion. The comparative aspect of Neville's project is even more evident in *NC* in terms of ethical praxis, the role of ritual in civilized life, and the need for the diverse civilizations of the late twentieth century to learn to talk to each other across the great divides of language, religion, and culture.

Neville believes that the proper definition of God is a problem for any serious thinker. "For most people who turn to theology, the chief problem is whether there is a God" (*TP,* 25). This being the case, Neville does not waste any time honing in on what he considers to be the most important root metaphor for trying to unravel this problem: the notion of "God as the agent of the creation of the world" (*TP,* 25). In this regard, Neville shares a common problem with Whitehead and the process tradition. What is the nature and function of God? In both cases the main emphasis falls on divine creativity, with the main argument regarding the nature of this creativity. For Neville, the divine creativity is expressed as *creatio ex nihilo,* while for Whitehead it is likened to the divine eros that ceaselessly creates the universe as an urge for the evocation of ever more complex and harmonious creatures.[10]

Neville proposes that the best way to address this problem is to state "the primacy of divine creation." The notion of God as creator in an ontological sense has been one of the themes of Neville's theology since its inception, and it is one of the main points of disagreement with the revised Whiteheadian process philosophy of this essay.

> Cosmological creation takes place *within* the created world, and illustrates the laws and measures defining closure within the world. Ontological causation is God's creating of the world as such, and is different from the cosmological. . . . The hypothesis to be put forward technically in the next sections is that divinity is best understood as the creating of the world *ex nihilo*. This is the root notion. (*TP*, 29)

Neville notes that this is a problematic way of stating the issue after the Enlightenment and the rise of modernity as a distinctive philosophic culture. "For the purposes of theological discussion, 'modernity' can be defined precisely. It is that culture whose basic senses of the world have closure" (*TP*, 26). For the theologian, the main question is whether God is closed into or out of the natural system. Whitehead and the process tradition accept the enclosure of God; Neville rejects divine closure as restricting God to the cosmos as modernity defines it. In *ETF*, Neville specifies the notion of closure even more narrowly in his analysis of the modern Western philosopher's typical move to restrict any analysis of time and eternity to the present moment, that is, that the present is basically all we can know and that it defines all that can be. For Neville this is both a mistake and yet another example of the detrimental aspects of the philosophy and culture of closure on modern thought. Even Whitehead, who was interested in process and the future, fell prone to this mistake by focusing too narrowly on the present moment of self-creation in the concrescence of the emerging new actual entity.

Nonetheless, Neville lauds the process tradition for trying to deal with the problem of closure. At least Whitehead knew he had a problem; often the beginning of wisdom is the recognition of the real nature of the problem at hand. The difficulty is that Neville believes that the process tradition, even with what he acknowledges as a highly creative view of cosmology, does not answer either the metaphysical questions of philosophic closure or the religious issues involved in this characteristic move of the late Enlightenment that identifies everything that is with only cosmological causation, the self-referencing of each agent with other cosmologically defined agents. Nor, according to the argument about eternity and time in *ETF*, does it go very far in explaining the complicated relationship of past, present, and future.

According to Neville, the analysis of the modern world as a world of closure is an important point to remember in both its Western and Chinese modalities. It is at this juncture that Neville parts company with Whitehead and that part of modern culture that opts for a world of closure. This is a point we will need to ponder in terms of comparative thought. For instance, it may well be the case that the Neo-Confucians also share a sense of the world of closure with modern Western thought. This may well be yet another reason why so many sinologists have marked the beginning of early modern China with the rise of the Neo-Confucianism in the Northern Sung. The recognition of the modern aspect of the Neo-Confucianism movement in part relates to the Neo-Confucian sense of closure in Neville's terms.

Neville does not like this aspect of modernity because he believes it closes the world off from divine creative influence and reduces the role of divinity to just one more limited aspect of cosmological causation. There is no real source for ontological creation if closure is the last word, philosophically speaking. But does closure really mean being closed, even in Neville's own terms? This is an important question even if it is based on a quibble about the best way to define modernity.[11] I believe that neither the Sung Neo-Confucians nor Whitehead felt confined by the closure of the world. In this the Neo-Confucians are at one with some of the most enduring aspects of Chinese thought.

However, in *ETF,* Neville disputes my reading of the Sung Neo-Confucian tradition as one that shares the modern Western proclivity for closure. Although his remarks are short and do not form a complete reading of the early Neo-Confucian texts, Neville argues that Chou Tun-i's crucial "An Explanation of the Diagram of the Great Ultimate" expresses a sense of eternity and time that shows that "Underlying the flow (of the Tao) there is a deeper sense of genesis that is not temporal" (1993, 174). Neville's main point here is that

> Time's flow is badly represented by the analytical placement of creation in the temporal modes. . . . But all that the analytical depiction can show is the systematic interconnections and changes that take place as present moments become past, changing the future possibilities and giving way to new moments of decisive creativity. Chunk, chunk, chunk go the droplets of becoming. (1993, 172)

This is not what Neville takes the Tao to be for Chou Tun-i or any of the later Neo-Confucians (see chapter 4). While I agree with part of Neville's analysis, namely that chunk, chunk, chunk is not at all the impression that Chou provides in his Neo-Confucian manifesto on the Tao, I do not accept all the rest of the Nevillian analysis as it pertains to the nature of Neo-Confucian closure and creative synthesis. In fact, one of the main reasons that Chu Hsi appreciated Chou's short treatise is that it embodied a primal Confucian sense of real creativity as a manifesto against the Taoists and Buddhists. I do agree with the direction of Neville's analysis of principle where he states, "Principle directs the reconfigurations, not so much by supplying Platonic-like forms but by defining what harmoniousness would be. Principle is normative and always addresses every swirl of changes uniquely" (1993, 175). But still, both I and the Neo-Confucians rather like the chunk, chunk, chunk of the creative synthesis of each object–event as an expression of the realistic pluralism of the cosmos; at least we know where the sounds are coming from. Knowing the directionality of creativity has its rewards.

Neville continues his sketch of the divine reality by noting what kind of world is created and what this implies for divine creation per se. The world is a determinate place created *ex nihilo* by a God characterized as indeterminate as creator, except as we can ascertain from the marks of creation per se. Once dealing with the created order of our world, we do indeed confront a determinate divine reality. Before Neville deals with what we can know of the creator God by means of the marks of determined creation, he addresses the prior issue of what it means to be determinate at all. The notion of determinateness is a crucial philosophic issue for Neville. Unless we understand what it means to be determinate, Neville argues that we will not be able to comprehend what it means to be part of the creation. For according to Neville, determinate beings have only each other to analyze in the world as created by the creator God.

The first point Neville makes involves the metaphysical level where determinateness is defined as the harmony of essential and conditional features. Every determinate thing has essential features of its own and conditional features that connect it to other determinate things. It also is important to remember that the two sets of conditions are linked internally in each determinate thing and with other determinate things such that the essential features of one thing may be the conditional features of some other thing and vice versa. The whatness of the things is the realized harmony of its essential and conditional features.

> By "thing" I mean substance, event, change, situation, condition, whatever. By "harmony" I mean that things are mixtures of their components and the patterns according to which the components are integrated in them. . . . A harmony is a mixture of its components and patterns, requiring each and giving each equal importance. (*BMG*, 61)

Second, Neville recognizes that the notion of harmony is vast, yet he is clear that "A harmony is a mixture of both essential and conditional features" (*BMG*, 62). In the Nevillian scheme of things, God is rather like Derrida's *différance* as the font of all the multifarious things of the created order or disorder as the case may be. Or, on an even more radical reading such as proposed by David Hall, the divine creativity is like Lao Tzu's notion of the Tao as the mother of all determinate things altogether, the indeterminate sum of orders is chaos itself as the font of sui generis creativity of each and every object–event in this or any cosmic epoch.

Returning to the origins of more traditional Western religious thought, Neville believes that, under the impact of Hellenistic thought, Judaism adapted the religious concept of Wisdom or the Logos for philosophic usage to try to specify a determinate image or metaphor of the indeterminate creator of all that is. One does not always need to quote Lao Tzu or Chuang Tzu to find images for creative chaos. Simply put, through the Logos or Wisdom all that was made was created. Working with Plato's *Philebus*, Neville goes on to point out that the Judeo-Christian Hellenistic vision of the Logos used four elements to explain the determinate nature of reality. These are form, components to be formed, their actual mixture and the value of the mixture in terms of the essential and conditional features of the determinate thing.

This fourfold ordering of the Logos or Wisdom as the determinate image of the indeterminate creator in the *Philebus* demonstrates how Neville incorporates his Platonic sensibility into his modern Christian systematic theology. In *BMG* he spells out the Platonic roots of his fourfold schema in terms of an exegesis of Plato's *Philebus*. Neville believes that this Platonic speculation about the nature of the divine reality is superior to all other Western alternatives, including Aristotle and Whitehead as representatives of the ancient and modern Western tradition.

> Plato's earlier theory in the *Philebus*, however, has a more accurate generality. Plato argued that the concrete world of temporal change must be analyzable in terms of Limit or order, the Unlimited or things-to-be-ordered, the actual Mixture of these two, and the Cause of Mixture. (BMG, 17)

According to Neville, these are the Platonic specifications of the religious notions of Wisdom or Logos. In chapters 4, 5, 6, and 7, I will return to an alternative tripartite schema based on the traits of form, dynamics, and unification in place of Neville's short list of the four Platonic elements of conditional and essential harmony based on his reading of the *Philebus*.

The process-related triad of form, dynamics, and unification achieves the same cosmological and analytic ends as Neville's Platonic fourfold analysis for a reformed Whitehead discourse but with a more supple and spare list of prime elements. The triad of form, dynamics, and unification also may be a better match for Christian trinitarian speculation than Neville's Platonic quartet. But then, one of the perennial games of Christian theology has been to make Christian revelation fit into Platonic schemas. It is an honorable game and Neville plays as well as anyone ever has. We will return to Neville's notions of Limit, Unlimited, Mixture, and Cause of Mixture in chapter 5, where this quartet will be contrasted to the triad of form, dynamics, and unification.[12] Furthermore, in light of cross-cultural philosophic interests, the triadic formulation also takes into consideration the Chu Hsi school of Neo-Confucian organic thought—although it also is clear that Neville's quadrilateral can include and interpret Chu Hsi as well. In this regard, the specifics of the triad of form, dynamics, and unification can claim joint parentage from two distinct versions of relational process/organic systems. While an appeal to a Neo-Confucian master such as Chu Hsi may not presently count for very much in intra-Christian debates, it may help throw a new light on an ancient debate. At least Neville himself has found the Chinese case illuminating as an aspect of comparative theology.

After his presentation of Plato, Neville returns to his defense of ontological creation. Put simply, he wants to argue that we can never adequately explain the creativity of the determinate order by merely referencing the creatures to each other, regardless of how complicated such cosmological causal self-referencing may become. The closed world of cosmological causation can never explain why there is something rather than nothing or why there is creativity per se as a key feature of the world. Something novel really does happen here in the mundane world, and Neville maintains that this creativity needs an explanation that is ontological and dialectical in the Platonic sense, and not merely cosmological in nature. "Therefore, we need to find something that explains why there are these determinate laws and principles, and not others or none" (*TP*, 34). If we take creativity seriously, then the determinate things themselves cannot provide an answer to the harmony of the essential and conditional features of each determinate thing. "But it is not possible to understand how the essential features of different things can be together if the only kind of togetherness is conditional, constituted by determinate cosmological causation" (*TP*, 34–35). My counterargument in the later chapters of this study is that a reformed Whiteheadian position, with some assistance from the Neo-Confucian tradition, can indeed give just such a plausible answer.

Neville is quite clear that in the role of creator qua creator we can know nothing about God, for there is nothing at all to know beyond the world so created by God as creator. What we can know is the world God creates, a world entirely dependent on God's creation. This then, at least, tells us what kind of world we have as created by God *ex nihilo*. Any further religious or mundane attributes of the creator God can be specified only on the basis of what we can know of the determinate order. Neville, as a Christian theologian, then quickly moves to an analysis of Wisdom as the Logos in order to begin to talk about what we can know about the God who created this cosmos. This does not mean that this would be the only cosmos God could have created. The problem is that all we can know about God is drawn from the evidence of the present determinant order. Given that we are determinate beings in this cosmos, that is enough. We can, through the specifics of our own religious traditions, learn quite a bit about the nature of God's creation as it impacts us and our fellow creatures.

NEVILLE'S ONTOLOGICAL QUEST

As we have already seen, the argument between Neville and the Whiteheadians revolves around Neville's contention about the notion of cosmic closure, a characteristic theme of modern Western sensibility that he wishes to refute. On the other hand, Whiteheadians believe that only something can reference something else. Neville affirms this to be true as far as it goes for contingent worldly affairs, but *only* as a contingent cosmological hypothesis. For Neville there are *a priori* ontological reasons, based on his interpretation of the proper role of Platonic dialectic, for holding that we cannot adequately explain the ultimate reasons of being merely by running from one finite thing to another, or even taking all of the determined things altogether as representing some kind of systematic order. According to Neville, we need some kind of dialectical explanation of order itself, hence his desire to refurbish the ontological question as being crucial for speculative philosophy. On the other hand, for Whiteheadians and certain Neo-Confucians, this running around from thing to thing is all there is—although we must remember that it is game without limit regarding the number and complexity of the players involved, much less the rules of the game itself. I shall make the case that the comprehensiveness of the Neo-Confucian vision fuses with Whitehead's emphasis on creative principle, giving rise to a creative synthesis that does justice to both the openness and the closure of the world.

In some respects, the Neville–Whitehead argument is between two ships that pass each other, not in the night, but in the bright daylight of an ongoing Western debate about ontology and metaphysics. I say they pass in the daylight because theirs is such an ancient quarrel in the Western religio-philosophic tradition. Neville expresses well a modern version of the classic appeal to the ontological arts, whereas Whitehead is stubbornly committed to what we are calling an *ars contextualis* that takes cosmology to be the prime data for metaphysical speculation.[13] There are moments, and we will come to them in later sections of the essay, when one wonders how much of this argument is verbal and how much is based on a truly different vision of reality.

In *HAM* Neville continues his revisioning of the theological tradition (1992). His main focus is on the American pragmatic tradition, most profoundly expressed in Peirce, as a way around the problems of later modern thought. He charts his way around the shoals of the "interpretation" debate and suggests that the American pragmatist tradition gives some interesting answers to the perennial problems of philosophy and religion. For instance, Neville notes that Peirce (in an essay from 1898) provides a theoretical background for a theory of religion requiring objective knowledge of the history of human religion, as well as the need for intersubjective communication about these truths in order to have an adequate understanding of religion. As far as the modernist debate goes, Neville notes that

> Speculative philosophy for Whitehead cannot be modernist, any more than it could be for Peirce. It cannot be foundationalist if it always has the status of an hypothesis subject to further revision. It cannot be intelligible in a self-contained manner because it necessarily makes external reference to fields it envisions and unifies, both being informed by them and informing them. (*HAM*, 93)

Neville continues that "For all its brilliance and legitimating force, Whitehead's conception of systematic philosophy is limited by its inability to ask the basic ontological question, why is there something rather than nothing" (1992, 94). Neville speculates that Whitehead was unable to carry out this necessary ontological analysis because of his lack of interest in what Platonic philosophy considers the ontological art of dialectic. Hence the problem is methodological as well as systematic. This lack of Whiteheadian interest in ontology and dialectic generates a grave problem for the theological use of process thought for religious purposes. "The result is that we are forced to what the Hebrew scriptures called 'idolatry,' that is, the attempt to make some cosmological parts of the world play those ontological roles" (1992, 96). These are words of judgment for any theologian and philosopher. We will have to answer these questions in the later sections of this essay if we are to defend successfully a Whiteheadian vision of natural theology against Neville's charges.

Here again the Chinese case is illuminating. One of the curious things about most non-Buddhist Chinese philosophic speculation is the lack of any overtly ontological analysis. There is a great deal of cosmology in classical

Confucian, Mohist, Taoist, Legalist, Neo-Taoist, and Neo-Confucian thought, but not a great deal of material that appears to be ontological in the Western sense. It is not the case that someone like Chu Hsi could not carry out this sophisticated task, it is just that it was not an issue, not a set of questions that were of great interest. Chad Hansen argues that early Confucian philosophy, along with all other pre-Han schools, simply did not approach intellectual exposition and disputation with the ontological question in mind (1992). According to Hansen, what the Chinese were always and everywhere interested in were questions of the nature of language and how it guides human conduct and forms character—hence the persistent belief on the part of Western scholars that Chinese thought is ethical and pragmatic in form and function. While Hansen may have overstated some aspects of the case, his argument is plausible in that it points to an area of difference between the typical Western philosophic quest and the Chinese search for wisdom and proper conduct. If Hansen, and by extension scholars such as Graham, Yearley, Ivanhoe, Birdwhistell, and Hall and Ames are correct, then ontology is simply not as important a comparative issue as Neville wants to assert, even if it remains of concern for Western intellectuals.

NEVILLE ON CREATIVITY AND GOD

While it is true that Whitehead's separation of creativity and God in *PR* has always been a philosophic issue for Neville, his most specific challenge to the tradition is found in articles assembled in *CG*. Ultimately, Neville holds that the separation of these two key elements is not warranted and leads to incoherence for the entire system. Typical of Neville's general approach, he states the problem, offers a critique of Whitehead and other process thinkers, and renders an appreciation of the genuine contributions of process thought when separated from its problem of creativity and God *and* confined to cosmological concerns. He then goes on to show that the problem cannot be answered on purely Whiteheadian grounds. And while *CG* is a good place to begin, we must remember that Neville has published numerous works in the 1980s and early 1990s that also bear on this question.[14] Along with Whitehead and Hartshorne, Neville distinguishes himself by being willing to learn from criticism and further reflection on almost any topic. Because Neville has a systematic vision still in the process of full expression, we should expect revision from time to time.

Nonetheless I will maintain that there is a pattern in Neville's critique of process thought that remains consistent from the 1980s (and even from the 1960s when we remember his early criticism of Whitehead in *God the Creator*) through the 1990s. For instance, *ETF* extends his creationist and Platonic critique to the analysis of the relationship of eternity and time. He argues that we cannot really understand the nature of time without linking it to eternity and hence to God's creation of all that is.

It also should be noted that Neville follows MacIntyre's suggested pattern for a responsible comparative philosophy. Neville is careful to show how the problems found within process thought cannot be solved with the resources of process thought by itself. He hopes that his critique is based on an internal reading of the Whiteheadian system and that Whiteheadians will recognize themselves in the discussion. He tries to present the Whiteheadian philosophy in the best possible light. Furthermore, Neville's desire to demonstrate the steps that must be taken to reform the system by the addition of material taken from his modern vision of ontology and axiology should make sense to Whiteheadians on the basis of their own system.

In the preface to *CG,* Neville writes that his own philosophic critique is one framed " . . . from a standpoint at one with Whitehead in appreciation of speculative philosophy, neighboring in general cosmology and opposed regarding the conception of God" (*CG,* x). He ends his essays with the following reaffirmation of the potential of process thought, however sufficiently revised. "The philosophical cosmology of which process theology is a part is a rich enough matrix to nurture other and perhaps more viable conceptions of God" (*CG,* 146). As with many other students of process thought, Neville is moved by the grand sweep of Whitehead's vision but is profoundly troubled by the conception of God found therein in terms of the modern urge for a premature closure of the world. Our first question is, has Neville gone far enough in his Whiteheadian explorations? A second question is, even if Neville has gone far enough in his critique, are there suggestions in *PR, AI,* and *MT* for a more coherent Whiteheadian response to the question of closure and the separation of creativity and God?

On the surface the answer would seem to be yes. As I have pointed out, Neville has been a careful critic of Whitehead, Hartshorne, and the rest of the process tradition, a movement to which he is so philosophically indebted. Further, as we have shown, Neville is correct in his strategic attack as far as it goes as focused analysis of Part V of *PR.* The potential problem is, does this attack give up too quickly? And even if it is successful, are there more subtle Whiteheadian defenses? By this I mean does Neville stop, as do so many other process thinkers, with the conception of God in Part V of *PR* without giving due attention to *AI* and *MT*? My general conclusion is that Neville has done just this, and for good reasons. This is the place that everyone else stops, so why should Neville proceed? Perhaps because the traditional defense does not go far enough.

As we have noted, Neville sees himself as a philosophically independent thinker indebted to process thought; therefore, he does not need to do for process thinkers what they have not done for themselves. Neville is justified in stopping where the majority of Whiteheadians have left the argument, because he wants to make his own argument. Fair enough. Except that Neville is an honest thinker, and I believe he should be reminded that there is perhaps yet another way to nurture a Whiteheadian vision different both from his, Hartshorne's, Ford's, Cobb's, or Nobo's replies that may answer some of his questions. The point is not to refute Neville's own philosophic project; it is probably not even a profitable one for a Whiteheadian who has much to learn from Neville. As close neighbors, Neville and the Whiteheadians are more in need of dialogue than impassioned invective. As Richard McKeon was often fond of pointing out, philosophers are most interesting in what they assert and less interesting in what they attack in others. The task here is much more modest, namely the defense of a revised Whiteheadian defense of the process vision of God as an actual entity.

A brief examination of the various essays that comprise *CG* confirm this point. Neville carries out most of his disputation with process thinkers such as Hartshorne, Ford, and Ogden, as well as with Charles Wimquist, who introduces transcendental modes of discourse into the mixture. It is most instructive to note that Neville frames his argument by beginning with an analysis of Lewis Ford's defense of Whitehead's notion of God. Neville quotes Ford to the effect that the uniqueness of Whitehead's theological approach is that Whitehead separates creativity from God.[15] Neville counters that "My own alternative is that God is creator of everything determinate, creator of things actual as well as of things possible" (CG, 8).

A Whiteheadian will not have a problem with the Nevillian notion of God the Creator as far as it goes. The problem is that it understates the role played by the object-events of the world in the determination of their own values. There is a creative aspect to each creature that only proximately owes its basis to God. God is the divine co-creator of the world along with the creatures of the world, or any world if this one is not vast enough. One of the things all Whiteheadians insist upon is an understanding of the real, concrete role that the creatures play in the co-creation of the world. From the Whiteheadian perspective, if there is no such freedom then all creaturely freedom is some kind of sham.

As we have noted before, Neville's point is that he agrees with Whitehead's analysis of cosmological creativity but not with Whitehead's lack of an account of ontological creativity. Neville believes that cosmological creativity is all that Whitehead will acknowledge, and that this is the root of the problem for all process thinkers who follow Whitehead in this major mistake.

Neville believes that if we cannot give a radical account of ontological freedom, creativity, then Whitehead's cosmologically limited God becomes rather like " . . . a smother-mother, structuring all possibilities and continually insisting on values of her own arbitrary choice" (CG, 9). Hence the much-vaunted Whiteheadian commitment to creaturely freedom is a counter-sham in the end.[16] My contention is that it is Neville's God that is the ontological smother-mother or at least the sole real, actual, and potential source of all creativity.

Neville is as careful a critic of Ford as he is of Whitehead. However, in the midst of his general criticism, Neville indicates where his real critique lies. "In essence, I think that nothing short of the ground or principle of the whole of things is supreme enough to be worshipped" (CG, 14). Neville's complaint is that if creativity is separated from God, then God is not supreme enough to be the focus of worship. Here again there is nothing novel about this kind of criticism; theologians have worried about God being merely one more thing among other things in the world and hence not a suitable object of veneration by the faithful from the beginning in their analysis of Whitehead.[17] But there is another potential problem here, even if we are able to show how creativity and God can be reunited on viable Whiteheadian grounds. This problem resides in Neville's claim that no determinate thing, however divine, noble, self-surpassing in excellence, or vast, can explain the ontological foundation of all things.

Even if we can show how God and creativity are intimately coimplicated in theory and practice, Neville will still have yet another major objection about the coherence of this notion of God's finitude. Neville's second critique focuses on Whitehead's notion that God is an actual entity among all other actual entities. While it is true for Whitehead that God is a very special, and in fact, unique kind of object-event, this is still a major problem for Neville. Neville, as we shall see, argues that the ground for all determinant things cannot itself be just another determinant thing. In short, Neville argues that determinant things can define cosmological creativity but cannot define ontological or ultimate creativity. Neville has repeatedly argued that only a doctrine of God as creator ex nihilo will satisfy coherently the need for demonstrating ontological divine creativity. For Neville, no thing can be the divine creator—for this would not allow it to be the ontological source of all creativity and being; whereas for Whitehead, some thing, the truly divine object-event, must be the locus of divine agency. For Whitehead, framing this concern in terms of his ontological principle as expressing the real agency of all actual entities indicates that the locus of agency must be some actual entity. For supreme reasons, ultimate ends, and creative agency, this is God.

Whitehead, as opposed to Neville and most Christian theologians, was convinced that any agency, any creativity, must be found in some thing, some actual entity or concrescing occasion—although he denied, in technical terms, that God was an actual occasion per se. What Whitehead meant by this distinction is that God has not achieved a final or definitive satisfaction as would be the case for all other actual occasions. Hence God is an actual entity but not a closed, completed, exhausted occasion with nothing more to contribute but its final determination to the ongoing process of the cosmos. This was his way of stating that God is infinite while the creatures in their determinateness and final satisfaction are all finite.

To ask the reasons why for Whitehead was to ask about the location of agency in some actual agency. This is one reason why many Whiteheadian scholars, along with orthodox theologians, have been nervous about the apparent separation of creativity within the category of the ultimate from the essential nature of God. This would seem to imply, at least on the level of verbal symbols if not cosmologically, that creativity is somehow prior to or separate from God.[18] This is one persistent interpretation of the Category of the Ultimate. We need to remember that God is defined as an actual entity and hence also a creature manifesting divinely this free floating creativity. In discussing his notion of actual entities, Whitehead notes,

> They differ among themselves: God is an actual entity, and so is the most trivial puff of existence in far-off empty space. . . . The final facts are, all alike, actual entities; and these actual entities are drops of experience, complex and interdependent. (*PR*, 18)

Neville and other scholars argue that Whitehead's doctrine of the ultimate flies in the face of Whitehead's often-repeated assertions, as defined earlier, that all agency must be resident somewhere in an actual entity. Hence there is an internal contradiction in Whitehead's own vision of God and creativity, because it violates the intent of the Ontological Principle. The question then becomes hermeneutic and exegetical—do we read the Category of the Ultimate in terms of the Ontological Principle or vice versa? But even if we can show how Creativity and God can be reunited, we will still have Neville's challenge about the impossibility of anything determinant being God *a se*. In this vision of God, Neville is certainly much more of a traditional Christian than Whitehead. Interestingly enough, much the same kind of deep structural criticism was made of Chu Hsi because of his apparent separation of principle from the dynamic agency of material force, the matrix of all of the object–events of the Neo-Confucian metasystem. Here again, an examination of the Chu Hsi tradition in East Asia may suggest some new readings of the Whiteheadian canon.

Whitehead's defense of God being an actual entity among other entities throws down a gauntlet to orthodox Western understandings of divinity. God is seen as being complex and interdependent. This is hardly the stuff of traditional speculation about the omnipotent and omniscient Lord of all creation. But on the other hand, it is fertile ground for dealing with that perennial challenge to Christian theology, the doctrine of the Blessed Trinity. The true challenge is, as Neville reads it, both systemic and spiritual. Neville's first major complaint is fundamentally focused on Whitehead's ontology. The second has to do with the relationship of the divine reality to the creatures. In a spiritual sense, this second complaint is as serious as the first.

Neville notes that Whitehead's God can only know the creatures when they are literally finished, having achieved their final satisfaction and whatever harmony they can achieve by means of the Whiteheadian analysis of concrescence (*CG,* 15). According to Neville, there is no way for the Whiteheadian God to know or love the creatures until their concrescence is over. It may be the case that God is indeed the fellow sufferer who understands, but not a fellow pilgrim walking on the way to salvation in terms of a living and loving participation in the essential decisions of the emerging creature. When Whitehead talks about God being a companion, Neville is dubious (*PR,* 351). Such companionship would seem to imply a kind of relationship with God that Whitehead cannot allow in terms of the mutual independence of concrescing object–events. Neville holds that the language of fellowship and companionship is more poetic than systematic. Without the ability to relate to each creature as it becomes in the ontological act of pure creation, God must stand on the sidelines of creativity as far as the creatures are concerned. Neville also does not believe that Hartshorne's definition of God as a social creature helps the matter much either. God is still not able to play a role in the spiritual development of the creature as explicated by the great spiritual literature of the Western tradition. God, to use a Muslim metaphor, is not as close to us as our own jugular vein *if* we embrace either Whitehead's or Hartshorne's vision.

SHIPS PASSING IN THE DAY

Although it may seem obvious at this point, we still must ask, where is the *philosophic* location of the quarrel between Whitehead and Neville? Are they really talking about the same things, theories, intellectual maps of the universe, or are they like ships passing in the night? Or is the argument more linguistic than substantive? Are Whitehead and Neville using the same kind of language but moving conceptually in different directions?[19] For instance, Neville sees his argument with Whitehead primarily in terms of general or dialectical ontology. Neville believes that Whitehead's cosmology is the most interesting part of his system; the flaw in Whitehead's vision is found prior to the self-referencing of the things of the world because of the lack of an adequate ontology that can explain the reason for the relations and existence of the self-referencing object–events in any adequate sense of explanation of such things. This may be a correct Nevillian analysis, but the prior question is: Is this what Whitehead was trying to do?

Many scholars have written about Whitehead's metaphysics in terms of his cosmology. They then go on to infer that this "metaphysics" implies a certain ontology. In Neville's case, it is this implied Whiteheadian ontology as cosmology that is taken in error. From Neville's point of view, the problem is that Whitehead never explains the "why" of things, the *scientia ontologia* of things, but rather always refers to other object–events within the cosmological frame of reference. According to Neville, this kind of self-referencing is perfectly acceptable as cosmology but not as ontology or general metaphysics, much less as a natural theology. One of the problems of interpretation is that Whitehead is never quite as clear about his metaphysics, ontology, and cosmology as we may want. As many scholars have noted, Whitehead can be precise when he wants to be; at other times he uses less technical language, even poetic or rhetorical language. It is my contention that, for the most part, Whitehead is indeed more interested in cosmology than in what Neville would take to be ontology or metaphysics. As we shall see in chapters 4 and 5, much the same thing holds for Chu Hsi's version of Sung Neo-Confucianism.

Stanley Rosen (1989) has suggested another way to diagnose Neville's complaint about Whitehead. In the chapter on dialectic and logic in *The Ancients and the Moderns*, a work also concerned with the question of modernity, Rosen argues that logic as interest in consequences can never logically explain itself in terms of its own technical manipulations of its own discourse. Rosen's formal definition of logic in this chapter is: " . . . logic is the study of those formal structures that exhibit one or another sense of *follows from* obeying the principle of noncontradiction" (1989, 153). What formal logic lacks is what Neville wants to express by the ontological dimension, namely a more holistic explanation of everything that is, including logic itself. What both Neville and Rosen seek, and that which Rosen defends, is the art of dialectics. "Dialectic is rational speech about the whole" (Rosen 1989, 152). For Rosen, if there is no dialectic, then there is no explanation of logic itself. Logic, according to Rosen, cannot define itself, although dialectic can encompass the whole by rational speech. By extension, Neville argues that Whitehead lacks a dialectic, a vision of the ontological per se that allows him to speak rationally about the whole, and hence is limited by the closure of things, of the self-referencing of one thing to another with a narrative concerning why this is so.

Whitehead and Neville do agree on the basic purpose of the philosophic enterprise. As Whitehead said, "Speculative Philosophy is the endeavour to frame a coherent, logical, necessary system of general ideas in terms of which every element of our experience can be interpreted" (1978, 3). At least for Whitehead, true metaphysics would be that set of general ideas describing not only this cosmos but all possible worlds. There is always a problem trying to frame such a general set of ideas. Human finitude, ignorance, and error should always make us suspicious about these theories. One need not be an analytic philosopher worried about metaphysical news from nowhere to be concerned about our ability to frame truly metaphysical statements.

Among all of the statements that Whitehead loosely calls metaphysical, the most general arise in his discussion of the extensive continuum. As far as Whitehead can tell, the relations of any entities in any possible cosmic epoch would have to be " . . . united by the various allied relationships of whole to part, and of overlapping so as to possess common parts, and of contact, and of other relationships derived from these primary relationships" (1978, 66).[20] I will argue later that this way of putting the issue of metaphysics is allied to certain Chinese notions of *ars contextualis* as defined by Hall and Ames in their study of Confucius (1987) and Chinese philosophic discourse (1995).[21] For instance, the classical and Neo-Confucian philosophers often frame their speculative systems in terms of the relationships of whole to parts.[22] Hence we almost always find the Neo-Confucians referring to the unified world continuum as a pattern of the alternating yin–yang forces as ordered by principle through the agency of the human mind-heart. Depending on the lineage of the Neo-Confucian school in question, the picture becomes even more specific in terms of the cosmological details concerning such things as the human mind, nature, and emotions.

This exposition of Whitehead's notion of the extensive continuum is a highly abstract metaphysical system of parts, wholes, and their contacts and overlaps; it is certainly much less detailed than the rest of Whitehead's cosmological schema. It also may be much closer to certain primal patterns of Chinese philosophic speculation than previously anticipated or noticed by Western scholars. But as Whitehead notes, metaphysical principles never take a holiday; they are always present in this or any other world. That is the reason we call them metaphysical: they obtain in any possible world whatsoever. According to this understanding of metaphysical principles, they must be extremely vague as to concrete specification. Here I agree with Neville about the abstract nature of any metaphysical claims. In fact, any kind of specification, according to the event pluralism of Whitehead's cosmology, is the result of the interaction of actual entities in any particular world. We can know little of the specifics of the object–events until they have achieved their final values and forms. This may not be a very exciting metaphysics, but it is general and vague enough to embrace different and more complex cosmologies. It is certainly vague enough to include the Western and Chinese branches of process thought.

AI also has another short list of metaphysical principles, this time reduced to three in number. First, "One principle is that the very essence of real actuality—this, of the completely real—is *process*" (1933, 354). Second, "It is the doctrine that every occasion of actuality is in its own nature finite. There is no totality which is the harmony of all perfections" (1933, 356). Finally, "The third metaphysical principle may be termed the principle of Individuality" (1933, 360). There is nothing revelatory about the first two principles; they are restatements in a slightly different and nontechnical language of Whitehead's reflections on process and reality beginning with *SMW* and concluding with *AI* and *MT.* The third principle, however, is of a different and intriguing, suggestive nature. It speaks about a certain kind of organization, the notion of the individuality of the object–events, a kind of internal definiteness that did not previously serve to define the nature of actual entities as the harmony of achieved value. Such a principle also reinforces Whitehead's commitment to a pluralistic cosmos.

One key feature of Whitehead's philosophy is the attempt to embrace all of the items of human experience. He believes that philosophy does itself a disservice when it tries to explain away persistent features of common experience. For instance, in *AI,* Whitehead returns to the question of the soul. Having come to a seemingly Humean or even quasi-Buddhistic view of the human person as being ultimately empty of self-being or reference, Whitehead revisits the question in *AI.*

> Thus, the basis of a strong, penetrating experience of Harmony is an Appearance with a foreground of enduring individuals carrying with them a force of subjective tone, and with a background providing the requisite connection. . . . There is a real conflation of fundamental feeling. (1933, 363)

This may not be a typical Western definition of an enduring soul, yet it is different in significant ways from the previous account of the soul given in *PR.* It serves as a warrant for Neville's notion of a discursive person with essential and conditional features. In *AI*, Whitehead is trying to explain the nature of enduring individuality rather than explain why it does not exist. Interestingly, Hartshorne sometimes comes close to formulating a similar triad of concepts. He often asserts that metaphysical analysis must always deal with the questions of existence, actuality, and concreteness (1970, 74–75). The way Hartshorne habitually frames the issue is in terms of the contrast between concepts such as existence and actuality and the difference between relatively abstract and fully abstract terms.[23] In many ways this is a more traditional Western method of defining metaphysical ultimates. While this may be useful in connecting process thought to other forms of Western metaphysical discourse, it suffers when applied to the broader comparative world of speculative thought. For instance, what would be Chu Hsi's analogs to these very Western metaphysical concerns? In some ways Whitehead's more imprecise notion of the triad of process, occasions of finite achievement, and the individual definition of harmony point toward the Chu Hsian triad of mind, nature, and emotion—or so I shall argue in chapters 4 and 5.

The source of confusion is found whenever we try to distinguish between *ars contextualis, ontologia generalis,* and *scientia universalis.* Sometimes I have a great deal of sympathy for the great early Taoist Chuang Tzu, who maintained that all we have is our own perspective on things. Contrary to popular opinion, Chuang Tzu was not a complete relativist in that he took some perspectives to be more useful than others. Neville himself tries to be clear in distinguishing these related systems. In fact, a great deal of the power of his critique of process thought comes from his charge that process thinkers habitually confuse these various levels of speculative discourse. As we have already seen, Neville argues that process thinkers take their general cosmology for an adequate account of what should more properly be an ontological account of reality. The issue becomes even more complicated when we introduce the distinctively Neo-Confucian desire to frame systematic discourse in terms of *ars contextualis.*

I am convinced that the distinction between cosmology, ontology, and *ars contextualis* would have been comprehensible to the Sung Neo-Confucians if they had time to digest the Western intellectual tradition in its broad outlines.[24] Chu Hsi might have objected that the attempt to analyze reality in cosmological and ontological terms removed the living vitality of the process of self-creation from the richness of his contextual analysis. While I am not sure that this is merely a question of intellectual taste as opposed to a significant speculative departure, it does matter how you go about framing the basic issues. As every tyro debater knows, she who sets the parameters of debate controls the discussion. Or as Chuang Tzu noted, it is all in the perspective.

Neville never wearies of making the point that the process tradition cannot adequately deal with God in terms of *creatio ex nihilo*. Given that process thought takes creativity to be a supreme category of analysis, Neville believes that process thinkers must take creation *ex nihilo* seriously as the most divine manifestation of creativity per se. Most Western process philosophers, at least those still interested in metaphysical issues, feel uneasy when facing Neville's charge because they have been trained to sense the weight of this kind of ontological analysis. Interest in systematic, constructive philosophy is tantamount to being able to give the reasons for the "why" of things. However, to be fair to those interested in philosophic questions, some analytic philosophers argue that one can be interested in a topic without being able to give metaphysical reasons for this interest; one can also simply still be working through the complicated epistemological issues involved in proposing answers to these kinds of questions. Or even more radically, someone like David Hall (1982b) argues, from a process perspective, that to seek reasons is part of the problem itself. What if, as Hall argues on the basis of his reading of the Taoist tradition, there simply are no reasons at all?

Nonetheless, to be accused of not being able to give good reasons for something so basic as the ontological question is supposed to reveal a true lacunae in the system for those who still prize adequacy in speculative philosophy. Most speculative philosophers, East or West, hate gaps in their systems— save for the wonderfully ironic Chuang Tzu. But perhaps, just perhaps, Whitehead and the Neo-Confucians are correct when they suggest that this may be the wrong way to approach the issue. *Creatio continua* may be the more important key to understanding than *creation ex nihilo* in philosophic systems that are realist, pluralistic, contextualist, organic, and process oriented.

METASYSTEM, ONTOLOGY, DIALECTICS, OR METAPHYSICS

In terms of the schema I am proposing, is it really profitable to continue discussing these metasystemic second order issues *and* cross-cultural forms of conceptualization in terms of the hallowed label of metaphysics and its constant companions of ontology and cosmology? While it is true that Whitehead uses the terms *metaphysics, ontology,* and *cosmology,* does he really stipulate the same thing here as the Western tradition has usually meant?

> The metaphysical characteristics of an actual entity—in the proper sense of 'metaphysics'—should be those which apply to all actual entities. It may be doubted whether such metaphysical concepts have ever been formulated in their strict purity—even taking into account the most general principles of logic and mathematics. (*PR*, 90)

Whitehead is not merely being modest at this point. We need to remember that metaphysical principles never take a holiday. "The metaphysical first principles can never fail of exemplification. We can never catch the actual world taking a holiday from their sway" (*PR*, 4). And since what we know we know by the method of difference, of contrast, of the comparison of what is with what is not, it is very, very hard to say that we ever reach real metaphysics in the strict sense. Whitehead noted that we notice elephants when they are there and when they are not, if we know what elephants are. The problem with metaphysical principles is that they are not like elephants, even if they are some of the most important intellectual tools for human civilization. This was one reason why Whitehead called *PR* an essay in cosmology.

Nonetheless, in the discussion of the extensive continuum, Whitehead expresses what he calls "two metaphysical assumptions."

1. That the actual world, in so far as it is a community of entities which are settled, actual, and already become, conditions and limits the potentiality for creativeness beyond itself (*PR*, 65).

2. The second metaphysical assumption is that the real potentialities relative to all standpoints are coordinated as diverse determinations of one extensive continuum. . . . An extensive continuum is a complex of entities united by the various allied relationships of whole to part, and of overlapping so as to possess common parts, and of contact, and of other relationships derived from these primary relationships (*PR*, 66).

This is a suggestive pair of assumptions in light of our investigation of the general problem of the separation of God and creativity. At least in these passages Whitehead does not suggest that one can separate any one item, even an abstract notion like creativity, from another except where the mutual standpoints are separate. There is no hint that creativity can be understood apart from the allied relationships outlined in the second assumption; in short, creativity is not some kind of ontological surd free floating without connection to anything else in the Whiteheadian cosmos. If this is the case, then we must seek to find a way to reunite God and creativity.

On the Confucian side of things, Chu Hsi also indicates that principle can never be found separated from matter-energy. Chu notes that we can, for heuristic purposes of analysis, differentiate principle and matter-energy, but different modes of analysis do not indicate a different level of ontological reality. Analysis indicates a second-order level of cognitive investigation, but not some kind of cosmological or ontological dualism as far as Chu Hsi or his school are concerned. Hence what we are dealing with in a revised

Whiteheadian *ars contextualis* are assumptions about what a system would have to express in order to be a true metaphysics. And as long as God and creativity are separated as they seem to be in Part V of *PR*, then we cannot have what Whitehead would acknowledge as a coherent metaphysical system.

Even if some kind of revised process *ars contextualis* can be drawn from Chu Hsi and Whitehead, this will still not satisfy Neville's essential complaints about process philosophy. In *HAM*, Neville restates both his great appreciation for Whitehead's contribution to philosophy as well as his grave reservations about process thought as being a corrective to the problems of modernity and its evident present state of decay. In terms of Whitehead's accomplishments, Neville believes that "Perhaps the most important and surely the most liberating contribution of Whitehead has been the construction and legitimization of speculative philosophy" (*HAM*, 92). In doing this, Whitehead assists in building the Anglo-American highroad around the problems of modernism that Neville himself seeks to address.

According to Neville, Whitehead's very success in escaping some of the characteristic problems of the modern project also leads to a strange sense of incompleteness that haunts the Whiteheadian program. While Neville is very much in favor of the interdisciplinary and public nature of the philosophic enterprise, he believes that Whitehead does not go far enough and was misled by what can be accomplished by Whitehead's own desire to see speculative philosophy as framing speculative hypotheses subject to further public revision. While this is an aspect of his thought that Whitehead shares with Peirce, it is not the most appealing part of the ensemble as far as Neville is concerned. The problem with this methodological perspective is that Whitehead, according to Neville, is then unable to ask *the* ontological question because of the empirical nature of the method: "Empirical generalizations simply cannot express the peculiar combination of necessity and contingency required of a treatment of the ontological question" (*HAM*, 95). The reason for this is that speculative philosophy, according to Neville, must deal with questions that move beyond the merely empirical, that is to say, to questions that not only describe the empirical reality but give reasons for it.

This is a very important point for Neville. As he notes, "Some thinkers, of course, take this to be a meaningless question and therefore believe it to be no limitation to Whitehead's system to be unable to answer or even to raise it" (*HAM*, 94). Neville believes that Whitehead failed to move from the framing of hypotheses to the practice of dialectic on Plato's model of "climbing upon them to see their own genesis and assumptions" (*HAM*, 95). If Whitehead had been willing to employ a Platonic dialectic, he might have been able to at least ask the ontological question. No doubt this is an astute observation from within the traditional matrix of Western metaphysical speculation, but does it make as much sense if Whitehead is proposing something more akin to Chu Hsi's Neo-Confucian *ars contextualis*? In fact, how does Neville understand Chu Hsi and the Neo-Confucian tradition in terms of his challenge to the process tradition?

SHIPS PASSING IN DIFFERENT SEAS BUT WITHIN HAILING DISTANCE

From the perspective of comparative philosophy and theology, one of Neville's strengths (and it is another that he shares with Whitehead) is a willingness to consider the history of human thought beyond the confines of the North Atlantic world. The most recent example of this talent is found in *BMG*, a series of essays devoted to Neville's formulation of a comparative philosophy and theology. Along with his attempts to defend speculative philosophy and theology in the Western tradition, he has written extensively, consistently, and with informed appreciation about the Chinese intellectual tradition, with a growing emphasis on the Neo-Confucians. Before I move on to an examination of the Neo-Confucian tradition, we need to ask, how does Neville interpret Chu Hsi on the issue of creativity and the role of ontology and cosmology in the Neo-Confucian synthesis? Is he as critical of Chu and the other Neo-Confucians as he is of Whitehead and the Western process movement?

In *TD* (1982), Neville defines the Neo-Confucian movement, for good historical reasons, as "It is sometimes said that Neo-Confucianism combines the metaphysical naturalism of Taoism and the process psychology of Buddhism with the moral concerns of Confucianism" (*TD*, 147). Although Neville is mainly concerned with an analysis of Wang Yang-ming in *TD*, he does provide a general interpretation of the primary Sung-Ming Neo-Confucian worldview: "Within the Chinese cosmology of vibratory motion, ascending and descending the waves is called yang and yin, respectively" (*TD*, 151). In his later works, including *ETF* and its analysis of time, Neville continues to be impressed with the ability of the Chinese vibratory primary cosmology to avoid some of the characteristic pitfalls of Western metasystemic discourse such as the mind–body or matter–spirit dualities.

Just as with the Western process tradition, Neville finds a paradox in this generalized vibratory Neo-Confucian cosmology. No one will be surprised at this point when Neville tells us that the paradox for the Chinese system is the following:

> Let me suggest that a way around the paradox is to acknowledge that all functional, vibratory yin–yang relations are cosmological relations; they are matters of the conditioning of one thing by another. Further, such conditioning presupposes that the conditioned and conditioning thing are in a context

of mutual relevance more fundamental than the particular condition. (*TD*, 169)

It is this "more fundamental" condition that fascinated Neville in his search for the ontological root of creativity. Here again he finds the Neo-Confucians informative as far as they go, which is pretty far concerning a general cosmology, but not far enough in terms of finding the proper dialectical ontological reference for all such cosmological self-referencing. Neville's early interest in Wang Yang-ming was in Wang's ability to go farther toward an ontological style than the other major Sung-Ming Neo-Confucians.[25] Of course, my argument is that such a search for something or even some reason beyond the object–events of the world that reference each other is to look for something beyond what is warranted in either the Neo-Confucian tradition or in Western process thought. Be this as it may, Neville may still want to embrace his own vision. My purpose is not so much to refute Neville but to answer some of his charges against Whitehead and engage him in reasoned debate. That much is warranted from the Chu's and Whitehead's perspective.

Slightly later in *TD*, Neville makes it crystal clear where the problem lies.

> Although there is little warrant in Wang or in Chinese thought for attributing agency to creative ground by calling it God, there is a metaphysical necessity to acknowledge a ground that creates diverse substance–functions together as they can mutually influence one another. (*TD*, 170)

I agree that the Neo-Confucian tradition is not very interested in the analysis of any analog to the typical West Asian notion of God as a divine theovolitional first principle or creator. Nor is there anything much like Artistotle's unmoved mover either. I also am less than enthusiastic to subscribe to the theory that there is a metaphysical necessity to describe the creative ground of the beings of the world in light of my defense of the Whiteheadian Ontological Principle: to ask for a reason is to ask for an object–event as the Neo-Confucians would thematize the analytic issues involved in such worldview construction.

In *BMG* (1991), Neville again returns to the Chinese case to prove his point that even the Neo-Confucians, renowned agnostics though they may be, still need to account for the creative ground of object–events in terms of some kind of reflective ontological analysis. Here in the work of the Northern Sung master Chou Tun-i (1017–1073), Neville finds a doctrine of the ontological grounding of the Neo-Confucian cosmology. Neville argues that we can read the opening line of Chou's famous and terse "An Explanation of the Diagram of the Supreme Ultimate" as expressing this "asymmetrical ontological grounding" (*BMG,* 77).[26] Neville takes the relationship of the Uncontrived Ultimate (*wu-chi*)[27] and the Supreme Ultimate (*t'ai-chi*) to express the Neo-Confucian understanding of the relationship of the ontological ground of being and the beings themselves as cosmologically conditioned. This shows, for Neville, that " . . . ontological creativity is not merely vertical asymmetry of generation running through levels of determinate organization, but the original creation *ex nihilo*" (*BMG,* 79). Neville has a real genius for finding a plausible way to discover his favorite theme in any tradition; but then, this is what any good comprehensive thinker does in order to read or interpret all of reality in terms of her or his system. Chu Hsi did nothing less in his appropriation of Chou Tun-i in the Southern Sung.

Neville assumes, correctly I believe, that Chu Hsi was faithful to Chou Tun-i's insights as expressed in the Diagram of the Supreme Ultimate. Furthermore, Neville then offers a interpretation of Chu's famous "Treatise on *Jen* (Humanity)" cognate with his ontological reading of Chou's Diagram based on Chu's own understanding of the primary Confucian axiological virtue, humanity. What Neville believes gives him his warrant to read the "Treatise on Humanity" in this fashion is "The emphasis on the controlling and pervasive power of origination as such, not antecedent causes but generativity, indicates a powerful commitment to ontological asymmetry as a dimension running crosswise through immanent definition" (*BMG,* 78). In conclusion, Neville asserts that "Chu Hsi, after Chou, gave a profoundly ontological rendition of the harmony or Mind of Heaven and Earth" (*BMG,* 79). There is no higher philosophic praise within the Nevillian corpus than to acknowledge such a vision on Chu's part. In this regard, Neville believes that Chu avoids Whitehead's lack of a proper ontological interpretation of the cosmos, because Chu does indeed have a Neo-Confucian ontology of creation based on Chou's Uncontrived Ultimate. The question that must be addressed is: Is this a sound reading of Chu Hsi? And even if it is sound, is it the best, most fiduciary reading we can give?

In some fascinating ways Neville parallels a method of reading Chu Hsi that mirrors Mou Tsung-san's modern critique of Chu.[28] However, in Mou's case he is unhappy with Chu's outcome for just those reasons that Neville applauds Chu. Mou argues at great length, being philosophically more in agreement with Wang Yang-ming and Liu Tsung-chou, that Chu misreads Chou and the other Northern Sung masters rather dramatically and decisively. Nonetheless, Mou agrees that Chu's is a most inventive and creative misreading, and in fact, a misreading that comes to dominate the history of Neo-Confucian discourse because of its sheer intellectual genius. Chu's genius was rather like that of Hsün-tzu's equally brilliant interpretation of the Confucian Way—too analytic, too rationalistic, and ultimately too formalistic to capture the real meaning of the mind–heart. But genius is not enough when you have misunderstood the real basis for creativity within the Confucian Tao, which is just what Mou assumes Chu has done. Mou is much less impressed with the transcendent, formalistic, and ontological reading of the Uncontrived Ultimate than Neville is because it again detracts from a proper understanding of the cultivation of the mind–heart. It is the cultivation of the living mind–heart that Mou holds to be the essence of the Confucian Way as a lived tradition and not just an aspect of the intellectual history of human-kind. Yet both Neville and Mou are equally concerned with the notion of creativity or generativity in the Neo-Confucian tradition. Mou argues that the idea of creativity is an absolutely crucial and foundational notion in what Neville calls the primary cosmology of China.

I agree, but the key question then is: What does this creativity mean in Chu's process thought, a Chinese form of that tradition not committed, as Neville is metaphysically and methodologically, to a Platonic dialectical and ontological analysis? Is Neville correct in asserting that Chu offers a Neo-Confucian corrective to Whitehead's excessively cosmological reading of ontological creativity? We need to turn to Chu Hsi to see if this is a correct guess on Neville's part.

NOTES

1. Neville sees himself primarily as a constructive and systematic philosopher interested in the classical metaphysical questions. Among other things, metaphysics is an attempt to state a hypothetical system that can be tested against our experience of the world. In this regard, Neville locates himself in the classical Western philosophic tradition and more specifically identifies with that Anglo-American strain of thought interested in constructive metaphysics, ontology, cosmology, axiology, ethics, and the practice of wisdom. He often traces his intellectual origins to pragmatists such as Peirce and Whitehead, though his appreciation of Whitehead is more limited. And behind all of his philosophy stands the example of Plato as the master dialectician.

He also is a philosopher of religion as well as a Christian systematic theologian writing from the perspective of natural theology. However, he argues that these are heuristically separate tasks and has tried to be clear about the boundaries between these allied disciplines. He believes that we cannot isolate philosophy from religion. This is also in agreement with Whitehead's view of the relation of religion, science, and philosophy.

2. Neville has written more than thirteen books, almost all of which deal with the process tradition in one way or another when dealing with metaphysics, social theory, comparative thought, and the analysis of time. One consistent theme in all of his works has been an attempt to continue Whitehead's task of framing a modern speculative metaphysics, albeit in a Platonic key. Neville surely agrees with White-

head in arguing that every thinker has a metaphysics, even if unacknowledged. One of Neville's own tasks is to try to reintroduce a Platonic voice into modern philosophic discourse. Neville has also continued the interest in comparative religious, philosophic, and theological issues, which has been a trademark of the process tradition. Whatever his criticism of Whitehead might be, Neville agrees that we now need a more globally responsive approach to theological and philosophic issues.

3. At least part of this interest is also professional. In 1988, Neville assumed the deanship of the Boston University School of Theology. Although always interested in religious and theological questions, the assumption of a deanship in a school long known for its tradition of philosophic theology only incited Neville to a more detailed examination of theological issues.

4. Recently, Walter Watson (1985) developed and David Dilworth (1989) applied and extended just such a hermeneutic system for exposing the differences in worldviews. They call their work an "architectonic of meaning," which I will hereafter define as "archic analysis." While offering a hermeneutic for reading texts drawn from most of the literate world's major intellectual traditions, Watson and Dilworth are careful to point out that there is no such thing as an ahistorical or value neutral approach to such analysis. Their architectonic analysis is firmly rooted in the Aristotelian tradition of the West. The basic structure of their method will be outlined in more detail in chapters 5 and 6.

By the use of its categories of archic variables, archic analysis is often a useful tool when trying to differentiate the arguments that occur within one tradition or between closely allied traditions. I believe that this is the case in the debate between Neville and more orthodox Whiteheadians. Archic analysis can help distinguish between real and verbal disagreements and show where Neville and a reformed, but still orthodox, Whiteheadian cosmology have their real quarrel.

5. I used the language of disputation rather than logic because of A.C. Graham's seminal *Disputers of the Tao: Philosophical Argument in Ancient China* (1989) on the history of disputation in classical Chinese thought. Graham has demonstrated that the classical Chinese philosophers were masters of the arts of disputation, although they did not follow the path of classical Western logic, a cultural subset of the universal human inclination to argue and to try to give warrants for these arguments. Good disputation is found everywhere.

6. One process thinker who has continued to respond to Neville has been Lewis S. Ford. For instance, in his 1991 article, "Contrasting Conceptions of Creation," Ford tries again to show how, with some modification, he can present an alternative Whiteheadian answer to Neville's criticism. In doing so, Ford modifies both Neville and Whitehead to articulate a more adequate understanding of creation.

7. Neville has been appreciative of Charles Hartshorne, as he has been of Whitehead. For instance, see Neville's 1991 contribution to Hahn's *The Philosophy of Charles Hartshorne*. Just as with Whitehead, Neville both applauds and criticizes Hartshorne at the same time.

8. As Jacques Gernet (1985) has shown in his study of the early impact of Christianity in China, the Chinese believed that the Christian missionaries were quite confused about their presentation of the faith. One of the major theoretical problems of the Western study of religion is the generation of categories allowing for the interpretation of the East Asian religious scene in something like its own understanding of tradition. As W. C. Smith has so often argued, you have not really described a tradition until members of that tradition tell you that they can see themselves in your description.

9. I have discussed the question of the religious nature of the Confucian tradition in *All under Heaven* (1994).

10. No one should assume that this is always a successful project for God according to Whitehead or Neville. There is room enough for tragedy, ignorance, and evil in their philosophies. Yet, according to Whitehead, God's initial aim is always to create the best that can be, that is to say, the most intense choice that can be made, in relation to the lives and actions of free creatures. Neville is dubious of all such claims because he believes they lead to a form of anthropomorphic idolatry. While the Neo-Confucians did not thematize their ultimate concerns in terms of a divine theovolitional agent, the Tao as the matrix of all creativity seeks, if such agential language is stretched to its limits, the good. The good for the Neo-Confucians is the normative nature of the Heavenly Principle.

11. There is a whole cottage industry devoted to the analysis of the definition and meaning of modernity. For instance, there is intense debate about whether or not we are living in a later modern or early post-modern world. Humorously, Neville has occasionally been heard to mutter that he would prefer to live in a paleo-galactic era rather than to be "post" anything.

12. It is interesting to note that Edgar Sheffield Brightman, one of Neville's great predecessors at Boston University, had a distinctively different reading of the *Philebus*. As we have seen, Neville launches his ontological speculations on the basis of his reading of Plato's analysis of the unlimited and the limited.

Brightman notes, quoting Socrates, "As Socrates puts it a little later, it is 'the infinite bound by the finite' (27D) that creates the 'victorious life.' Thus, all meaning, goodness, and order are limitations on infinity by the finite" (1946, 287). Brightman understands that Plato wants to make this move because of the problem of evil in the created order. "God is a will for good, not infinite but finite, limited on the one hand by rational principles or order and control (*Philebus*), and on the other by "discordant and disorderly motion" (*Timaeus*) which he finds in existence" (1946, 288).

Neville's most recent interpretation of his use of Plato's fourfold analysis is found in *HAM*, pp. 264–273. He here defends this form of analysis on ontological and cosmological grounds.

13. Chad Hansen (1992) has recently argued that reading Chinese thought as *ars contextualis* is even a misleading way to state the issue if we take this to be yet another cosmological debate. According to Hansen, Chinese philosophy in its classical

pre-Han articulation is simply not interested in questions of ontology, cosmology, and epistemology. Rather the focus is on a very sophisticated philosophy of language as a pragmatic guide for human conduct. Hansen does admit, however, that by the Sung the Chinese had learned to deal with these questions because they were part of the Buddhist package imported from India and Central Asia and then digested in the form of the T'ang schools of Hua Yen and T'ien-t'ai. In some respects, Hansen's argument about the nature and role of language in Chinese thought parallels the argument made by Hall and Ames (1987, 1995) about the lack of transcendence in early Confucian thought. In both cases they argue that any notion transcendence or an informed interest in cosmological or ontological issues marks a late arrival in Chinese thought. Such modern New Confucians as Mou Tsung-san, Tu Wei-ming, and Cheng Chung-yin demure and find a cosmological element in early Chinese thought, especially in the *Doctrine of the Mean* and the *Book of Changes*.

14. As noted before, *BMG* and *HAM* both return to the general issues of natural or philosophic theology and continue to presuppose Neville's critique of Whitehead. In *HAM*, Neville refines his criticism of Whitehead's failure to establish an ontological vision sufficient to ground a modern speculative philosophy.

15. Lewis Ford has continued his side of the debate with Neville by placing, and I truncate Ford's argument, creativity and God in a future key. One could say that this is a process version of proleptic eschatology. See Ford (1987).

16. There has been a great deal of debate in the scholarly community about how much actual freedom for the emergent creatures Whitehead really allows. Here again Neville is very much in line with some of the main points of contention in Whitehead scholarship. For one careful summary of the problems involved, see David Basinger's *Divine Power in Process Theism: A Philosophic Critique* (1988).

17. One of the first and still most cited critiques along this line was made by Stephen Lee Ely in 1942. Although originally only fifty-eight pages in length, it expresses orthodox Christian frustration with Whitehead's notion of God.

18. It is fascinating to remember a similar problem in Chu Hsi's metasystem. Chu Hsi had a problem trying to explain how principle is one with *ch'i*/matter-energy without confusion but also with essential features that allow human beings to make the distinction analytically, and for good reasons, between the two concepts. Chu Hsi's students often wanted him to state which of these two notions was really ultimate, although Chu himself refused to frame the question that way. For Chu Hsi, it did not make any sense whatsoever to try to separate principle from matter-energy. If you like, these are dipolar traits analogous to the primordial and consequent nature of God in Whitehead. Another analogy is Aristotle's distinction between matter and form.

19. I remember talking a number of years ago to Hans Küng about a similar problem in meaning. He told me that as a young theologian he was delighted with the reforms begun at Vatican II. However, as the years went on, he noticed that things were not changing as quickly as they might. His enlightenment about this non-process

came during a conversation with a very old Italian cardinal in the Roman Curia. As he and the cardinal had a very cordial conversation, he realized that even though they were using the same language, they did not mean the same thing at all by what they were saying. This was the beginning of Küng's continued fascination with paradigm shifts in theology. As members of a religious tradition, Christians continue to use the common language of faith but mean different things in different times and places.

20. It is just this kind of speculation that has stimulated Nobo to propose his creative interpretation of Whitehead's metaphysics of extension and solidarity. Both Nobo and I agree on the centrality of the whole–part relationship. This is also a key to understanding the Chinese proclivity for *ars contextualis*.

21. Both A.C. Graham (1989) and Chad Hansen (1983) have made a similar argument in terms of the nature of the way classical Chinese philosophers order their world. Graham and Hansen are interested in how classical Chinese as a language makes such an analysis possible and likely.

22. This agrees with Hansen's (1992) suggestive analysis of Chinese philosophy as a debate about the nature of language as a means to guide conduct.

23. While I do not want to imply that Hartshorne would agree with my formulation of form, dynamics, and unification, I do believe that without too much violence being done to his work there are analogs in his work to my thematization of the metasystemic issues involved. What is not immediately present in much of Hartshorne's philosophy is the easy connection to the notion of process or dynamics that is so clearly a crucial emphasis for Whitehead. But then, as Hartshorne has always argued, he is not a scholastic follower of Whitehead.

24. In fact, a number of modern Confucians such as Tu Wei-ming and Cheng Chung-ying are engaged in such a search for a way of characterizing the Confucian tradition. There also is a renewed interest in Neo-Confucian philosophic methodology among younger scholars in the Peoples Republic of China, such as Zhang Liwen and Zheng Jiadong.

25. There have been many scholars of Neo-Confucianism who might agree with Neville about Wang Yang-ming. Wang certainly goes farther in Neville's direction with his four-sentence teaching and his speculations on *liang-chih* than do most other Neo-Confucians. Wang's search for the ultimate root of the things moved him in the general direction of the Western ontological quest, albeit in a distinctive Neo-Confucian voice.

26. I agree with Neville that, at least for Chu's school, Chou's *Diagram of the Supreme Ultimate* is the foundational cosmological document. It was taken as the metasystemic manifesto of the Northern Sung philosophic movement and was interpreted as announcing all of the characteristic themes that would serve to thematize the tradition for the rest of its creative life. As with all such short and multivalent texts, it is indeed open to many, many creative readings.

27. I have chosen to translate *wu-chi* as the Uncontrived Ultimate rather than as the Ultimate of Non-being, as Neville does, because I believe that invoking the notion of Non-being loads too much Western Platonic and Neo-Platonic freight on a perfectly good Chinese philosophic term. If the notion of *wu-chi* really has something of a Taoist heritage, which is what many later Chinese scholars have argued, then it certainly makes more sense to translate it as the Uncontrived Ultimate in respect to one of its parents. In this way we can serve filial piety and Taoist sensibilities at the same time.

28. For those interested in some of the details of Mou Tsung-san's critique, see Berthrong (1994). In this work I try to explain the nature of this ongoing Neo-Confucian and New Confucian debate about Chu's contribution to Confucian discourse.

4

Introducing the Neo-Confucians

Just as there is an expanse of Western philosophic history spreading out over centuries and regions before Whitehead shaped his problems, categories, and solutions, the Confucian tradition had a complicated and rich history before Chu Hsi's synthesis during the Southern Sung dynasty (1127–1279). There is a persistent philosophic folk myth in Western intellectual circles fostered by the Hegelian and Romantic reaction to the Enlightenment infatuation with Confucianism as a nontheistic ethical lifeworld. This myth asserts that there was little philosophic development in traditional China from the classical period of the late Chou dynasty (480–221 B.C.E.) to Chu's Southern Sung.[1] However, as we shall see, a great deal happened between the fall of the Chou (249 B.C.E.) and the rise of the Sung (960). Paraphrasing Whitehead's remark that the history of Western philosophy is a series of footnotes to Plato, the permutations of the Confucian Tao after Confucius were a veneration and interpretation of the First Sage. Whitehead's witty remark was never intended to be a complete description of the history of Western thought after Plato, nor was everything in Confucianism a mere repetition of Confucius's own vision of the Tao. One of the worst criticisms that can be made about the Confucian Way is that it is only one tradition rather than the proliferation of perspectives and research projects.

In at least one aspect, the nineteenth-century European philosophers can be forgiven their rush to judgment on the Confucian tradition's seemingly frozen state of intellectual development. From a non-Chinese (and East Asian) perspective, this seeming inertia is the result of the constant recycling of philosophic terminology and texts that was the hallmark of Confucianism till the modern period. Of course, this is not how Confucian discourse was understood throughout traditional East Asia. Until the twentieth century, all educated persons in East Asia knew how to read classical Chinese, the lingua franca of Confucian studies. Moreover, many Korean, Japanese, and Vietnamese intellectuals were comfortable in composing their works in classical Chinese. It would be as if all educated Europeans retained a high level of fluency in Latin until 1900. The convention would have been that any serious philosophic work ought to be composed in classical Latin (or classical Chinese, as was the case in East Asia), even if the contemporary problems and situations were radically different. What happened in Confucian discourse was that old terms were given new meanings as time went on; old meanings also were retained, making for a very complicated hermeneutic situation.[2] Any student of Confucian philosophy has to be aware of the generally accepted philosophic meanings of a term *and* pay careful attention to how an individual philosopher either affirmed the traditional readings or added a new twist, a new layer of sedimentation to the history of Confucian semantics.

Two examples of this modification of meaning will suffice. For instance, the most important of Confucian virtues is *jen*/humaneness. In early Chou China, *jen* meant something like noblesse oblige of the aristocratic person for the commoner levels of society. Confucius accepted this meaning but expanded it to mean an inclusive humaneness, a quality of concern and care for others that should be the hallmark of any civilized person, regardless of their class background or civil rank. Another example is the transformation of *ch'eng*/sincerity by the Sung Neo-Confucians. The term started out meaning sincerity or personal integrity. The Sung Neo-Confucians built on this base and incorporated into the classical meaning the notion of self-perfection or self-actualization. *Ch'eng* came to mean the perfected state that arises from the cultivation of the self and engagement with the social lifeworld; of course, the older meanings were retained and no one ever believed that the newer abrogated the older virtue of sincere integrity. If we do not pay careful attention to the expansion of meanings over time, it is easy to overlook the growth of Confucian discourse.

I refer the reader to the appendix on archic analysis for another interpretation by Watson (1985) and Dilworth (1989) about how to differentiate the use of Confucian terms over the centuries. While taxonomies are never able to capture the living vitality of a complex philosophic system, the extended use of classical Chinese as the medium for Confucian discourse makes archic analysis a handy tool for helping to see how different philosophers used the same terms to mean quite distinct things. Arguments between Chu Hsi and proponents of Wang Yang-ming fall into focus when we realize that some, thought not all, of the debate hinges on the different meanings or shades of meanings applied to their common philosophic vocabulary.

In fact, there are roughly 1,600 years of momentous change from the beginnings of reflective thought in China from Confucius (551–479 B.C.E.) to Chu's birth in 1130. Without a doubt, Chu is second only to the First Sage in influence in Chinese philosophic history. Of course, not everyone agreed with Chu either in the Southern Sung or in the later developments of the tradition. Chu has often been compared to St. Thomas Aquinas, and the analogy is apt. No one can safely study the history of Western philosophy and theology without recourse to St. Thomas; equally, no one can ignore Chu when trying to understand the growth of what has been called Neo-Confucianism by Western sinologists.

The specific nomenclature invented by Western scholars (now adopted by East Asian intellectuals as well) in order to differentiate the two great periods of Confucian intellectual history testifies to the major transformations of the tradition. The first term, *Confucianism,* designates the work of the three great Chou dynasty masters, Confucius, Mencius, and Hsün Tzu, and constitutes the classical period. In terms of Chinese thought, this is called the period of the Hundred Schools in recognition of all of the various schools that arose prior to the founding of the great Ch'in empire in 221 B.C.E.. This was indeed the period of contending schools of philosophy and has been compared with the rise of Greco-Roman thought in the classical world of the West. In both cases, the thinkers of this great Axial Age set the agenda for their respective cultural areas.

From the Confucian point of view, there are two pivotal periods in the development of the tradition. The first is the classical age of the three masters and their students and disciples (ca. 551–221 B.C.E.). The second is recognized as beginning with the great Confucian revival in the Sung dynasty (960–1279), 1,100 years after the death of Hsün Tzu, the last of the classical Confucian founders. Western scholars, in order to distinguish this second period from the classical age, gave it the name "Neo-Confucianism." I should note that there is a good deal of debate regarding the adequacy of these Western terms of reference; there is nothing in the Chinese tradition that corresponds to the Western usage. For instance, the term *Confucian* was used in the classical period to designate what Chinese historians called the *ju* or *ju* school. While Confucius would have recognized himself as a *ju,* that is to say, someone skilled in the study and application of classical rituals and their theory, it probably would have struck him as impious to call himself the founder of a school. Confucius constantly reminded his students that he loved the ancients and was seeking to restore the wisdom of the sages as codified in the culture of his beloved Chou dynasty.

The term *Neo-Confucian* is just as contentious. It designates a group of T'ang and Sung intellectuals who perceived themselves as reviving classical Confucian culture after the arrival of Buddhism during China's long medieval period (ca. 200–900). However, there was no single name that all of them would have accepted as a proper designation of their movement. In fact, the Neo-Confucian movement was divided into a number of different schools. The most dominant Sung school, at least philosophically, called itself *tao-hsüeh,* or the Teaching of the Way. Needless to say, many contemporary scholars thought that this was a highly pretentious name and made fun of these scholars for making such outrageous claims for purporting to rediscover

Confucian orthodoxy and orthopraxy. Nonetheless, through the efforts of a group of Northern and Southern Sung teachers, the name of *tao-hsüeh* stuck, and the Chinese intellectual world was never the same after Chu's account of the rise of the Teaching of the Way.

Western and Asian scholars have grumbled, and not without reason, that all too often the entire history of post–Sung thought is read hegemonically in terms of Chu's account.[3] These scholars point out that there are all kinds of other accounts available as well. By the end of the imperial age, the great Confucians of the Ch'ing dynasty (1644–1911) made their philosophic careers by demonstrating errors of logic and history in Chu's account.[4] Of course, it did not hurt that Chu's version of the teaching was made the basis for the entire civil service examination system from 1313 to 1905. This meant, for good or ill, that every Chinese student was forced to learn Chu's philosophy well enough to pass an extremely demanding series of regional, provincial, and national examinations if they wanted to join the imperial civil service. The social pressure to take the examinations was enormous. The examination system was the only sure way a family could enter and remain in the early modern Chinese cultural and political elite, the literati class.

For our purposes, the terms *Confucian* and *Neo-Confucian* will suffice. They work perfectly well if we remember that, as with all such conventional labels for the development of thought, they obscure as well as illumine important features of the history of Confucian discourse. For instance, one can ask, what happened to the Confucian Tao between the death of Hsün Tzu (ca. 220 B.C.E.) and the Northern Sung Neo-Confucian masters (1020–1060)? A great deal. For instance, there was the mere matter of the arrival of Buddhism in East Asia and the dramatic transformation of all East Asian culture caused by the indigenization of the *dharma*. For almost six centuries, many of China's most able intellectuals took part in Buddhism's golden age across Asia.

To put Chu Hsi's thought in perspective, we need to determine those periods and materials that were most important for the Sung synthesis. The history of the tradition can be periodized as follows:

I.   The Classical Period (551–221 B.C.E.)—defines the fundamental axiology and inclusive humanism of the Confucian Way;

II.   The Han and the Rise of the Commentary Tradition (206 B.C.E.–220)— incorporation of cosmological theories and creation of the Confucian canon;

III. The Defense of the Way (Three Kingdoms to the fall of the T'ang, 220–906) and the Rise of Neo-Taoism and Buddhism—cosmology, ontology, and self-cultivation are debated;

IV. The Neo-Confucian Revival (Late T'ang to Sung, 845–1279)—the rise of systematic and speculative philosophy in a Confucian modality.

Whatever their lineage or school, all later Confucians looked back in awe to Confucius, his students and disciples, and the other Chou dynasty masters. These are literally the founders of the tradition as we now know it. And whatever else can be said about the early tradition, from Confucius to Hsün Tzu, its prime focus was on social ethics or axiology. The major problem faced and question asked by Confucius was, with the times so full of social decay and conflict, what must be done to restore human flourishing? Confucius's simple answer was to restore the rites, disciplines, and rituals of the early Chou as exemplified in the lives of Kings Wen, Wu, and the Duke of Chou. All that must be done is for people to practice *jen,* or humaneness, as the primordial virtue of the early sage kings and ministers. Of course, this was easier said than done, and Confucius knew this as well as anyone else. Confucius's students were always commenting on the fact that seeking humaneness with the Master was an arduous process, and whenever one goal was realized the Master prodded the weary student on to yet another task. The message that the students took from this was that the road to true virtue was long, in fact, unending, and in need of constant renovation.

Of course, Confucius and the later Confucians were in constant dialogue with other thinkers within the fertile and heady matrix of the classical Chou philosophic world and borrowed from them both consciously and unconsciously as they debated points of history, political theory, aesthetics, and philosophic method. However, Confucians have pointed out that Confucius, Mencius, and Hsün Tzu provided a wealth of suggestive insights, a richness internal to Confucian discourse that gives a remarkable continuity to the Confucian project over the centuries. Confucians recognize stimulation from other sources but defend the premise that the response to outside stimulus is founded on primordial Confucian insights. Confucians have defined themselves as scholars committed to the integral vision of the Master as codified in the classic texts. The pious Confucian tradition maintains that Confucius was the collector and editor of the basic classics of the Confucian canon. Of course, in their more critical moments, the later Neo-Confucians were aware that the proposed authorship and editorship of Confucius for the early canon was highly dubious. Long before the Western higher criticism of the Bible, Sung, Ming, and Ch'ing Neo-Confucians exegetes demonstrated on impeccable textual and historical grounds that Confucius was not the author and editor of the canon. However, in no way did this detract from their admiration for the very human scholar who emerges from the records of his disciples in the *Analects.*

Over the centuries the canon expanded from the original five classics until it reached its terminus with the thirteen official classics in the Sung period. It was not that the Confucians had a doctrine of open revelation that allowed for the composition of new classics after the Chou, but rather that the canon was expanded to include classical material that supported the earliest stratum of texts such as the *Book of Poetry* and the *Book of Changes*. If a commitment to the classics is a necessary part of being a Confucian, it is not sufficient for self-definition. To be recognized as a true Confucian by other scholars, a person must learn to embody the transcendent dimension or ultimate reference point of the tradition. Self-cultivation of the mind–heart was crucial for taking the burden of culture upon oneself. A person must get the Tao for oneself in order to be of service to oneself and others.

Mencius and Hsün Tzu continued the defense of the emerging Confucian vision against a backdrop of an increasingly dangerous world and in the face of other philosophic visions. This was the period of savage warfare, of large states devouring smaller states, which resulted in the destruction of the Chou dynasty and the unification of the Chinese world under the first emperor of the Ch'in. Rather like Socrates, the steadfast concern of the early Confucians was to probe the means and ends of human flourishing. This led, as the philosophic debate between and among the Confucians and other philosophic schools intensified, to the consideration of theories of human nature, cognition, disputation, epistemology, the role of government, poetry, music, ritual, and the cultivation of the mind–heart.

The early Confucian masters were noticeably distanced from concerns for what the Western tradition calls "cosmology," or the question of the organization of the cosmos or the question of ontology concerning why is there is something rather than nothing at all.[5] However, there were other early schools of thought, such as the Mohists and Taoists, who evinced more interest in these kinds of ontological and cosmological issues. Another fertile arena for the development of early Chinese cosmology was thinkers that were related to the medical sciences, including the arts of physical self-cultivation and the preservation of health. Works such as the *Kuan Tzu* and the *Lü-shih ch'un-ch'iu* represent the results of these speculations on the nature of the cosmos.[6] From the Confucian point of view, the appendices of the *Book of Changes* became the most important reservoir for their appropriation of late Chou and early Han cosmological reflections. Pan-Chinese concepts such as yin–yang, the five phases, the Supreme Ultimate and the perennially elusive *ch'i,* or matter–energy, were the most important elements of early Chinese cosmology.

It was the task of the great Han dynasty Confucians such as Tung Chung-shu (ca. 179–104 B.C.E.) to weld the ethical bedrock of the classical masters onto the pan-Chinese cosmology of the late Chou and early Han. Because the

Han scholars followed their illustrious classical masters, and because of their penchant for writing in a commentarial mode, not enough recognition has been given to thinkers like Tung for forging a Confucian tradition that combined the best of their school's thought with the emerging pan-Chinese cosmology. The Han Confucians also were successful in commending their tradition to the new Han rulers as the ideological basis for Han imperial rule. Such a linkage proved to have two edges; on the one hand, Confucianism reigned supreme as the civil ideology for the imperial state, but on the other hand, such a close connection with imperial power often compromised the ethical integrity of the Confucians.

With the fall of the Han dynasty in 220, an event as traumatic for the Chinese as was the fall of Rome on the other side of Eurasia, Confucianism was again challenged by new and renewed religions and philosophies. There was a noteworthy revival of Taoism with both religious and philosophic movements. The great Neo-Taoist thinkers of the third and fourth centuries evinced a fascination with ontology, the question of why there is something rather than nothing, and in the Chinese case, a special enchantment with the relationship of being and non-being. One interesting track of Neo-Taoist speculation led to questioning how the cosmos was creative of the myriad creatures. This was yet another important speculative element for the Neo-Confucianism synthesis.

However important the Neo-Taoist contribution to Chinese thought was, and it was major, it pales in significance when contrasted to the arrival of Buddhism in China, sometime in the second century of the common era. The contributions and stimulus of the *dharma* were manifold: the *dharma* emerged to challenge cherished Chinese social ideals as well as to established patterns of philosophy. For instance, no culture has lavished more attention on the role of the family as a metaphor to live by than the Confucians; yet the Buddhists audaciously suggested that there was a more exalted way of life, that of the celibate monastic order. The Buddhists imported all of the various schools of Indic thought along the Silk Road for centuries to the delight of Chinese intellectuals

Along with the translation of the vast range of Buddhist literature into Chinese, by the sixth century the Chinese began to create their own schools. The litany of the names of these schools echoes around the world to the present day, from Central Asia to the shores of California and the hills and valleys of Europe. T'ien-ta'i, Hua Yen, Pure Land, and Ch'an/Zen have become the ecumenical property of the world due to the Chinese desire to preach the liberating *dharma* with their own cultural sensibility. No other tradition so challenged the Confucians at the core of their beliefs as did the Buddhists.

If the Neo-Taoists had introduced Confucians to the joys of ontological reflection, the Buddhists proposed that even being and non-being were not enough. The true nature of the world was emptiness. Nothing could have been more shocking to the resolutely axiological, realistic, and naturalistic Confucian sensibility. By the end of the T'ang dynasty, there arose a generation of thinkers, the most famous being Han Yü (768–824), who rallied to the defense of the Confucian Tao. Stimulated by their exchanges with Buddhists, Han and his friends sought to find in the classical Chou tradition a way to respond to the Buddhist challenge to their fundamental philosophic beliefs and social institutions.

The encounter was remarkable because it was the first time the Chinese had extensive literary contact with another high, literate civilization with a different worldview. Although Western philosophers and theologians perceive Buddhism as a strange creature, it was a religious sensibility elaborated in various philosophic positions common to the broad Indo-European linguistic world. It is this pan-Indo-European philosophic world that has brought forth ontology, cosmology, metaphysics, and epistemology wherever it has flourished. Although it flirted with these kinds of issues during the height of the Chou classical period through the work of the Taoists, Mohists, and Logicians, the Chinese tradition tended not to emphasize these characteristic Indo-European concerns for thinking about being itself and its relationship to human flourishing.

Part of the reason for this resides in the nature of the Indo-European and Sinitic language families. The languages used by the early Buddhist philosophers, Pali and Sanskrit, had the wonderfully flexible Indo-European verb "to be." Classical Chinese, on the other hand, does not have one verb system to express what normally would be signified by the protean verb "to be" and all of its other Indo-European cousins. Chinese has a range of verbs that cluster around the normal functionings of the Indo-European "to be," but is forced to make choices whenever confronted with the various shades of meaning that "to be" can assume in philosophic discourse. For instance, Chinese philosophers will use the verb *"yu"* when they mean something like "to be" as to have some feature or characteristic. On the other hand, they would use the verb *"shih"* for distinguishing this from that, when in English we would say it *is* this or that. As I noted earlier, there was nothing in classical Chinese that prevented Chinese philosophers from dealing with the philosophic issues caused by the various functions of the Indo-European verb system of "to be."[7] It was novel for them to have to take these questions as seriously as they did after the sinification of Buddhism and the rise of the great Chinese schools in the sixth century. However, after the rise of Chinese Buddhist philosophy, Chinese intellectuals were faced with these kinds of issues; and the Neo-

Confucian synthesis, in part, is an answer to what it means to be in the Chinese case. What is of particular interest to us is that the Neo-Confucian sense of what it means "to be" is always linked to a theory of cosmic generativity and process.

The work begun by Han Yü was renewed by a remarkable group of scholars in the Northern Sung dynasty beginning in the 1020s with the reform program of Fan Chung-yen (989–1052).[8] One wing of this fellowship of committed public intellectuals eventually took the name *"tao-hsüeh,"* or Teaching of the Way. The standard Western designation of the group is Neo-Confucianism. While the Neo-Confucians were united in their desire to revive the Confucian Tao, they were a highly diverse movement. They ranged from social reformers to prime ministers to great essayists, poets, and historians to recluse cosmologists to moral and speculative philosophers. Some thought well of Buddhism and Taoism; some believed that these two alternative traditions needed to be confronted and refuted in the strongest possible terms. However, they were the heirs of the previous epochs of the development of the Confucian Way, and this included their ambiguous relationship with Buddhism and Taoism as well.

The group of reformers inspired by Fan Chung-yen's example knew that they were proposing something new. Of course, like so many great reformers, their battle cry was based on an impassioned plea for a return to the classical sources of the tradition. In the case of Ch'eng I (1033–1107), Chu Hsi's most influential teacher, this meant the theory that the Way of the Sages had been obscured since the time of Mencius. According to Ch'eng I, the true teaching of the Way was eclipsed from Mencius' death down to his teacher Chou Tun-i (1017–1073). According to Ch'eng I, Chou and his colleagues began the process of uncovering the true principles of orthodox Confucian teachings, teachings that had been obscured by the mistakes of the Han and T'ang commentators. Needless to say, these orthodox Confucian teachings also were refutations of the heretical works of the Taoists and Buddhists as well. With a fervent Confucian sense of familial piety, Ch'eng I believed that only with the insights of his beloved older brother Ch'eng Hao (1032–1085) was the real richness of Confucian teaching available to students of the Way. The general outlines of Ch'eng I's restoration theory were later supplemented and completed by Chu in his theory of the orthodox transmission of the Way.

This reconstruction of history and the Confucian way was audacious for a tradition such as Confucianism that reverenced the continuity of history as highly as it did. These Northern and Southern Sung scholars claimed that they had an undisorted insight into the true teachings of the sages appropriate for their generation. In Chu Hsi's reconstruction of the teachings of his Northern Sung masters, each of these scholars contributed a special segment of the restoration project, with the capstone being the contribution of *li*/principle theory by the two Ch'eng brothers.

If it were not enough to rewrite the history of the tradition, Chu made the momentous decision to edit and supplement the classical Confucian texts. One of the most important texts for the Neo-Confucians, and especially for Chu, was the *Great Learning*. The *Great Learning* had started life as one chapter of a longer ritual text, the *Li Chi*, but was singled out by Chu, along with the *Analects* of Confucius, *Mencius*, and the *Doctrine of the Mean*, to become part of the *Four Books*. These four texts were chosen by Chu to become a canon within a canon, the stepping-stones to a more accurate understanding of the Confucian classics as a whole. Chu not only selected these texts, he wrote definitive new commentaries on them for future generations of students.

Following Ch'eng I, Chu Hsi made the decision that the original text of the *Great Learning* as transmitted from the Han dynasty must have become corrupted and indeed lacked a whole section after the end of chapter 4. I should note that the chapter divisions in question were also added to the text by Chu. Chu's solution was to add a new section to replace the "missing" material in order to complete chapter 5.

> It would appear that the preceding, fifth chapter of commentary [by Tseng Tzu], elucidated the meaning of "fully apprehending the principle in things" and "the extension of knowledge," but it is now lost. Recently, I made bold to use the ideas of Ch'eng-tzu to supplement it as follows: what is meant by the "extension of knowledge lies in fully apprehending the principle of things" is that, if we wish to extend our knowledge to the utmost, we must probe thoroughly the principle in those things we encounter. It would seem that every man's intellect is possessed of the capacity for knowing and that every thing in the world is possessed of principle. But, to the extent that principle is not yet thoroughly probed, man's knowledge is not yet fully realized. Hence, the first step of instruction in greater learning is to teach the student, whenever he encounters anything at all in the world, to build upon what is already known to him of principle and to probe still further, so that he seeks to reach the limit. After exerting himself in this way for a long time, he will one day become enlightened and thoroughly understand [principle]; then, the manifest and the hidden, the subtle and the obvious qualities of all things will all be known, and the mind, in its whole substance and vast operations, will be completely illuminated. This is called "fully apprehending the principle in things." This is called "the completion of knowledge."
> (Gardner 1986, 104–105)

Of course, this becomes a precise summary of Chu's program of study based on the examination of things in order to find their normative principles.

Chu Hsi's own synthesis was known as the school of principle, or *li-hsüeh*, because of his insistence on the examination of things in order to discover the principles that made them what they were. Each of Chu's Northern Sung masters provided at least one of the building blocks for his system. Chou Tun-i contributed the idea of the Supreme Ultimate, the principle of principles as the organizing form of the ceaselessly responsive and generative cosmos. From Chou's *Diagram of the Supreme Ultimate,* Chu appropriated the notion that the whole cosmos was pervaded by a principle of creativity and unity that was manifested in each particular emergent object–event as its own principle. This was the formal side of reality as the search for the principles of order and definiteness.

From Chang Tsai (1020–1077), Chu borrowed the notion that principle always resides in *ch'i*/matter–energy. Matter–energy was the dynamic, ever-changing side of reality in which form or principle gave a pattern for the emerging object–event to follow. For human beings, the mind–heart was the highest form of matter–energy with the particular ability to recognize principle and hence the organizing center of the emerging person. Chu owed as much to Chang for the pan-Chinese cosmological concept of matter–energy and the particular Sung Neo-Confucian understanding of the mind–heart as he did to the Ch'eng brothers' theory of principle.

The third of the great Northern Sung masters, Shao Yung (1011–1077), was a problem for Chu. Shao shared all of the typical Northern Sung conversational topics, but approached them from a direction that forced Chu to exclude him from Chu's own list of major masters. The problem with Shao is that, according to Chu, he became too enamored of the pseudo-science of numerology. Shao certainly was an astute student of the *I-ching* and of the role of "broad comprehension" that flowed from the tradition of the interpretation of the *Classic of Changes.* Chu simply felt that Shao had gotten too close to what can only be called a Sung version of the occult. It did not help that Shao also was known as the recluse of Loyang and refused to sit for the civil service examinations. However, Chu was definitely stimulated by Shao's epistemological reflections, which were no doubt among the most sophisticated Northern Sung deliberations on the ability and methods of knowledge.

The fourth and fifth Northern Sung masters were Ch'eng Hao (1032–1085) and Ch'eng I (1033–1107). They are the most famous fraternal philosophic team in Confucian history. What Chu derived from them was a theory of principle as a form of definiteness. The Ch'engs saw principle everywhere and understood comprehension of principle to be the key to knowledge and ethical action. According to them, everything in the world had a principle that made it what it was, that gave it a specific form of definiteness. For the

Ch'eng brothers, form or principle was ultimately moral, a primordial axiology of becoming that infused the whole cosmos.

Chu's personal contribution to the mix of Northern Sung philosophy was to provide order to the various elements that lent them a harmony not articulated by his revered masters. In short, this was the analysis of object–events in terms of form (principle), dynamics (matter–energy), and their unification (self-actualization). This process of self-actualization, often described through of the terms such as *jen*/humaneness and *ch'eng*/self-actualization, allowed Chu to depict not only how the world (and humanity) works but how it should function in accordance with the teachings of the ancient sages. Along with Chu's thoughts about harmony and the ultimate good, these elements were fused into his comprehensive teaching of principle. No thinker since Hsün Tzu had provided such a robust defense of the Confucian vision of the ultimate good in so many dimensions of human life.

Chu's Neo-Confucian discourse occupies the boundary between philosophy and religion, because Chu always linked analysis with self-cultivation and social action. In terms of the *Doctrine of the Mean*, Chu argued that the end of human flourishing could only be found in harmony or the perfection of goodness/*chih shan*. Consonant with Whitehead's paean to peace at the end of *AI,* Chu would have agreed that it all comes to naught if there is not some kind of sense of harmony, of a life well spent in search of human excellence. The grand historian of Chinese science, Joseph Needham, remembering the end of a sermon he once heard, suggested the following paraphrase as an excellent summary of both Christian and Confucian views of harmony and peace: "Finally, my brethren, for well-conducted people life presents no problems." We are now prepared to view Chu's contribution to our discussion of creativity in light of his own philosophic background.

NOTES

1. For an excellent summary of the history of Confucianism, see Tu Weiming's account of the development of the tradition in Arvind Sharma, ed., *Our Religions* (San Francisco: Harper San Francisco, 1993).

2. For an examination of how this works, see the appendix on archic analysis. Archic analysis is a taxonomy with its controls derived from the work of Richard McKeon. Many comparative philosophers and theologians have grave reservations about taxonomies. The main quarrel, expressed cogently by Hall and Ames (1995), is that a taxonomy imposes a categoreal schema that has little to do with the target philosophy or theology. This of course is true when you think of the Aristotelian roots of the fourfold analysis of texts used by Watson and Dilworth. But taxonomy does have one benefit. It is a controlled experiment in that the method is held constant. This

works well, I argue, when you are trying to understand how one tradition (Confucianism) makes use of a set philosophic vocabulary over 2,500 years by means of adding new shades of meaning to established terms over time. By asking the same set of questions, archic analysis can ferret out new or different meanings for the same term. Of course, the Neo-Confucians themselves were well aware that they were adding new layers of meaning to older terms. Ch'en Ch'un (1159–1223), one of Chu's best students, often remarks about this active sedimentation in his philosophy glossary (1986).

3. Along with his commentaries, Chu and his good friend Lü Tsu-ch'ien also edited a collection of the works of his Northern Sung masters that became the "gateway" to the study of the Sung movement. See *Reflections on Things at Hand: The Neo-Confucian Anthology,* translated by Wing Tsit-chan. For additional selections from the justly famous *Chin-ssu lu,* see Chu (1991), edited by Allen Wittenborn. The *Chin-ssu lu* is a brilliant example of creating a new synthesis out of the work of previous thinkers.

4. Other Korean and Japanese thinkers also came to doubt Chu's program. For one of the most interesting challenges to Chu, see Mark Setton's (1997) account of the life and thought of Chong Yagyong (1762–1836). The Korean case is particularly fascinating because of the great reverence the Koreans felt for Chu.

5. For an extended meditation on why the Chinese did not engage in cosmology or ontology, see Hall and Ames (1995). One does need to agree with the entire sweep of their argument in order to get their point about the difference between classical Greek and Chinese ways of world making.

6. For two magisterial studies of early Chinese thought, history, and textual studies, see A. C. Graham (1989) and Benjamin Schwartz (1985). For a critique of these two positions, see Chad Hansen (1992).

7. Again, for the best summary discussion of the question of the role of language in Chinese thought, see Graham (1989, 389–428).

8. For a rich account of the rise of the Neo-Confucian philosophic fellowship, see Peter Bol's (1992) study of the Neo-Confucian revival of their philosophic culture.

5

A Neo-Confucian Interlude: Chu Hsi on Creativity

It is now time for a more extended Neo-Confucian interlude in the midst of a debate over the nature of creativity, God, and the world—a Whiteheadian and Western disputed nexus of questions located securely in the world of late modern North Atlantic philosophic and theological debate. The intrusion of a Neo-Confucian voice is not quite as strange as it might seem at first glance. For instance, both Whitehead (1978) and Neville (1982, 1987b, 1991a, 1992, 1995) have demonstrated a proclivity for comparative philosophy and theology. Whitehead often mentioned, albeit without a great deal of specific detail, his interest in Indian and East Asian forms of religion and philosophy, while for his part Neville has evinced a growing interest in the Neo-Confucian tradition as a resource for his own constructive ventures. *Mutatis mutandis*, it would only be fair to see if the Neo-Confucian tradition in the persona of Chu Hsi (1130–1200) can play a role in the formulation of a Whiteheadian response to Neville's challenge.

The introduction of Chu Hsi, Ch'en Ch'un (1159–1223), and the other Neo-Confucians necessitates an exposition that foregrounds and backgrounds the Neo-Confucians against the Western perspective of Whiteheadian process thought. Comparative philosophy, at least in its beginning stages, is a hybrid discipline, a combination of intellectual history, cross-cultural hermeneutics, translation, and philosophic analysis. Because of its mixed disciplinary nature, it will always appear somewhat sketchy. There will be issues that need to be expanded, explanations of terminology from other cultures that do not quite fit contemporary English usage, and a host of other problems simply derived from the act of comparison. Yet, as the Chinese proverb goes, a trip of a thousand miles begins with a single step. At least we can hope to head in the right direction.

Besides considerations of proclivity and comparability within the emerging process or organic traditions, there are historical and philosophic reasons for demanding such a comparative model for responsible metasystemic reflection. As Gordon Kaufman has pointed out in his *In the Face of Mystery: A Constructive Theology*, we live in a time of emerging global consciousness,

111

itself a product of the dialogue of diverse religious, philosophic, and cultural systems of discourse (1993). This emphatically does not mean, however, that the inherited particularities that have defined the great Eurasian cultures will disappear; what it does mean is that the cultures of Europe, Islam, India, and China will be mutually transformed.[1] Especially since World War II, no intellectual can retreat from the confrontation with the global reach of the modern historical process. At the beginning of this new historical era, we need to experiment with novel forms of cross-cultural comparison in order to generate worldviews and theological explanations adequate to the task of sustaining any kind of civilized human life in the twenty-first century.

A comparison of Chu Hsi and Whitehead is especially useful for a number of reasons that will become clear later. These reasons range from the fact that the two philosophies seem to belong to a particular family of philosophic systems called the organic/relational or process thought. Beyond this rather broad characterization of organism as a form of generative relationality, in the case of Chu and Whitehead at least two other key features draw comparative attention as well. For instance, both systems have important places for the notion of creativity, relationality, or what G. H. Mead called sociality (1932). Given that creativity is the focus of my response to Neville on behalf of process thought, it is entirely sensible to review at least one non-European system of thought to see if we can find a suitable answer to the problem of the separation of God and creativity. As we shall see, Chu had a similar potential problem with the coherence of first principles when trying to explain the linkage of principle and matter–energy to his students and critics. Many other Confucians argued that Chu Hsi's explanation of the relationship of principle and matter–energy sounds wonderful but makes less and less sense when you tease out its philosophic implications.

We also need to remember that this comparison of Whiteheadian thought with Chu Hsi's Neo-Confucianism is not a new venture.[2] The great Cambridge biologist and historian of Chinese science, Joseph Needham, commented on the striking affinity of the two traditions in the second volume of *Science and Civilisation in China*, a work devoted to a history of Chinese philosophy and religion (1954–). To be sure, Needham was not concerned with the interplay of creativity, God, and the world as technical comparative questions or as significant markers of the emergence of a global philosophic theology and philosophy. What he did note was that some of the Sung Neo-Confucians, especially the great Chu Hsi, were organic philosophers whose systems bore fascinating comparison with Whitehead. Needham was well aware that Whitehead himself called his system of thought a philosophy of organism. In this regard, Needham asserted that Chu Hsi also represents such a tendency in the history of global philosophy. Subsequent study of the two philosophers has confirmed Needham's initial insight into the affinities of the two organic, processive, and relational systems.

It is important at this point not to make too much of the comparison. Chu Hsi was not some kind of Sung dynasty (960–1279) precursor of the Anglo-American Cambridge and Harvard don. The differences, as we shall see, between their systems are as interesting as the similarities. Nonetheless, when all is said and done, there is a relationship between the two based on certain deep perspectives concerning the world, such as the often-mentioned emphasis on process and relationship. I believe Needham was correct in suggesting that the potential comparison has to do with the organic and relational nature of their projects rather than the details of the two philosophic positions. Whitehead also believed this to be the case. "In this general position the philosophy of organism seems to approximate more to some strains of Indian, or Chinese, thought, than to western Asiatic or European thought. One side makes process ultimate; the other side makes fact ultimate" (1978, 7).

Needham's discussion of the relationship of Chu Hsi and Whitehead is embedded in his description of Chu Hsi's philosophic synthesis.

> Indeed, I shall suggest that Chu Hsi's philosophy was fundamentally a philosophy of organism, and that the Sung Neo-Confucians thus attained, primarily by insight, a position analogous to that of Whitehead, without having passed through the stages corresponding to Newton and Galileo. (1954–, 2:458)

In a later part of his exposition, Needham clarifies where he believes we can find the analogy that makes sense of the comparison.

> With regard to Chu Hsi's organicism, it is well also to bear in mind that thesis of a modern Chinese philosopher, Chang Tung-Sun, that while European philosophy tended to find reality in *substance*, Chinese philosophy tended to find it in *relation*. (1954–, 2:487)

The most suggestive aspect of the comparison has to do with the organic, relational, processive, and pluralistic features of Chu Hsi's thought.

There are two intersecting points that make the comparison relevant for the question of God and creativity within a Whiteheadian framework. The first is that both Chu Hsi and Whitehead had a problem with the notion of creativity, although in significantly different modalities.[3] We need to unpack this claim for just a moment. Neither the Anglo-American don nor the Sung literatus really had a problem recognizing the power of creativity, the generation of new object–events, in their process philosophy—the problem was how to explain the role and origin of creativity as part of their process/relational system. For Whitehead, this was part of the drama of his unfolding speculations on the complex nature of God and its relationship to creativity as one of his foundational cosmological categories.

For Chu Hsi, the role of creativity was a question that had to be faced when reviewing the history of the rise of his own Northern and Southern Sung Neo-Confucian movement as a new advance in Confucian intellectual history.[4] In Chu's case, the philosophic aspect of the problem has to do with his characterization of *li* or principle. Chu Hsi called this Sung movement *tao-hsüeh,* or the Study of the Way, and realized that it marked the beginning of something new in the history of the Confucian tradition. Along with Chu Hsi's own synthesis, this and all of the other creative late T'ang and Northern and Southern Sung philosophic Confucians have come to be labeled "Neo-Confucianism" in modern North Atlantic and East Asian scholarly discourse.[5] While no orthodox Confucian would ever want to claim too much individualistic originality, Chu Hsi was aware that his teachers, most specifically Chou Tun-i (1017–1073), Chang Tsai (1020–1077), Ch'eng Hao (1032–1085), and Ch'eng I (1033–1107)—the most justly famous philosophic brothers in Chinese history—had created something distinctive. Looking back at the Northern and Southern Sung achievement, Chu Hsi's assessment is accurate. The Northern and Southern Sung masters, as they have been known ever since in all of East Asia, inaugurated a new phase in the history of the Confucian Way.

Chu Hsi's interpretive problem was first how to defend the creativity of his favorite teachers and second how to explain how true virtue and renewed ritual found expression appropriate to the Sung situation. Chu was not at all interested in how creativity fit into a highly abstract philosophic theology; his aim was to defend a specific creative advance of Confucian culture as defined by his understanding of the correct transmission of the Confucian Way from the archetypal sages such as King Wen, the Duke of Chou, Confucius, Mencius, and, much later, his revered Northern Sung masters. What makes for an engaging comparison with Whitehead is that Chu went about his reconstruction of the Confucian tradition by means of framing an organic, relational, and pluralistic philosophic system without any direct reference to God.

Another point of interest is the fact that Chu Hsi's grand Sung construct was also indicted for a fundamental incoherence having to do with key elements within the system. In Chu's case, this is the charge of holding some kind of a quasi-dualistic structure because of the unwarranted separation of principle and matter–energy. Hence the problem of incoherence within the system is located in a different place for Chu when contrasted with Whitehead, yet the problem of the separation of key elements is also a difficulty that Chu grappled with in his own lifetime. It is fascinating to see how often the question of the right relationship of principle and matter-energy comes up in discussions with Chu's students, friends, and critics. It seems that Chu and Whitehead are also connected by the controversial elements of their systems as well as their predilection for organic philosophy. This is a paradigmatic case of what G. H. Mead called the question of the emergence of the novel from the sociality of the present world.

CHU HSI'S CURRICULUM AND SOURCES

A study of the specialized problem of Whitehead's understanding of the relationship of creativity and God is not the place to launch into a long discussion of Chu Hsi's entire philosophy. There is already a growing body of literature in various East Asian languages and English that examines the background, development, and synthesis of Chu Hsi's thought.[6] Nonetheless, some short explanation of why the comparison is useful in philosophic terms is necessary. Such a juxtaposition may point to suggestive and alternative ways of viewing the Whiteheadian paradox of a God without creativity as an essential part of the divine reality, as well as commenting on some continuing problems with Chu Hsi's formulation of the Sung School of Principle.

The history of the development of Chu Hsi's system is complex in terms of the richness of both the ideas generated and in the development of these ideas in a constant dialogue of conversation and correspondence with his colleagues. As Hoyt Tillman (1992) has demonstrated so convincingly, there really was a fellowship of Confucian intellectuals seeking to realize the sagely way in the Southern Sung. While it is now clear that Chu Hsi was the master composer of the group, this does not mean that he somehow stood alone or was isolated from the larger political or intellectual issues of his age and his distinguished group of friends. Nor is there little doubt that Chu Hsi is the most important Chinese philosopher after Confucius in the great classical age of Chinese thought. Chu Hsi sets the agenda for Confucian discourse from the Southern Sung until the present; this is a fact that is alternatively praised or condemned, depending on the view of Chu Hsi held by other East Asian intellectuals. Yet, as Chu realized, none of this would have happened without the previous work of Chou Tun-i, Shao Yung, Chang Tsai, Ch'eng Hao, and Ch'eng I—just to list the most philosophically inclined of the Northern Sung Confucian revivalists that Chu considered his masters.

One of the real problems in attempting a comparison with Whitehead is that Chu Hsi never wrote a narrative summary of his philosophy.[7] Although some Northern and Southern Sung Neo-Confucians did write programmatic essays, extended expositions in systematic philosophy in the style of Aristotle,

St. Thomas, or even Hsün Tzu was not the way they normally sought to express the Way for themselves and to pass it on to their students. In many respects, the Neo-Confucians were more rabbinic in style, valuing commentary, exegesis, and explication of the classics above transitory individual creativity in terms of novel literary publications.[8]

Although Chu Hsi was quite a systematic thinker in his vision for the Confucian Way, like his fellow Neo-Confucians, he did not write systematic philosophy in any easily recognized medieval, early modern, or post–Enlightenment Western genres. For instance, much of his most influential work is found in famous commentaries on classical Confucian texts such as the *Four Books* (*The Analects*, the *Mencius*, the *Great Learning*, and the *Doctrine of the Mean*) and in correspondence with friends and students discussing his understanding of the classical texts. This is a literary style that takes the community of scholars very, very seriously. It is writing based on a dialogical model: commentary on the past classics and conversation with friends and colleagues in the present. However, there are certain parts of his corpus that are more systematic than others; that is to say, they better fit the Western disciplines of cosmology, epistemology, and metaphysics in terms of what Chu was seeking to explain to his friends and students. Certainly generations of Asian Neo-Confucians have taken comfort in Chu's philosophic speculations.

For instance, the first six *chüan* or sections of the *Chu-tzu yü-lei* (Conversations of Master Chu, Topically Arranged—often simply referred to as the *Dialogues* or *Conversations*) outline Chu Hsi's essential cosmological vision.[9] This material functions as a summary of Chu's mature thought insofar as it collects his reflections on what in the Western tradition would be considered ontology, cosmology, epistemology, hermeneutics, and metaphysics. From what we now know of the development of Chu Hsi's thought, his distinctive interpretation of the Sung Confucian tradition reached its definitive form by his mid-forties. While Chu continued to refine his system almost to the day of his death, by his mid-forties it was the coherent work of genius that made his reputation for all time.[10] Because most of the material in the *Conversations* was recorded after Chu Hsi was in his fifties, it is safe to assume that this material represents his considered opinion on the matters under discussion.

Another excellent source of systematically arranged material taken from Chu Hsi's major and minor writings and dialogues is Li Kuang-ti's (1642–1718) *Chu-tzu ch'üan-shu* [The Complete Works of Master Chu]. The title is something of a misnomer. Li was a famous Ch'ing dynasty Chu Hsi scholar, and the *Complete Works* is a carefully crafted collection of material taken primarily from Chu's dialogues and other literary works. It represents what the best Ch'ing *li-hsüeh* scholars understood to be the essence of Chu's thought. Of course, it is an edited work, but then all of Chu's works were edited by his disciples. Because of the dialogical nature of Chu Hsi's tradition as examined by Tillman (1992), there is nothing dishonest about the use of such material. We need to remember that much of Chu's best thought was generated in discussion and debate with his friends and students.[11]

A very different, though very useful, source for the comparison is the philosophic glossary of Chu Hsi's interpretation of key Neo-Confucian concepts prepared by one of Chu's most gifted students, Ch'en Ch'un (1159–1223). The use of material from a student honors the corporate fellowship that the great *tao-hsüeh* scholars tried to embody in their lives. This historically important text for the entire East Asian context has recently been translated by Wing-tsit Chan as *Neo-Confucian Terms Explained*. While not an exhaustive *summa* of Chu Hsi's cosmology, this short book has been widely recognized throughout East Asia as an invaluable and accurate interpretation of Chu Hsi's thought. Along with Ch'en's glossary, we also need to note that Wing-tsit Chan's translation of Chu's and Lü Tsu-ch'ien's great anthology *Reflections on Things at Hand* serves the English-speaking world as a sourcebook of Chu Hsi's thought because Chan has added so many of Chu Hsi's own comments on individual passages throughout the anthology that it becomes as much a study of Chu Hsi as of his favorite Northern Sung masters.[12]

In some respects, Ch'en Ch'un tried to do for his master Chu Hsi what Charles Hartshorne does for Whitehead, although Hartshorne justly claims much more originality than Ch'en. Ch'en sought to capture in his glossary the correct Chu Hsi school interpretation of many of the most contested terms of discourse in the Neo-Confucian philosophic vocabulary. The continuous publication and circulation of Ch'en's little classic throughout East Asia as a Chu Hsi school textbook attests to the success of his modest goal. Wing-tsit Chan, speaking for generations of Chu Hsi scholars, notes that "There is no doubt that he adhered to Chu Hsi's philosophy strictly. There is no single instance in which he contradicted or doubted the Teacher" (Ch'en 1986, 17). However, Chan is also quick to point out the unique talent that Ch'en brought to his task.

> Surely the *Tzu-i* is the best crystallization of Chu Hsi's thoughts and the best explanation of Neo-Confucian philosophical terms. But it is more. It is a commitment. Ch'en Ch'un wrote it with a far greater purpose than merely explaining terms. He brought his own philosophy to bear upon it. In other words, the work represents a fresh approach to Neo-Confucianism. (Ch'en 1986, 20)

Within the tradition, Ch'en has always been viewed as the most systematic of Chu's students, the disciple most eager to draw out coherent philosophic chains of reasoning from the work of his master. Traditionally, the glossary was divided into comments on twenty-six key Neo-Confucian concepts. Given the rigor, clarity, and elegance of Ch'en's scholarship, one can only wish that he has seen fit to expand the work beyond its modest size.

Therefore, for the purposes of a limited and focused comparison of the Chu Hsi school and modern process thought on the notion of creativity, I will primarily make use of material taken from the beginning sections of Chu Hsi's *Conversations/Dialogues*, the *Complete Works*, and Ch'en Ch'un's glossary.[13] While in no way is this limited selection an adequate representation of the richness of Chu Hsi or his school, it throws additional light on the question of creativity within the family of global philosophies recognized as process or organic philosophies.[14]

THE QUESTION OF CREATIVITY IN CHU HSI

The reason this comparison works is because the role the notion of creativity plays is a weighty philosophic problem in both systems. Beyond the details, and as we shall see, the differences are great, there is a common problem. This is the problem Neville has labeled "the ontological constriction of closure." Neville asserts that both Whitehead and Chu attempted to explain synoptically all that is or can be on the basis of a closed world, albeit a pluralistic world of self-referencing object–events, a referencing that precedes Neville's appeal to the creator *ex nihilo*. We have already explored the problem of the placement of creativity in Whitehead, and we will now review the analog in the Chu Hsi school.

Wherein lies the problem of creativity in Chu Hsi's account of the world? Or is it a problem at all? First, it definitely does not reside in Western theistic or categoreal definitions of the Category of the Ultimate as is the case for Whitehead. Whatever else Chu Hsi may be, he is not a theistic thinker in any typical Western sense of the meaning of theism as an appeal to a theo-volitional agent. However, this does not mean that there is no religious dimension to his thought; it only means that Chu Hsi's religious inclinations were not expressed in terms of a theism with a personalized theo-volitional focus so common to West Asian religious history. Second, as David Yu (1959) has argued in one of the first extended studies of Chu Hsi and Whitehead, Chu also omitted what could be called an analogy to Whitehead's theory of concrescence, a feature of Whitehead's thought crucial to the discussion of creativity in modern Western process thought. One of our key questions will be, without Whitehead's theory of the primordial nature of God and creativity, and without a theory of concrescence, how can Chu Hsi thematize creativity within his system? As we shall see, this is not an impossible task for the Sung literatus.

Actually, Yu's assertion that Chu Hsi lacks a theory of concrescence is a perfect example of the perils of seeking a perfect fit for concepts in comparative theory. Of course, Chu does not have anything as specific or technical as Whitehead's detailed exposition of concrescence. But on the other hand, Chu's discussion of the role, function, and cultivation of the mind–heart provides the analog to Whitehead's more philosophically technical discussion of concrescence if we attend to some other related concepts. This is especially the case when we add to the account Chu's theory of *ch'eng* as self-actualization of the mind–heart and the Supreme Ultimate.[15]

The main location of the question of creativity in the discussion of the mind–heart is because this is where Chu Hsi embedded his discussion of creativity within his system. Chu did so to explain how the sage is able to respond to the world in a timely, humane, and ritually correct fashion. Chu was not concerned with the concrescence of Whitehead's actual entities; rather, he was concerned with the ethical cultivation of the human mind–heart. Chu Hsi, because of his interpretation of the Northern Sung achievement, had to show how we, as ordinary human beings, can cultivate our minds in order to become sages—even if very few will ever realize this desired end. While it is true that only a real sage is creative in the ordering of civilization in any foundational sense, individuals of lesser talent can still be creative in their responses to reality as ordered by the instructions and insights of the sages as recorded in the classics. The Confucian record of creativity can be replicated in the lives of able and industrious students of "this culture of ours," as Peter Bol has so felicitously expressed the social nature of Sung Neo-Confucian discourse.

In addition to the notion of mind–heart and *ch'eng* as self-actualization, I also have become more and more convinced that Chu Hsi's notion of the Supreme Ultimate shows a striking similarity to some of Whitehead's analysis of the process of concrescence, at least on the functional level as an explanation of the coming into being of any object–event. Without the functioning of the Supreme Ultimate, nothing would become actual for Chu Hsi. While it is true that Chu does not develop anything like Whitehead's extended discussion of the process of concrescence in *PR,* the Supreme Ultimate does indicate how any object–event achieves its own specific form of definiteness. But then Whitehead is not nearly as interested in the cultivation of the mind–heart, either from the Confucian perspective or the Western point of view, as he is in the technical analysis of the emergence of new object–events.

As we have seen, Whitehead's analysis of actuality proceeded on the basis of three fundamental analytic elements: form, dynamics, and unification.

We shall discover that Chu Hsi formulated his mature system with analogous systematic elements. In Chu Hsi's case, most of his philosophic vocabulary is drawn from the early Confucian classics and the writings of his favorite Northern Sung masters, even though there are notable exceptions to this rule. This willingness to mix classical, modern, and even non-Confucian materials demonstrates the creative instincts of the Neo-Confucian tradition as it responded to the social changes of the Sung and the continuing challenge of Taoism and Buddhism.

One of the most important examples of an important term without a perfect Confucian petigre is the famous term *wu-chi*, or the Uncontrived Ultimate, immortalized for the emerging Neo-Confucian philosophic tradition in Chou Tun-i's *Diagram of the Supreme Ultimate* (Chang 1957–1962, 1:140–150). Most modern scholars now agree that *wu-chi* was more of a concept in philosophic Taoism than of Confucianism in Chu Hsi's time, and that Chu and his school were always having to explain to more conservative Confucians why they needed to use such a distinctly un-Confucian term for Confucian purposes.[16] Moreover, while almost all of Chu Hsi's technical vocabulary is drawn from the Confucian classics, his manipulation of key terms generates new meanings to fit the novel situations devised for them by the Sung Neo-Confucians.

For Chu Hsi, the first set of key analytic traits are those representing the formal side of reality. The formal analytic elements are his rational principles or modes of analysis of any object, event, or ritual in our collective universe. The most conspicuous of these is *li*, or principle. In terms of Chu Hsi's general contribution to Chinese philosophy, his analysis of principle was so important that his whole school was called *li-hsüeh*, or the learning of principle. We also can add *t'ai-chi*—the Supreme Ultimate as an even more specialized account of principle—one of the most important elements of Chu Hsi's formal analysis of reality. The Supreme Ultimate, as the most refined and comprehensive of principles, provides the locus for the lure by which the principle of a thing informs the actualization of any object–event. In Whitehead's terms, the Supreme Ultimate plays a crucial role in the concrescence of any object-event as it achieves its own form of definiteness.

The Supreme Ultimate, as a symbol of cosmic order, also provides a description of order as a generic ordering principle as found in the *tao*, or the Way of the cosmos. All of these formal terms indicate reality as real potentiality; they exist but they are not actual in and of themselves. They are not the concrete things or events, rather, they are the sources or lures for the possibility that events can achieve actuality in becoming what they should be. For example, principles provide the norms by which ethical actions can be judged humane and civilized, hence they are the potential models for all human conduct. *Li* are formal principles that have being or true actuality when they are actualized in some concrete event or entity—although they lack pure creativity without recourse to the other elements of Chu Hsi's system. As Mou Tsung-san has so brilliantly argued, they are the "mere" reasons for the universe (1968–1969, 1: 58). However, without this 'merely' potential quality, nothing could arise, flourish, perish, and contribute to the differentiation of the cosmos. At least for Chu Hsi, the "mere" of mere potential is extremely important.

The second set of traits is concerned with the dynamic side of object– events. Since Chu Hsi is concerned mostly with an analysis of human conduct in its moral aspects, the key terms for the dynamic side of his thought often deal with his moral anthropology. The obvious concepts are *hsin,* or mind– heart, and *ch'ing,* or feeling as manifestation of *ch'i.* And of course the grand pan-Chinese concept of *ch'i* or matter–energy itself, is always part of this aspect of Chu Hsi's thought. These dynamic elements refer to human life through self-cultivation, a series of classical Confucian ethical disciplines that produces moral excellence. All of the dynamic traits refer to object–events or to the observable activities and dispositions of human beings. The mind– heart, for example, refers both to the agency that is the seat of human personality as well as to the mechanism by which the other human capacities are regulated. Thus, as Chu Hsi so often said, the mind–heart unites human nature (the principle of humanity) and the feelings (Li 1973, 1: 329).

The third set of traits signifies the unifying elements of reality. The most important of these are the ethical virtues of *jen,* or humanity, and *ch'eng* as self-actualization (Berthrong 1993). These terms have a descriptive content because they refer to the process by which things become or reside in some particular state. As the highest human ethical norms, they define what it means to be fully human. Both of these terms carry the strongest positive connotations in the Confucian tradition—they are the ideal states or moral virtues that all persons should seek to emulate. Only a sage can truly be said to achieve humanity and self-actualization. While a person can be described in terms of principle and matter–energy, the process by which the principle is unified into a human life is called *ch'eng,* or self-actualization. However, *ch'eng* is more than a mere description of the process by which a person appropriates culture and virtue; it is a statement of what this process should be and points toward the ideal realization of all actuality in the life of the sage. It moves in the direction of being the unifying definition of the ideal actualization of principle (Li 1973, 1: 350). *Jen,* or humanity, indicates another direction of ethical perfection. It describes the moral intentionality of a person that gives unity of purpose to all civilized human conduct.

It is always important to remember that for Chu Hsi all of these virtues can only be discussed in terms of the cultivation of the mind–heart. As in many other aspects of Chu's thought, one cannot escape the need to focus on the role, definition, and functions of the mind–heart. As Ch'ien Mu has commented throughout his huge study and commentary on Chu, if there was ever a school of the mind–heart within Neo-Confucianism, Chu Hsi deserves to be considered its exemplification (1971, 2:1–38). One of the most crucial things that happens in the mind–heart is the actualization of virtue and true humanity of human beings, hence the true topos of unification. Of course, this means that there is nothing simple about the analysis of the concept of the mind–heart for Chu Hsi. It is that feature of humanity that combines both the qualities of principle and matter-energy.

In summary, we can say that Chu Hsi often thematized his analysis of the world in terms of form, dynamics, and unification. This is even the case when Chu is working with various inherited dyadic concepts, as has been so carefully elucidated by Donald Munro in his study of Chu Hsi's theory of human nature (1988). Chu Hsi loved to pose questions in terms of dyads that find their mediation through some third term that does not belong directly to either term of the dyad per se. There is a comprehensive, self-reflexive synthesis at play that Chu Hsi found compelling that balances the creative act of the mind–heart between human nature (principle as form) and human emotion (matter–energy as dynamic action).

In his use of these dyads and triads, does Chu Hsi affirm anything like Whitehead's Ontological Principle? Does Chu Hsi believe that without any actual entities there is no reason for anything at all? I believe that anyone who has read Chu's commentary, subcommentaries, and other remarks on the *Great Learning,* where the question of the investigation of things occurs, can have no doubt on this score.[17] In his commentary on the *Great Learning,* and in other places in his writings where he deals with the same question, he states that without objects or events there would be no principles to investigate or understand, hence nothing for the mind to consider.[18]

The phrase *ko-wu,* or the investigation of things, indicates a method of discovering the reasons for things, including the ultimate principles of the writings of the sages. Chu Hsi argues that only by examining the various objects of the world can we find the reasons for the way the world is as it is. His definition of what comprises this world of evidence as objects and events is quite broad. The things Chu Hsi is willing to analyze are more properly understood as tangible objects, events, actions, rituals, or human ethical cultivation and conduct, *not* glassy essences or atomic monads, modalities of being unconnected to anything else save through the mystery of the mind of God.[19] The things of Chu Hsi's analysis are the world of people, their cultural institutions, their science,[20] their politics, their art, and the instruments of their daily lives. The search for reasons is always an examination of things that exist in the concrete, not an intuitive leap into a realm of nothingness or emptiness where there are no guideposts or reference marks—to seek in emptiness or nothingness would be to follow the Taoist or Buddhist path of enlightenment. Of course, given the scholarly nature of Sung Confucianism, much of Chu Hsi's own research was textual in nature. He sought to understand the tradition as it had been delivered to him in the Confucian canon.

Chu Hsi's understanding of things also points to an element of growth and development within these object–events. He constantly refers to the first four characters of the *Book of Changes* as symbols for the growth of any object–event.[21] While not directly comparable to Whitehead's theory of concrescence, the stages of growth of the mind–heart, symbolized by the text of the *Book of Changes*, do indicate the complex nature of any object of analysis or discourse (Bruce 1923, 171–83).[22] In his commentary on the *Analects* passage concerning the flowing river,[23] Chu Hsi drives home this point by insisting that the dynamics of the universe are like the flow of a river—it never pauses so that things are produced without exhaustion of the primal generativity of the Tao (Chu 1971, *chüan* 5: 4a–5b).

Once Chu Hsi has defined what he means by things and events, he is careful to provide an explanation for their fundamental relationality or relativity. In his definition of *ch'eng*/self-actualization, he indicates that there is no object-event in the universe that does not find its proper and necessary place and connection to all other object–events. If self-actualization is a necessary process by which any object–event achieves its true nature, then the creativity necessary for such actualization never takes an ontological holiday (Ch'ien 1971, 1: 349–50). There is no disconnection of things and their principles for Chu Hsi.

Nor are there any object–events so elevated that they escape this general role of relational relativity. Humanity participates in the universal structure of reality and actuality. A person's excellence rests in the fact that the human mind–heart can think, speak, and act correctly (Mou 1968–1969, 1: 486; Ch'ien 1971, 1: 372). According to Chu Hsi, a human being is the most noble and perfect exemplification of virtues found in all levels of the natural world. He points out that even the birds and the beasts seem to have some of the cardinal virtues that find their final perfection in the mind of the sage. When pressed to the extreme, Chu affirms that even the dried and withered things of the world have their own proper functions and principles, just as human beings and heaven have.

While Chu Hsi constantly proclaims that human beings have the potential for perfection, he also is aware of the evil humans do, blinded as they are by inordinate self-interest (Chan 1969, 88–116). While the principles of object-events are all interrelated, this is no guarantee that they will all be consummated in a timely or appropriate fashion. There may be no perfect world. While matters of fact are the reasons for all experience, they are not the total realization of the possibility for perfect self-actualization. The potential principles of virtue or the values of humane life are not granted an easy victory. The very act of actualization gives both meaning and tragic limitation to human life. The model of the sage is just that—a model that can be sought and rarely achieved only by a few.

Even the achievement of sagely wisdom is not always enough to project good into a corrupt world. Chu Hsi constantly had the example of Confucius, much less all of the other Confucians who struggled throughout history against injustice and indifference, in mind when he thought of sages who were unable to undo the evil of their own ages. More directly, Chu Hsi had the examples of his Northern Sung masters in mind when he contemplated the vagaries of the historical process. Confucius was a true sage according to Chu Hsi's understanding of sagehood, yet he personally had little influence on the course of the history of even his own small state. Confucius's ideals were lures for future generations. Chu Hsi knew that ignorance and error all too often find their reasons and seasons in actual things, historical situations, and social institutions that defy any melioristic vision of human destiny.

Nonetheless, things finally do cohere for Chu Hsi, regardless of the question of worldly success because of the example of sage virtue. Relativity qua interconnection means order, at least in terms of human relationships. Chu has a vision of unity, and it finds expression in many of his favorite natural images. He often likens principle to the moon that shines on many streams and rivers and yet is essentially one (Li 1977, 2: 1066). He understands by this what we might call in Western philosophy the vision of the form of the good. His argumentation does not run to metaphors drawn from the natural sciences or mathematics, but rather indicates the incipient feelings of moral judgment, or perhaps the aesthetic intuitions of fitness and beauty that haunt the minds of civilized people. That some people are paragons of moral depravity does not vitiate the fact that the world ultimately is axiological in character. Depending on the group of terms he is using, his overall definition of the form of the good is most often called *t'ien-li,* or Heavenly Principle. That these principles are conditioned by each other is never in doubt, nor is the fact of their universal applicability.

One classic example of Chu Hsi's affirmation of the principle of relativity is found in his exegesis of Chang Tsai's (1020–1077) notion of *shen,* or spirit.[24] Chang Tsai, perhaps one of the more neglected of the great Northern Sung philosophic masters in terms of his contribution to Chu's thought, held that within the world of *ch'i* as dynamic matter–energy, one actual object–event implies many actual entities and that the many, in turn, imply one (Li 1977, 2: 1076). Chu Hsi agreed with the general thrust of this judgment and offered a discussion of the theory that makes it clear that he saw the universe as growing together into one related synthesis and then having the actualized one give itself again to the many that follow it because of the ceaseless productivity of the generative yin-yang forces. Because of the self-limiting nature of the individuating process, Chu Hsi thought that the dialectic of growth involved in the productive process was unending and uniform as far as it reflected the balance of yin–yang energy (Li 1977, 2:1076–77). This kind of dialectic never makes any kind of purely quantitative or qualitative ontological leap that would produce elements so novel that they could not be accounted for by the means of yin–yang or five phases analysis.[25] In short, there is no possibility for something utterly transcendent entering into the process qua the natural process of growth, because there is nothing that is transcendent from some kind of relationship to everything else.[26]

In all his discussion of creative process, Chu Hsi never resorted to anything like Whitehead's notion of God's primordial envisagement of principle. For Chu, the principles have an order about them that is always phrased in terms of self-determinate or inherent order rather than some kind of lure for order located beyond human sagely wisdom. There is no actual entity, such as Whitehead's God, that has a mental pole prior to the physical pole.

However, are the principles one or many? That is a difficult question for Chu Hsi. One of his favorite expressions that expresses the balance of the one and many is that *li-i fen-shu*/principle is one but its manifestations are many. On the one hand, he is unqualifiedly a pluralist in his natural philosophy, as he felt any Confucian must be if one is not to fall into the monistic or empty heresies of Buddhism and Taoism. There are a plurality of things, as has been stressed already, and they are in many ways self-referencing in that they select their own mode of self-actualization. However, we must never forget the role of *ming* as destiny or *t'ien-ming* or the Heavenly Mandate as an element in the actualization of all object–events. There is always an element of choice, even if this choice, as the *Doctrine of the Mean* notes, is unfathomable in its full richness in terms of both self-actualization and the destiny of the specific situation. Each thing has its own principle that it can exemplify with varying degrees of success (Li 1977, 2: 1064–65).

On the other hand, there are ample indications that Chu Hsi understands an axiological unity to be the essential cosmological feature of principle (Li 1977, 2: 1064–70). For Chu Hsi, there is a vision of the perfect mode of action and society that is definitely coherent, even harmonious. This is what Tu Wei-ming (1989) has called the fiduciary community as the Confucian ideal of the *Doctrine of the Mean* for humane civilization. Whether this reading is the result of Chu Hsi's cultural conditioning or whether it is built into a system that lacks Whitehead's concept of God's primordial nature is another question. Again the question is, without some kind of Nevillian creationist ontology, wherein does creativity arise? Chu Hsi's emphasis, as with the rest of the Neo-Confucian tradition, is primarily on the life of the person seeking to become a sage, the moral effort needed to live in trust with other people.

Ch'en Ch'un has a rather interesting way of looking at this bipolar aspect of principle in his *Glossary*. After explaining that principle, something without a physical form or shape cannot be perceived by the senses, Ch'en goes on to make the following point: "It is simply the specific principle of what a thing should be. A specific principle means a standard. As such it has the sense of being definitely unchanging" (Ch'en 1986, 112). The Neo-Confucians rather happily move between is and ought, and in fact argue that the very nature of principle is such that it defines what should be by means of the standard of what a thing ought to be. For instance, Ch'en goes on to show how this is linked to moral purpose. "Principle is the specific principle of what the thing should be, while righteousness is that according to which principle is applied" (1986, 113). Hence principle encourages creativity but is not creativity itself as some kind of separate metaphysical realm or object–event. This is the case because, as we have seen, principle by itself is not capable of action independent of *ch'i*.[27]

As we shall see, there is a theory of creativity in Chu Hsi, but it is located in a different part of his theoretical analysis of principle qua principle as pattern. The locus of creativity is identified with the classical teaching about the mind–heart of heaven being the unceasing production of things, as is taught in the *Book of Changes*. However, typical of Chu Hsi, he modifies the account of creativity derived from classical sources. Chu Hsi discovers creativity in the dynamic side of his speculative system, with the primordial power of *ch'i* when linked to the axiological power of principle. It is not principle that is actually creative by itself, for it functions as the model of things, but the restless *ch'i* that gives birth to the universe of things when it is informed by principle (Li 1977, 2: 1061–63). Chu Hsi never tires of making the point that, as far as an account of creativity goes, you simply cannot ever separate an account of principle from *ch'i*.

First, the fact that principles exist means that they exist in things, for we have already seen that to ask for reasons in Chu Hsi's system is to ask for the investigation of particular object–events. In this regard, Chu Hsi agrees with Whitehead's commitment to the Ontological Principle. When this investigation is carried to its final conclusion, it results in the illumination of the principles that inform the particular object–events under investigation. The process is from investigation to understanding, from particular things to particular reasons, from particular object–events to particular principles. It is only at a later stage of the analytic process that comprehension and the particularity of principle is fully understood.

The complexity of the interrelationship of principle and *ch'i* in any particular concrete object–event is demonstrated in the intricacies of the process of actualization. That the principles of things exist as potential does not mean that they are not also part of a living process.[28] In fact, for there to be such a process at all there must exist principles of process for Chu Hsi, or we would end up in an inconceivable world indeed, a world without models, directions, moral actions—a world without standards, rules, or civilized conduct. If there were only one thing, how could it distinguish itself from its own principle? As Ch'en puts it,

> In actuality, principle does not lie outside material force, because in the operation of the two material forces, the production and reproduction (*sheng-sheng*) has gone on without cease from time immemorial. It is impossible for there to be nothing but material force. There must be something to direct it and that is principle. Principle is in material force and acts as its pivot. (Ch'en 1986, 38)

Second, what would it mean for principle to be inactive, inert? Does this mean that the system becomes a mechanical movement at best? Hardly. What Chu Hsi is getting at here is the timeless quality of principle that Ch'en Ch'un already noted. Principles do not move in time as do actual object–events. In this sense, principle resembles Whitehead's eternal objects that ingress in actual entities that are located in time and space as actual entities, but are not literally in time and space themselves as eternal objects. Eternal objects are atemporal and have relational essence. Much the same thing seems to be in Chu Hsi's mind too. His principles are "before" time and "above" space as the Chinese idiom describes the apriori nature of principle (Li 1977, 2: 1061–63). I take Chu Hsi to be arguing that the space–time continuum itself is constituted by the object–events and is not some form of Newtonian receptacle eternally awaiting mundane action.

W. Mays has suggested that Whitehead's eternal objects are propositional functions used to elucidate the structure of experience (1959, 74). Eternal objects serve as an abstract logical structure taken from the relations of extensive connection obtaining between events. Chu Hsi, of course, does not have this kind of quasi-mathematical background or interest in the formulation of formal or informal logic (if this is indeed what Whitehead was doing).

Very rarely does Chu Hsi use models or illustrations that suggest this kind of abstract interpretation of principle. But on occasion he does imply that principle is something like the straight and horizontal lines of a segment of bamboo, showing that such abstraction is entirely possible based on Neo-Confucian interpretations of principle (Ch'ien 1971, 1: 252). However, this kind of geometrical analysis is not the primary focus of his work, which is always located in the realm of human ethical action and moral reflection.[29]

Chu Hsi's defense of Chou Tun-i's concept of *wu-chi*, or the Uncontrived Ultimate, is a classic case of a theory of the creative advance in philosophic terminology, and hence creativity in general. Chu Hsi argues, and Ch'en Ch'un concurs, that there is a *kairos* moment in any philosophy when something new has to be generated in order to respond to the conditions of the times. A good part of sagely wisdom is learning to be timely. Sagely wisdom and the formulation of ethical norms did not end with Mencius as far as Chu Hsi was concerned (Bruce 1923, 79–82). For instance, Chu Hsi was convinced that the Northern Sung Neo-Confucians made real contributions to the Confucian Way. Chu Hsi had a doctrine of open if austere revelation in theological language: a sage expounds a vision of reality commensurate with the demands of the age. The Uncontrived Ultimate of Chou Tun-i is just such a case. Chu Hsi admitted that this term was relatively new in Confucian usage, but not contradictory to the established usage of the sages. When the notion of the Uncontrived Ultimate was linked to the older idea of the Supreme Ultimate, it lent a new precision to the conceptualization that made it part of the growth of the Confucian vision of reality. Thus, according to Chu Hsi, the sage can create new verbalizations when the need arises, and there is always a need for new vision to meet the needs of new days.[30]

The fact that Chu Hsi's analysis of principles as existent, if not independently active, does not mean, as we have seen, that he lacks an interpretation of the role and place of creativity and that principle does not play an important part in that creative process. The category of creativity includes in its scope all of the various kinds of concepts and symbolic resources Chu Hsi had at his disposal. The production of things may be unceasing, but there is an order to it that is conditioned by the relevance of the past and the pattern of the yin–yang forces.

The emphasis Sung Neo-Confucianism placed on the centrality of ethical behavior and the cultivation of the human mind ensured that concepts of creativity related to maturation and enlightenment were often stressed. Chu Hsi did not merely reflect on the newness of the changing seasons or Confucius's remark about the ever-flowing river, but also on the affairs of civil society. In fact, if Tu Wei-ming is correct, the Confucian concept of adulthood is in itself one of growth and process, a way of self-cultivation on the way to true humanity (1979, 35–36). Reflection on human maturation and relationships necessarily leads to a philosophy that gives a great deal of attention to the dynamic side of life with its subtle roots or inceptions of activity.

P. J. Ivanhoe, in his short study of Confucian moral self-cultivation, notes that Chu Hsi modifies Mencius' understanding of the original goodness of nature in a very characteristic way. Ivanhoe argues that Mencius believed that the prime metaphor for ethical self-cultivation was "the *development* of incipient tendencies" to proper ethical conduct. Chu, while accepting a great deal of Mencius' vision, moved his metaphor from development to the recovery of the original good nature (Ivanhoe 1993, 54). This act of recovery was based on Chu's theory of education and the examples of his Northern Sung masters such as Chou Tun-i, Chang Tsai, Shao Yung, and the Ch'eng brothers.

Ivanhoe outlines the basic structure of Chu's search for sagely wisdom in terms of a recovery model based on two primary activities and a mediating function that connects both part of Chu's curriculum (1993, 58–59). The first act for Chu is to preserve the mind–heart by means of honoring the virtuous nature (*ts'uan-hsin* and *tsun te-hsing*). This can often be accomplished by the meditation form known to the Neo-Confucians as quiet sitting (*ching-tso*). As Ivanhoe says, "The goal was to gather together and calm one's mind, and thereby protect it from the obscuring effects of agitated emotions and desires" (1993, 59). Once this was done, Chu then urged the student to complete the task by means of pursuing inquiry and study (*tao wen-hsüeh*). This was primarily accomplished by a commitment to the examination of things (*ko-wu*). And finally, the whole effort was then linked by the attitude of reverence (*ching*). As Ivanhoe indicates, "One of the great strengths of Chu Hsi's method of self-cultivation is that it provided students of the Way with a definite procedure and clear criteria for study" (1993, 60).

Furthermore, Chu Hsi also shares with Whitehead the hope of rationalism. It is the hope of rationalism that there is sufficient order in the cosmos for human beings to form civilized societies, even if our limited understanding cannot comprehend all of the order or disorder to be found in the universe. If Chu Hsi did not believe in a modicum of order, there would have been no reason for the discussion of the process of the investigation of things. For Chu, we start from something we know and probe on until we understand something that previously had escaped our attention. And we go from one thing to another till we reach a point where the total pattern begins to make itself clear to us, and it is the very nature of humanity to want to know and to be able to know (Ch'ien 1971, 2: 509–10).

Chu Hsi does not assume that we will be able to know all of the things of the universe. No one can know all of the particulars or principles of things.

Nor does he believe that this would be a very wise task to try to undertake, which is why he recommends certain specific and clear approaches to knowledge (Li 1973, 4: 3294–95). But on the central point he is clear indeed (Ch'ien 1971, 2: 495–96). Ch'ien Mu attributes the following saying to Chu Hsi: "Not to seek for the reasons why, but only to say that a thing is self-determined, is foolishness"[31] (Ch'ien 1971, 1: 270).

The methods by which Chu Hsi goes about seeking knowledge are very different from those of a modern Western philosopher.[32] For instance, Chu concludes that there is an adequate historical model for our behavior as potentially civilized human beings and that this model has been recorded in the words and deeds of the ancient worthies and sages. These men and their records have a canonical status for him that is very much like the biblical canon for Christian theologians. Chu Hsi affirms that knowledge can be found in many areas, but it is profitable to look at the historical records of persons who have achieved sagely excellence in the past as a first guide to learning and conduct. History is a model, a source of confirmed inspiration.

But this is not all. There is a need to appropriate this material for your own life. It must be made one's own. For instance, Wm. Theodore de Bary (1991) has shown how important this task is in his *Learning for One's Self: Essays on the Individual in Neo-Confucian Thought*. There is always an emphasis on self-cultivation that is central to Chu Hsi's thought. According to Chu, if a person really knows the good, then that person should try to be good and learn more about what goodness entails for civil society. It is not impossible for Chu Hsi to aspire to become a sage; it is only a very, very difficult lifelong task.

Chu Hsi's hope for rationalism is also an expectation for life. Human beings can understand the principles that inform object–events and in doing so can become co-equal to the power of heaven and earth in creativity. In this regard, Chu Hsi is in complete agreement with the *Doctrine of the Mean*. Chu Hsi, along with the rest of the Confucian tradition, affirms a depth dimension to reality, and even more so, he proclaims that human beings are an important, creative part of that reality. Not only is there hope for rationalism in Chu Hsi, there is promise of faith too; not a faith in some transcendent beyond all comprehension but in the mystery of the production of things and events that is common to all of the creatures that find their place in heaven's way.

SIMILARITIES IN PROCESS, DIFFERENCES IN STRUCTURE

The major difficulty in comparing Chu Hsi and Whitehead is that Chu is resolutely concerned with the middle range of human affairs; he also lived in a completely different world of discourse containing a different set of canonical texts as well as different religions, artistic sensibilities, economic systems, and political forces, just to mention a few of the factors that differentiate Southern Sung China from the modern North Atlantic world of Whitehead. Chu focuses his attention on human life as human relationship because this is the way the Confucian tradition operates; like Whitehead, his philosophy is axiological, but the focus is resolutely social in scale. However, he does develop, as we have seen, his own cosmological system, but its main features are found always linked to his work in moral philosophy rather than on reflections on epistemology, logic, or science, as was the case with Whitehead. However, it is well to remember that Whitehead, especially in *Adventures of Ideas,* was also passionately interested in what makes a civilized society.

Perhaps the historical explanation of the development of Confucian discourse is sufficient to explain the differences between Chu His and Whitehead. However, these differences can also suggest different subtypes within process philosophy, based on the relative points of emphasis of each thinker on the formal, dynamic, or unifying aspects of the world. In Whitehead's case, the formal side is heavily stressed, as witnessed by his interest in defining the function of God's primordial nature as well as all of the continuing mathematical sections of his work. Chu Hsi, following a different course, does not stress the formal side of his system as much, although we have seen that both he and Ch'en Ch'un are capable of analytic rigor when it is necessary to make their contested points. Chu is primarily interested in human personal and social ethical conduct and self-actualization, and because of this, he tends to stress the relational or unifying elements of process philosophy; these are theoretical tasks for the perfection of virtue.

Chu Hsi's comparative lack of interest in the formal or analytic side of process philosophy tells us a great deal about process philosophy as a global movement. For example, we can probably assume that not all relational process philosophies need to develop or formulate a theology or systematic philosophy to provide for an object–event that envisages all eternal objects or principles. Chu Hsi did not do so and yet is clearly a process philosopher. Chu stresses the relational aspects of the universe, and as such, develops a most robust pluralistic naturalism—but a naturalism with a religious dimension. We also need to be alert to the simple fact of comparative thought: Not all cultures organize their worlds after the pattern of the post–Enlightenment West.

However, I hesitate to extend the proposed triadic typology of form, dynamics, and unification beyond the confines of process philosophy. The reason is that both Chu Hsi and Whitehead are composing cosmologies rather than a general ontology, as Neville continually reminds anyone working within the process tradition. By admitting the Ontological Principle as a cosmological principle, process thinkers imply a philosophy wedded to a principle of ontological priority, to borrow a phrase from Justus Buchler (1966, 30–33). The principle of ontological priority states that some natural complex is taken to be superlative, to represent the really real, the standard by which all other natural complexes are to be measured. For Whitehead these are actual entities and for Chu Hsi these are object–events. All other natural complexes are only relatively real in comparison to actual entities and object–events.[33] Both philosophies are cosmologies, descriptions of the way things are in this cosmic era. What might hold universally for this cosmic era may or may not hold for all possible worlds, and hence is not a fundamental ontology or metaphysics.

Therefore, there is some doubt whether a typology for a comparison internal to process philosophy may be general enough to include philosophies whose main concern is ontology or metaphysics in the classical Western use of these sciences. The process principles of form, dynamics, and unification may prove an interesting methodological device for process cosmologies, but it may be less adequate for ontologies that deny the priority or primacy of actual entities or object–events. This is precisely the kind of question that Neville asks both Whitehead and Chu Hsi.

I have made the argument for creativity in exposition and substance for Chu Hsi's thought in other studies (Berthrong 1994). Furthermore, Mou Tsung-san, Tu Wei-ming, Liu Shu-hsien, and Cheng Chung-ying have all declared creativity to be an essential feature of Confucian moral metaphysics in all of its characteristic Sung, Yüan, Ming, and Ch'ing formulations. What about Whitehead and creativity? Does his cosmology become so encompassing that the category of creativity becomes a creative *and* comprehensive principle in terms of a Western hermeneutic such as archic analysis? Questions like this will drive the practitioners of archic analysis into deeper and more sustained meditations on the specifics of each tradition (see the appendix on archic analysis for an extended discussion of this issue). In our case, the resolution of such a question may help with the question of creativity in Whitehead's thought.

PROBLEMS OF COHERENCE

One of the main problems students of Chinese thought have had in interpreting Chu Hsi's thought has to do with the relationship of principle and matter–energy. The problem, although different from the Western dichotomy of monism and dualism, is discussed in terms of the unity or disunity of these two fundamental principles. Just as with Whitehead, one of the favorite features of Chu's thought is the promise of unity it brings to the analysis of the world.

If there is a fundamental element of incoherence in the formulation of the system, then the whole edifice becomes less appealing. The question is even more stark than a matter of mere authorial preference. Many later Neo-Confucians held that if Chu is really a quasi-dualist in the sense of the separation of principle and matter–energy, then he is simply wrong about the world at a very fundamental level. This was, for instance, the final judgment of the great Tai Chen (1723–1777) on Chu's philosophy.

Of course, as any student of Chu Hsi knows, he rejects such a simplistic labeling of his thought in regard to the notions of principle and matter–energy. For instance, when asked about the relationship of principle and object–events (always and everywhere constituted by matter–energy), he never wavers in stating that the two elements are always conjoined both *in se* and by any mode of analysis you want to apply. For instance, "In the world there is never *ch'i* without principle and never principle without *ch'i*" (Ch'ien 1971, 1: 238). In a characteristic passage in his commentary on the *Great Learning,* the unity of principle as the formal norm of all object–events is emphasized as the basis for our ability to know anything at all. "The myriad things each set forth one principle and the myriad principles commonly emerge from one source. This is the reason why we can extend from this and comprehend [everything]" (Chao 1973, 29). This is as straightforward a statement of clear exegesis as the history of East Asian Neo-Confucian thought teaches. Of course, Chu always claimed that the key to his theory of principle comes from a careful reading of the works of the Ch'eng brothers, the Northern Sung masters of the theory of principle.

Another problem with any interpretation of Chu Hsi's understanding of matter–energy is that he very rarely develops a sustained exposition of the concept. Although Chu is massively indebted to Chang Tsai, he does not expend the same effort explaining the theory of matter–energy as he does defending of principle. One reason for this could be that matter–energy is such an established idea that everyone assumes they know what they mean by it. *Ch'i* does serve as one of the foundational elements of Chu's thought, but he seems to assume that we all know what he is talking about or that he can refer to the authority of Chang Tsai where he needs to reference the notion more comprehensively. Even the ever analytic and eager Ch'en Ch'un does not include a separate section on matter–energy in the glossary, which indicates that he did not take Chu Hsi to be offering a provocative reading of the term. It is only in the Ch'ing that philosophers such as Wang Fu-chih (1619–1692), Yen Yüan (1635–1704), and Tai Chen (1723–1777) return to a careful examination of the suppressed or unexamined connotations of the theory of matter–energy.[34] In Korea Yi Yulgok (1536–1584) and in Japan Kaibara Ekken (1630–1714) also are famous for worrying about the problem of *ch'i* as well.

One of the most perplexing exegetical aspects of the analysis of Chu Hsi's thought is to figure out what he meant when he discussed whether matter–energy or principle has some kind of cosmological priority. Of course, this was just the kind of move Chu himself rejected. It was not that Chu did not make distinctions; he loved to do so when he thought it would serve the Learning of the Way. However, we need to step back for a minute to ask what kind of question this is from within the purview of Chu Hsi's system. When we do that, we discover the nature of the problem and also how it can be seen as an analog to Whitehead's problem with God and creativity.

One of the things Chu Hsi was very clear about was his own version of the Ontological Principle. For Chu Hsi to ask about the reasons for anything was to ask about the agency of some object–event. Nothing floats into the world from High Heaven unconnected with something concrete. As we have seen, Chu developed his theory of the interaction of principle and matter–energy as a way to explain the function of the human mind. It is important to note that the direction of the analysis is always from the concrete mind–heart to the principles involved and not vice versa. Living agency is a product of the mind–heart and not of the principle in and of itself. Principles are always manifested within the mind of a living person or remembered, commemorated, in the historical record of living persons. In fact, to be a Confucian scholar is to venerate one particular historical lineage as recorded in the classics and the scholarly writings of generations of Confucian commentators.

This was the crux of the problem. Principle did not, in and of itself, seem a very promising candidate for the Neo-Confucian locus of the creative advance into novelty because of its being the primus of order and determinateness. In fact, it was not where Chu Hsi placed the agency of creativity in object–events. Chu was adamant that it only became a lively principle within the medium of the mind–heart as the seat of the human person. So when students or friends asked about the independent qualities of principle, Chu Hsi would always refer them back to the cultivation and education of the mind–heart. For instance, the later questions or suggestions that principle acted like the trigger of a crossbow or a person riding a horse were misguided in that principle could never be separated from the living reality of the mind–heart.[35] Chu Hsi was always careful to distinguish the order of analysis from the order of agency qua *ars contextualis*, and he was equally clear which order was primary, even if his students, colleagues, and later interlocutors were not always equally clear in making this distinction. Speculation about the relationship of principle, matter–energy, and the mind–heart involved topics that were begging for category mistakes to happen.

In a striking parallel, Chu Hsi and Whitehead were constantly questioned about the separation of key elements in their systems, although Chu's system seems to have given others less reason to do so. In both cases, the problem was related to the question of creativity and what Whitehead called the Ontological Principle. Ch'en Ch'un sheds some light on the way Chu viewed the question.

> Principle is paired with nature. Principle is the principle in things, while nature is the principle in the self. Being in things means that it is the principle common to heaven, earth, man and things, while being in the self means that it is the principle possessed by the self to be his own. (Ch'en 1986, 113)

Here too Ch'en notes that principle only resides in the self, in the living person, or in other things. In the human person, it is identified specifically with human nature or *hsing*. In a preceding section, Ch'en demonstrates the inherently axiological nature of principle. "How can principle, which is without physical form or shape, be seen? It is simply the specific principle (*tse*) of what a thing should be (*tang-jan*)" (Ch'en 1986, 112). It is typical of the Chu Hsi school to offer paired or linked explanations of key concepts in order to signal the comprehensive range of the concept under discussion. It was a way to indicate that the concept to be analyzed was multivalent or played different roles in different aspects of the search for sagehood. As Donald Munro (1988) has shown, Chu Hsi often provided dyadic or correlative images to illustrate his philosophy. However, this deployment of dyadic or correlative imagery should not obscure that fact that principle always resides within the mind–heart of the person.

In Ch'en's discussion of the mind–heart, he definitively demonstrates the role of principle along with the mind. For instance, the very first definition is that "The mind is master of the body. . . . Only when principle and material force are combined can there be mind" (Ch'en 1986, 56). Slightly later he notes that "The mind has substance and function." This kind of correlative or dyadic formulation is Ch'en's way of signaling that the mind–heart is a truly comprehensive concept. This is especially so when he indicates that the mind–heart includes both substance and function, which serve as the markers for comprehensiveness throughout Chu's thought. Or, as Ch'en argues, "Nature is simply principle; it is perfectly good and not evil. The mind, however, involved both principle and material force. That the mind is lively is made possible by material force" (Ch'en 1986, 58).

However, none of this repeated set of explanations on Chu Hsi or Ch'en Ch'un's part had the desired effect. Generation after generation of Neo-Confucians in China, Korea, and Japan continued to worry about the relationship of principle, matter–energy, the mind–heart, and the role of creativity as a function of the unity or disunity of Chu's worldview. Or perhaps Chu's philosophy had precisely the effect that we should expect when this part of a process system is explained to colleagues who do not share its particular slant on the world. The comprehensive vision of Chu Hsi, especially in terms of its radical object–event pluralism and its cosmology as a form of *ars contextualis*, appears as difficult to comprehend in Sung China as was Whitehead's philosophy in Boston. This indicates that we need to clarify just what is going on in such philosophic discourse or admit that Neville may be right in arguing that there is a fundamental incoherence in the system. Obviously, I believe the first option is the correct one and that we can find some way out of the puzzle set by Neville.

We have now assembled the data we need to frame a proper response to Neville's challenge. It is the articulation of the answer to the question of the relationship of God and creativity that we turn to in chapters 6 and 7.

NOTES

1. One reason to deal with the Chinese case is that, at least in Eurasia, its culture developed in relative isolation from the rest of the great land mass. The only exception is the introduction of Buddhism into China. Today, Chinese intellectuals are increasingly becoming part of a larger ecumenical world culture dominated by the post–Enlightenment West. However, at Chu Hsi's time, the Chinse knew almost nothing about Europe. For a realistic evaluation of the potential problems of civilization encountered on the political, economic, and military realms, see Huntington (1996). Huntington agrees that civilizations need to dialogue in order to simply tolerate each other enough to live together peacefully in a complex world. If they enrich each other, that is fine, but Huntington is more concerned with ensuring human survival.

2. Along with Needham, others have also noticed the similarity of Chu Hsi and Whitehead. For instance, both T'ang Chün-i, in many of his magisterial studies of Chinese intellectual history, and Thomas Metzger (1977) have noted the similarity.

3. Cheng Chung-ying (1991, 537–58) has written an essay about the question of creativity in Whitehead and Neo-Confucianism. He argues that creativity is a much more radical concept among the Neo-Confucians than it was for Whitehead. We will return to this surprisingly strong claim in a later section of this chapter.

4. A. S. Cua, in his study of the notion of Confucian tradition, has done an excellent job describing the nature of Chu Hsi's understanding of how the tradition does indeed change over time (1992).

5. The nomenclature question within Confucian studies has heated up considerably over the last few years. For instance, there has been a great deal of debate (Tillman 1992b, Bol 1992) about the continued usefulness of the term *Neo-Confucianism*. While it is an English neologism, it has become the accepted designation of the

Northern and Southern Sung reformation of Confucian thought. To change the term at this point would probably just confuse the general educated public rather than enlighten the conditions of the debate.

Nonetheless, critics such as Tillman and Bol are correct in reminding us that no one Chinese, Japanese, Korean, Vietnamese, or English term will ever encompass the great scholarly, humanistic, artistic, political, and religious reality subsumed by the bland term *Neo-Confucianism.*

6. In Chinese, there is the excellent work of Ch'ien (1971), Zhang Liwen (1981), Liu Shu-hsien (1982); in English, there is Wing-tsit Chan (1987, 1989), Thomas Metzger (1977), Donald Munro (1988), and Hoyt Tillman (1992). I (1994) also have provided a short introduction to Chu Hsi's thought in my study of Confucian-Christian dialogue.

7. Of all the classical Confucians, only Hsün Tzu (ca. 340–238 B.C.E.) tended to write highly analytic, programmatic, and systematic essays on issues central to the Confucian project. As in so many other areas of the development of Confucian thought, it is a terrible shame that the Neo-Confucians did not model some of their writing style on Hsün Tzu. I should note that some later Neo-Confucians such as the great Tai Chen (1724–1777) wrote very systematic essays on Neo-Confucian themes. See Chin and Freeman (1990) for a translation of Tai Chen's famous philosophic study of Mencius.

8. John B. Henderson (1991) and Steven Van Zoeren (1991) both have demonstrated the role of commentary in the Neo-Confucian tradition. Van Zoeren devotes a chapter to Chu Hsi's commentary on the *Book of Poetry.* Furthermore, as Edward Farley (1983) has pointed out in his study of theological education, the earliest Christian theology was dedicated to commentary on the Holy Scripture. One sought, on the basis of a sound classical education, to provide a faithful exposition of the Scripture. But the final end of theological reflection was a pious life, the appropriation of the habit of virtue. Just as with Chu Hsi, mere technical brilliance was not enough if you did not realize "in the body" the intent of the text.

9. The question of adequate English translations of Chu's texts is a vexing one. Although more and more of Chu's materials are available in English, there is still very little compared to the scope of the Chinese texts. Part of the problem has to do with the question of scholarly style. Because Chu never wrote a systematic or complete philosphic testament, later scholars have all had to present edited material. While many of them, from his great student Ch'en Ch'un to Daniel Gardner, have carried out their tasks with exemplary scholarly integrity, there is always the nagging desire to be able to consult the unedited opinion of the master. Given the huge size of Chu's corpus, I doubt that this will ever happen in English.

10. In English, Munro (1988) and Tillman (1992) provide masterful expositions of the development of Chu's philosophy. In Chinese, Ch'ien Mu (1971), Mou Tsung-san (1968–69), Zhang Liwen (1981), and Liu Shu-hsien (1982) have documented the growth and maturation of Chu's scholarly achievement.

11. Another extremely useful modern source is Ch'ien Mu's monumental five volume *Chu-tzu hsin hsüeh-an* [A New Study of Master Chu]. Ch'ien provides introductions and commentaries on all of Chu Hsi's major and minor philosophic ideas. It is an invaluable source for orienting oneself to Chu Hsi's thought.

12. Allen Wittenborn (1991) has compiled, edited, and translated more material under the title *Further Reflections on Things at Hand*. This is a very useful supplement to Chan's translation.

13. I will, of course, violate my own short list of sources where necessary. For instance, along with material from the *Dialogues*, it is often very important to cite material from the more purely literary works of Chu Hsi called the *wen-chi*. This is often the case when working on the development of Chu's thought in his later thirties and early forties, when he carried on extensive philosophic correspondence with friends. We often find the first expressions of his subtle thought in letters to colleagues.

14. Nonsinological readers will no doubt be wondering by now why I have included such a lengthy discussion of the Chinese sources of Chu Hsi's thought in a comparative treatise. Part of the reason has to do with my frustration in being forced to make use of material drawn from different sources, almost all compiled long after Chu's demise. I sometimes have toyed with the idea of suggesting that Chu is the invention of his most clever students and editors. Since none of this seems to have upset generations of Chinese, Korean, and Japanese scholars, I will not dwell any longer on my textual discomforts. However, I do take solace that even the great Ch'ien Mu was forced to do the same thing in his presentation of Chu's thought. This mosaic of sources, at least, has good historical roots in the *li-hsüeh* tradition itself.

15. I (1993) have provided an extended explanation of the role of *ch'eng* in another article. The point I want to make here is that we often have to link different parts of Chu Hsi's thought in order to find a plausible analog to some of Whitehead's more technical theories. But once we have noticed that some of Chu's systematically related concepts, when linked as they already are in Chu, provide the context of Chu's exploration of parallel themes in Whitehead, then we can again see how a fruitful comparison can be made. In this case, we need to link the notion of mind–heart, self-actualization, and the Supreme Ultimate to find an analog to the Whiteheadian notion of concrescence.

16. Ch'en Ch'un also is interested in explaining how the Uncontrived Ultimate is merely used to explicate the true meaning of the Supreme Ultimate. "*Wu-chi* (having no extremity) means infinity; it merely describes principle as having no shape or appearance, spatial restriction, or physical form, very much like the operation of Heaven as 'having neither sound nor smell' " (1986, 116–17). The appeal here is the fact that the notion of the Uncontrived Ultimate serves to clarify an important Confucian point, and hence it is completely appropriate to use the term in this context. See Ch'en (1986), pp. 115–20; 188–92.

17. Chu Hsi, *Ssu-shu chi-chu* [Commentaries on the Four Books, *SPPY* Edition, *Ta-hsüeh*], 1b–2a, 4b–5a (1971). Daniel K. Gardner (1986) has provided us with a detailed study of Chu Hsi's commentary on the *Great Learning*.

18. Ch'ien Mu also makes this point in his study of the notion of the investigation of things in Chu Hsi (1971, 2: 504–5).

19. Yi Fu Tuan notes that the notion of the self as some kind of separate substance is a supreme cultural creation of the modern West. "In the West, the self has grown apart from others in prideful and nervous sufficiency. We are islands, each a world of its own; or, to use Goethe's metaphor, billiard balls, hard individuated objects that touch each other only at the surface" (Tuan 1982, 151). It is interesting to note that Tuan, a noted geographer, makes use of the notions of whole–part in trying to suggest ways to deal with the Western sense of personal isolation.

20. Chu Hsi was interested enough in the science of his day that one chapter of the Conversations is devoted to his remarks on astronomy and cosmology. See Li 1973, 1:161–202. For instance, as Needham (1954–, 3: 598) points out, Chu Hsi was one of the first observers to note and guess the nature of fossils.

21. This fact was noticed by the great Ch'ing Chu Hsi school scholar Li Kuang-ti (1642–1718) and duly recorded in his great anthology of Chu Hsi's thought, the *Chu-tzu ch'üan-shu* [The Complete Works of Master Chu] (1977, 2: 1063). Actually, it is not anything like the complete works of Chu Hsi, but it is a very useful and faithful anthology of Chu Hsi's more important comments. For a modern interpretation of the *Book of Changes*, see Lynn (1994). Lynn's translation is especially useful because he makes extensive use of Chu's own commentary. According to Lynn, the first four characters mean funamentality, prevalence, fitness, and constancy (1994, 129).

22. For one of the most compelling descriptions of the cultivation of the mind–heart in English, see Thomas Metzger (1977). Metzger is quite sympathetic to Chu Hsi's philosophic quest. So too is Bruce, although his translation is rather dated now. However, it is still the most extensive in English for the dialogues and the collected writings.

23. D. C. Lau translates the passage in Book 9:17 as "While standing by a river, the Master said, 'What passes is, perhaps, like this. Day and night it never lets up.' " (Confucius, 1992, 80–81).

24. Wing-tsit Chan collects some of Chu Hsi's comments on this aspect of Chang Tsai's philosophy in his translation of Chu's and Lu's *Reflections on Things at Hand* (1967, 33). Chang Tsai is remembered as the Northern Sung Neo-Confucian most interested in the theory of *ch'i* or matter-energy, as already noted in chapter 4.

25. Cheng Chung-ying (1991, 185–213) has some interesting comments about the difference between Chinese and Western dialectics. He traces this Confucian dialectics of harmony to the *Book of Changes*. Further, John Major (1991) has made a

positive case from translating *wu-hsing* as "five phases" rather than five elements. Major believes that the emphasis should be placed on the processive alternation of *wu-hsing* rather than on some elemental quality, hence the use of the term *five phases*. According to Major, this is the case certainly since the time of the composition of the *Huainantzu*. See Major (1991), pp. 67–78.

26. As John B. Henderson (1984) has demonstrated, there was room in classical Chinese cosmology for anomalies and strange happenings that do not seem to have a ready examination. However, for the most part, the Neo-Confucian world was an orderly one.

27. Mou Tsung-san has an alternative account of the Chu Hsi school interpretation of creativity. In the first place, Mou concludes that a pure principle of "active reason" is a distinctive feature of the philosophy of two of the most important of the Northern and Southern Sung Neo-Confucians, namely Ch'eng Hao (1032) and Hu Hung (1106–1162) (Mou 1968–69, 1: 58–61). The source of this creative principle is traced to its classical roots in the *Doctrine of the Mean* and the *Book of Changes,* where "unceasing production is what is called change." The question of what is produced by heaven is an internal argument in the Neo-Confucian tradition. Mou continues his analysis by pointing out that Chu Hsi's theory of principle was to interpret principle as merely existent and not as active reason itself (Mou 1968–69, 1: 68-69). For Mou, the question is clear and the issue at stake is great. If the mainline philosophic Neo-Confucian position on principle is to be identified with Ch'eng Hao and Hu Hung (which is just what Mou argues at great length in his monumental three-volume study), and if this tradition is predicated on the assumption of principle as creative reason, then how can Chu Hsi claim to have understood principle when he so openly disagrees with Hu Hung on just this issue? As always, Mou asks the right questions. Whether he has done complete justice to Chu Hsi will be addressed later.

28. To be fair to Mou Tsung-san, he argues that principle becomes merely a passive model for actualization and not the activity itself for Chu Hsi. Mou believes that for Ch'eng Hao and Hu Hung, the model and the activity are unified and not separated by Chu Hsi's analytic method. See Mou 1968–69, 1: 89; 3: 478.

29. The slightly more analytic Ch'en Ch'un (1986, 97–98), in his account of *ch'eng* as self-actualization, does give a list of characteristics such as taste, color, and shape that suggests a more abstract understanding of principle. I mention this because it was not that the Neo-Confucians could not understand the abstract point Whitehead made about eternal objects, but that they went about their philosophic construction with a different tradition in mind.

30. The ever scholastic Ch'en Ch'un (1986, 120), points out that Liu Tsung-yüan (773–819) and Shao Yung both used the term *wu-chi* before Chou Tun-i. However, Ch'en, just like his master, basically mounts a philosophic defense of the use of the uncontrived ultimate (1986, 115–20).

31. I have searched high and low to find Ch'ien's citation in Chu Hsi's corpus, but have been unsuccessful to date. Ch'ien's study is an invaluable sourcebook for the

study of Chu Hsi, but there are some mistakes to be found in terms of citation. However, the quote is so much in tune with Chu Hsi's approach, I have continued to accept it on faith, and because it seems so accurate in terms of Chu's opinion about the search for and respect for objectivity.

32. This is actually a bit rhetorical. Chu Hsi, just as his modern colleagues in any philosophy department or department of religious studies did, got most of his information from the same source we use today, books. It is interesting to note that Chu Hsi himself supplemented his income by running a publishing venture on the side of his more formal teaching duties (Chan 1989, 61–89). One has the definite impression that, like any good professor, he would have loved computers and CD-ROM access to the classics of his world.

33. Buchler did not approve of this kind of priority for metaphysics. He argued for ontological parity wherein all natural complexes, his term for anything that is, are equally real. Of course, Buchler went on to point out that reality comes in many forms and flavors. But a possibility is as "real" as anything else when you think of it as an element of a human situation. Possibilities can shape the future as surely as can tables and chairs.

Whitehead and Chu would probably agree with a great deal of Buchler's thesis, although they would contend that all such entities are to be found in some actual object–event. Of course, some object–events are possibilities, dreams, wishes, hopes, and anticipations, not just concrete, actual things.

34. For an informative discussion of the social role of the school of Han learning, see Benjamin A. Elman's two studies about intellectual change in late imperial China (1984, 1990).

35. David Gedalecia's (1971) discussion of the great Yüan Neo-Confucian Wu Ch'eng (1249–1333) addresses the nature of this question in great detail. As Michael C. Kalton (1988) notes, this issue was key to the philosophic development of Yi T'oegye (1501–1570) in Korea. This question also was crucial to the famous Four-Seven debate between T'oegye and Taesung, and later Yulgok and Song Hon. See Kalton et. al. (1994).

6

The World Reunited

FORM, DYNAMICS, AND UNIFICATION

Richard McKeon once remarked, echoing Leibniz, that philosophers are much more interesting when they explain their own positions than when they are attacking the theories of others.[1] Such a view is consistent with McKeon's interest in the convoluted history of pluralism as a theme in the development of philosophic theories and as a renowned historian of philosophy. McKeon was famous for insisting that his students at least correctly describe the philosophers they were discussing. According to McKeon, what is interesting about a philosophic system is its own essential features, its unique perspective on reality.[2] Following McKeon's wise advice, I will proceed in this and the next chapter to explain how a revised process philosophy and natural theology can resolve some of the difficulties disclosed by Neville's criticism of Whitehead's thought. While criticism has its place, an alternative hypothesis must be advanced about the nature of creativity and divine things in order to advance the debate within the emerging interdisciplinary matrix of a process-oriented comparative philosophy and theology.[3] I have been coy long enough.

I am acutely aware of the experimental and metaphorical nature of my project. While material drawn from the Chinese intellectual world is not as rare as it used to be in Western philosophic and theological literature, it is still unusual to make as much use of Chu Hsi and Ch'en Ch'un as I do.[4] A few selected quotes from Lao Tzu or an enigmatic Zen master flavoring the brew is much more common; the suggestion that Neo-Confucian scholars such as Chu Hsi and Ch'en Ch'un can materially assist in the apologetic improvement of a major Western philosophic and theological movement, much less cogently address a difficult philosophic problem, is still relatively rare. This mixture of Chu and Whitehead is a thought experiment, an interdisciplinary, cross-cultural invitation to explore what is essentially a Western intellectual problem from a Chinese perspective. Actually the question of creativity, albeit in a different conceptual world, was something the Neo-Confucians grappled with because of the very freshness of their own approach to their tradition. To bring some order to the comparison, I will make use of the comparative methodology of archic analysis as proposed by Watson and Dilworth (1985, 1989).

So far my strategy for trying to resolve the question of the relationship of God and creativity has been twofold. The first part of the defense, a combination of narrative and interpretation of the criticism, has been to outline the nature of the problem as expressed in Neville's critique of Whitehead's theory of God and creativity. In doing so, I have tried to avoid Hartshorne's gambit of redefining God as a society of actual entities and not as a unique actual entity per se, or by merely repeating Whitehead's statement of the issue as found in Part V of *PR* in different terms.[5] The inspiration for this move is based on a reading of suggestive passages in *AI* and *MT,* without ignoring *PR* and Whitehead's other earlier works.

The second aspect of the defense has been to adopt a comparative philosophic hermeneutic for the revision drawn from the Chinese Neo-Confucian school of principle founded by Chu Hsi as yet another different, though philosophically related, approach to the question. Chu and his followers were not interested in the Whiteheadian list of problems, so their solutions to the problem of the role of creativity and the relationship of principle and matter–energy suggest alternative approaches for process thought.

I have hinted at various possible revisions necessitated by Neville's critique without elaborating on the substance of the whole structure of the revisions to be presented. A narrative, historical review of the comparative problem of the location of creativity in process thought, coupled with a defense of Whitehead's own vision based on a new Chinese comparative gambit that promises to offer a solution to the problem, is not enough. Merely repeating the fact that Neville, Whitehead, and Chu Hsi disagree on the matter of metaphysical and ontological taste is not "coherent, logical, and, in respect to its interpretation, applicable and adequate" to the explication of a Sino-Western process position (*PR,* 3). While it may be commonplace that all Western philosophers are either followers of Plato or Aristotle and that all Neo-Confucians either accept or reject Chu Hsi's synthesis, this assertion does not address the philosophic and theological issues at hand; it does little more than suggest that what is at stake is a quarrel about philosophic taste between Western and Chinese intellectuals. Therefore, the enunciation of some kind of positive, constructive alternative position is in order, even if it remains just a sketch.

For instance, Neville has repeatedly argued for a fourfold analysis of any object–event in terms of his Platonic vision of reality.[6] He has offered this revised speculative system, inspired by Plato's *Philebus,* as an alternative to Whitehead specifically and to the rest of modern thought generally. In contradistinction to Neville's quadrilateral, what will a constructive Whiteheadian tripartite schema resemble if my thesis about the hints found in *AI* and *MT* holds at least some conceptual water? Is there a way to restate Whitehead's basic vision in terms that avoid the problems we have been struggling with in the previous five chapters? Does the Neo-Confucian version of process thought provide assistance and direction as well? What does Chu Hsi have to contribute to an analysis of divine things?

Of course, it also is necessary to comment on how unfashionable this kind of exploration of speculative philosophic concerns is in these days of logical analysis, ordinary language explanations, radical deconstruction, and the rupture of cultural criticism. Although they share very little else, both analytic philosophers and deconstructionists disdain systematic philosophy.[7] The appeal in this essay to systematic elements in organic thought is yet another area of general agreement with Neville, who also is interested in defending the place of large-scale thought and even theological issues in the grand Western tradition. Any constructive (and systematic) comparative proposal, according to the proponents of post–modernism, smacks of the ancient Greco-Roman, medieval, and early modern Western search for secure philosophic foundations, for the *logos* at the center of all reality. The main burden of a great deal of contemporary philosophy and cultural criticism has been to question the validity of this search for foundations or the presence of being, much less order or rationality in the cosmos.

Most contemporary professional schools of philosophy argue that such a search is futile, misguided, and even perverse. The analytic school moves from seeking a comprehensive vision toward the need for greater clarity and precision in dealing with questions of philosophic details.[8] While the founders of the second phase of modernism in the seventeenth century, Descartes, Hobbes, Spinoza, and Locke, sought the sure foundations of epistemology, ontology, and cosmology, their modern heirs seek to deconstruct any potential system that could possibly interpret the person and the world in terms of first principles or patterns, if there is even a common world at all in terms of Being standing over against beings. According to one important contemporary reading offered by the neopragmatic critic Rorty, the best we can accomplish is to suggest a new vocabulary for a fallibilistic vision of the world, an edifying discourse to guide humane social conduct. We cannot pretend that this new vocabulary has any purpose beyond being a set of hypotheses to be tested in debate within the scholarly community.

From the skeptical perspective of deconstructive post–modernism, the Whiteheadian and Neo-Confucian tripartite schema of form, dynamics, and unification can be read as a quaint suggestion for a new vocabulary, a linguistic tool for the examination of comparative philosophy and religion. Furthermore, it has the added benefit of being quaint in at least two different discredited cultural and philosophic modes, the process thought of Whitehead and the *li-hsüeh* of Chu Hsi. In the less jaundiced terms of my own constructive project, it is offered as a method for reading the formative classics of Chu and Whitehead as expressions of closely related *ars contextualis* qua process thought. As I have stated before, the value of the schema must be tested in a disciplinary fashion by those able to judge whether it brings more clarity to the study of these texts or whether it simply muddies the water by imposing an alien structure between the texts and the audience. It is an empirical, hermeneutical proposal in that I know of no way this question can be decided prior to the application of the proposal to the interpretive reading of the texts.

I believe that the revised Whiteheadian system based on form, dynamics, and unification presents a tripartite articulation of themes derived from a coherent internal reading of *PR, AI,* and *MT,* as well as the mature thought of Chu Hsi. Furthermore, I hold that this tripartite schema is especially useful in terms of a revised Whiteheadian natural theology, as well as comparative philosophy. Naturally, Christians will always find tripartite schemas appealing because so much Christian thought has been given to grappling with the mysteries of the Holy Trinity, a truly primordial tripartite schema if ever there was one. In a cross-cultural comparative mode, I have formally labeled these three elements or traits[9] of divine and mundane reality form, dynamics, and unification because such terminology connects the great Neo-Confucian synthesis represented by Chu Hsi and his school in East Asian Confucian thought to the modern process movement of Whitehead.[10]

The term *trait* could also easily be equated with metaphor and prototype as suggested in the collaborate work of George Lakoff and Mark Johnson (1980).[11] In their collaborative and individual works, Lakoff and Johnson have offered an alternative view of category formation. They make the clear argument that categories cannot be reduced to a neat, clear, distinct, and coherent set of verbal or even mathematical propositions. Basing their work on modern linguistics and the philosophy of mind and language, Lakoff and Johnson argue that the hallowed world of metaphors provides us with a better way of understanding how we use concepts. In fact, they argue that we live more by the extension of metaphors than by the cold and precise dictates of instrumental reason.

According to Lakoff and Johnson, we reason about major things in our lives by means of metaphors. Metaphors functions as prototypes for organizing the objects of our world. One of the beauties of the Lakoff–Johnson model is that it explains how different cultures can live with different metaphors and yet, through cross-cultural exchanges, learn new metaphors and extend old metaphors. They ask us to think about metaphors as prototypes of meaning. For instance, Lakoff (1987) and Johnson (1987) note that for native speakers of English, the robin is commonly accepted as a prototypical instance of a bird. We then extend our notion of what it means to be a bird metaphorically to other creatures such as owls, who are distributed farther from the core image of the robin as the prototype of birdness. In fact, there is no ultimate or absolute birdness ever to be uncovered, because we move freely from metaphor to metaphor, bird to bird.

Metaphors, as the culturally sophisticated traits of elite world making, are wonderfully vague general categories in Peirce's sense of vagueness. Metaphors point beyond themselves while remaining themselves, and when alive, have a power that cannot be reduced or captured by more logical forms of discourse.

Within Christian theology it has always been fashionable to describe how hard it is to deal with the Holy Trinity. While there is a great deal of truth to the claims for historical complexity for the attempts of Christian theologians to deal with this important Christian symbol and theme, some of the problems may not be as grave as the faithful have been given to believe. For instance, if the process tradition is correct in its hypotheses about the processive, organic, and relational nature of reality, then even mundane human beings have a much better chance of describing the riches of the Trinity than would be possible for some alternative speculative schemas that do not allow for the careful reworking of the concept of transcendence and immanence, creativity, and God–world relations that process thought offers. While humility is always in order when dealing with the internal workings of the Blessed Trinity, at least some of the purported mystery may reside more in human philosophic limitations and conventions than in God's revealing grace. Here too the theistically agnostic Confucians have some interesting observations to make in assisting their Christian dialogue partners.

In addition, I argue that the traits of form, dynamics, and unification closely cohere with the basically tripartite nature of Whitehead's thought, even though he obviously never used this technical vocabulary.[12] However, fear of a new set of neologisms has never bothered Whiteheadian thinkers. In the Chinese case, the three traits also find analogous symbolization in Chu Hsi's version of Neo-Confucian thought. The verbal formulation of the three traits is indebted to both Chu and Whitehead as an extension of their thought and not as an exact imitation of their own texts or vocabulary. Last, but not least, we need to remember that Whitehead did thematize his basic metaphysical position in terms of three principles in the chapter on adventure in *AI* (354–65) in a fashion that warrants this particular usage. Although I have departed from the exact wording of the texts, I hope I have not departed from their spirit and vision.

The three metaphysical principles (see chapter 2 for an extended discussion of metaphysics and/or metasystem) expressed in the discussion of adventure in *AI* are: (1) "One principle is that the very essence of real actuality—that is, of the completely real—is *process* " (354); (2) "I now pass to the second metaphysical principle. It is the doctrine that every occasion of actuality is in its own nature finite" (356); (3) "The third metaphysical principle may be termed the principle of Individuality" (360). Whitehead immediately links the third principle of individuality to "the doctrine of Harmony," as he calls it. He states that "Thus, the basis for a strong, penetrating experience of Harmony is an Appearance with a foreground of enduring individuals carrying with them a force of subjective tone, and with a background providing the requisite connection" (363). I believe my formulation of form—as the mark of the completely real, dynamics (as the mark of process), and unification—as the mark of individuality, can appeal to Whitehead's three principles.

Neville also proposes a similar way of describing the features of his metaphysics when he says,

> In sum, things are harmonies of both conditional and essential features, conditional ones in order to be determinately related to other things with respect to which they are determinate, and essential ones in order to be determinately different from those other things. (1993, 75)

To account for the reality, the actuality of any object–event, Neville postulates essential and conditional features of the emerging creature, features that are always harmonized in some fashion for good or ill. He shares the axiological bias common to Whitehead and Chu Hsi, an essential feature in his terms for a processive, generative *ars contextualis*. As we shall see, this Nevillian schema can be translated into the language of form, dynamics, and unification without overextending either vocabulary.[13]

There is nothing more Whiteheadian than inventing some new nomenclature to try to describe metasystemic conceptualizations to illustrate the novelty of the vision being propounded. If one were dealing with Whitehead only within the Christian part of the European world then we could call this a Trinitarian description of reality. But this specifically Christian designation obscures the broader reach of a reformed Whiteheadian system as a form of *ars contextualis*, a form of thought, with connections to Chinese thought and other forms of global natural theology or philosophy of religion.[14] Such a system will be useful in describing features of the divine reality outside of Christian-influenced circles of thought, because it hypothetically claims to describe certain basic elements of all that exists—or more modestly, to be a vocabulary that can describe all that is believed to exist. In short, it claims to be a global comparative philosophic vocabulary and, by extension, a comparative theology when applied to divine matters.

One of the provocative features of Western process thought has been its apparent ability to link modern philosophy, science, and theology. What is more, it also claims that these linkages should include material taken from outside of the classical North Atlantic intellectual world. While there is nothing novel in trying to link philosophy and theology in the praxis of classical, medieval, or even early modern Western thought, there is something subversive about the mixture of non–Western and Western material in the eyes of many contemporary philosophers.[15] But if Whitehead expresses a nondual vision of reality, such as discussed in great detail by David Loy (1988) in terms of Hindu, Buddhist, and Taoist Asian thought, then the conjunction of theology and philosophy is not hard to understand. Loy argues that all nondual philosophies are closely allied to soteriology because the typical nondual strategy is not only to thematize how we describe and perceive reality but to suggest that we can overcome the errors of dualistic thinking. Most nondual thinkers, according to Loy, develop methods for human beings to deconstruct their false perceptions of reality. Better thinking is one key to better living. Whitehead also argued that one task of philosophy was to help us live better and better still.

Furthermore, it is significant that Whitehead chooses to include his three metaphysical principles in the chapter on adventure, the zest for life in *AI*. Adventure embodies creativity in the generation of human civilization. Truly civilized life, according to Whitehead, must manifest creativity to remain alive to the ever-changing nature of a pluralistic world in which creatures make choices for value, for the ordering of definiteness that is the hallmark of object–events. These choices may be for good or ill; often the choices are for the worst and express human perversity in all of its ugliness. Philosophy itself is an attempt to give voice to the coherent, logical, and necessary features of this adventure. The problem is that we, as finite creatures, can never be sure that we have gotten it right. As Neville has often stated, there is no one to tell us if our slip is showing or if our fly is open in terms of perfected metaphysical insight.

On the Chinese side, Mou Tsung-san, the great modern Confucian philosopher and intellectual historian, has argued that all such rationalistic attempts to state, describe, or define the ultimate nature of reality are limited because their data is drawn from the past achievements of human experience and not from the living, creative, and adventurous present of living reality.[16] According to Mou, there is a real philosophic problem when philosophers such as Chu Hsi and Whitehead offer a retrospective vision of reality without realizing the nature of their error because of their interest in the analysis of object–events as the cosmological building blocks of all that is.

Mou believes that if we focus our attention on a retrospective rationalism, such as was the case for Chu, driven as he was by his fixation on
principle rather than the living mind–heart as the matrix of principle, we will
miss accounting for creativity as the foundation of the moral mind, the real
agent of change in the cosmos. According to Mou, great rationalists such as
Chu Hsi and Whitehead think they achieve too much because they are mes-
merized by the formal structure of the settled past rather than by the living
creation of the present creative advance into novelty, an advance generated
out of the potentiality of the agent intellect, the moral mind–heart of the sage.
All such formalistic rationalism is retroactive; Chu and Whitehead try to
reach farther back in order to move forward. This does not mean, Mou would
hasten to add, that Whitehead and Chu Hsi are useless or even uninteresting
thinkers if we are careful to note their limitations. But without the living heart
of the matter, the Neo-Confucian *hsin* as mind–heart, philosophy is merely a
pedantic exercise in intellectual history.[17]

Without being concerned with Mou Tsung-san's rejection of Chu Hsi's
retrospective rationalism, Charles Hartshorne has made much the same point
about the necessity for a tripartite formulation of reality, especially where it
intersects with speculation about the divine reality (1965, x–xi). Hartshorne
argues, in the context of his larger analysis of continuing relevance of a
revised version of Anselm's ontological proof of God's existence, that the
triad of essence, existence, and actuality is necessary for the adequate description of the divine reality. "An important point of the analysis is the
inadequacy of the dichotomy of *essence–existence*. A third term is needed,
'actuality' " (1965, x). Hartshorne passionately believes that anything less
than this triad will not be acceptable in terms of the real complexity of the
world that must be so described.

> Essence, existence, actuality—this triad is the minimum of complexity which
> must be considered if the famous Proof is to be correctly evaluated. As
> Peirce said, the thinker in mere dichotomies is a crude fellow, trying to
> make delicate dissections with an ax. So long as philosophers persist in
> confusing existence and actuality, just so long will they be but bumbling
> amateurs in a matter in which they have long been claiming competence.
> (1965, xi)

In terms of my version of process thought, Hartshorne's list of essence,
existence, and actuality is translated as follows:

1. essential = form
2. existence = dynamics
3. actuality = unification

For Neville (1993), my translation is:[18]

1. conditional = dynamics
2. essential = form
3. harmony = unification

Whitehead, at various points in *PR,* also indicated a certain preference for tripartite formulations of speculative concerns. For instance, in commenting on what endures and what changes in the world, Whitehead states

> We have certainly to make room in our philosophy for the two contrasted notions, one that every actual entity endures, and the other that every morning a new fact with its measure of change.
> These various aspects can be summed up in the statement that *experience* involves a *becoming,* that *becoming* means that *something becomes,* and that *what becomes* involves *repetition* transformed into *novel immediacy.* (*PR,* 136–37)

What Whitehead is driving at is the notion that the experience of the object–events (actual entities or occasions) informing and constituting the world demands an analysis of the actuality, the unity, and the becoming of the object–events. It also implies a notion of the dynamics of the process of the becoming of the actualities as well as a recognition of the repetition of the forms that are also present in all object–events.

In the discussion of the extensive continuum, Whitehead provides his most generalized notion of the triad of form, dynamics, and unification. He does so, as we have noted in chapter 2, in terms of the specification of the second of his metaphysical assumptions concerning the philosophic argument of *PR.*

> An extensive continuum is a complex of entities united by the various relationships of whole to part, and of overlapping so as to possess common parts, and of contact, and of other relationships derived from these primary relationships. (*PR,* 66)

The notions of whole, part, and contact, and their allied relationships, are about as abstract as one can get for Whitehead, even more abstract than the traits of form, dynamics, and unification. Whitehead is also careful to note that his own pictorial illustrations in the text of *PR* make the notions merely two-dimensional and hence become hopelessly inadequate and static. Whatever else the notions are supposed to indicate, static formalism is not one of their features. My traits of form, dynamics, and unification are more specific (that is, less abstract in Neville's terminology) in that they are suggested by an examination of the modern Western process tradition and the Chu Hsi school of Sung Neo-Confucianism. This is a good example of overlap in order to present some common features of the Western and Chinese forms of processive thought. The greater specificity of my triad is to be expected due to the greater content implied by the dual Western and Neo-Confucian terminological heritage.

Philosophic humility is demanded whenever anything as pretentious as ultimate triads are proposed for all object–events. The history of global thought is littered with such attempts to state metaphysical truth. All such claims are provisional, hypothetical, and heuristic—from my own archic perspective, such usage is always disciplinary, to be tested and corrected by others. The heuristic element I am appealing to here is the usefulness of this schema in revising a problematic aspect of Whitehead's notion of divine reality when contrasted with Chu Hsi's Neo-Confucian vision for comparative purposes *and* challenged by Neville in terms of philosophic coherence. As Whitehead pointed out, metaphysical principles never take a holiday. This persistence makes such principles terribly hard to recognize from the perspective of finite creatures. There is always the chance that some important and obvious aspects of reality have been elided, and the problem is that no other finite creature is liable to tell us where we have gone wrong. Nonetheless, the contrast between Whitehead and Chu Hsi does guard against hasty overgeneralization based on the civilized experience of only one philosophic culture within the emerging global discourse of late modernism.

I obviously believe that the elements of form, dynamics, and unification can be specified of certain Sung, Yüan, Ming, and Ch'ing Neo-Confucian systems of thought; the most obvious candidates are those Neo-Confucian forms of discourse systematically allied to the Chu Hsi school.[19] As we have seen in chapters 4 and 5, it has long been recognized, beginning with Joseph Needham in the 1950s, that there are some Neo-Confucian thinkers who manifest fascinating structural similarities with Whitehead's process thought. The application of these three traits creates at least one coherent reading of Chu Hsi's version of the Confucian *tao*. This is especially true when we consider the maturation of Chu's unique intellectual synthesis in his late thirties and early forties along with an explanation of his philosophic breakthrough as defined and recorded in his conversations with his students in his fifties and sixties.

At this point we can ask one very pointed question. How can such a systematic judgment be made about two great thinkers at different ends of the intellectual world, much less men separated by over 600 years of philosophic, artistic, religious, economic, social, and political differentiation? The simplest claim is that both Chu Hsi and Whitehead present systems that can be called species of process philosophy as a representation of *ars contextualis*. What this means, without putting too fine a point on it, is that both the Cambridge don and the Southern Sung Confucian worthy believed that creativity, pluralism, coherence, and relationality are key elements for any adequate systematic description of the world.

In fact, the traits for form, dynamics, and unification first emerged during studies of the proposed intellectual affinity of Whitehead (with a contribution from Tillich as well) and Chu Hsi in terms of organic thought as suggested by Joseph Needham. It struck me that one of these correlations resides in the fact that both Chu Hsi and Whitehead often organize their philosophy in a tripartite manner. My further claim is that form, dynamics, and unification, at least in English, indicate the range of meanings that both Chu Hsi and Whitehead sought to express in terms of their profoundly axiological *ars contextualis*. I continue to want to use the language of speculative system rather than metaphysics because I am convinced that Chu Hsi's deepest philosophic concerns cannot be described as metaphysics in any highly unqualified sense arising from the Western philosophic and theological world. There is indeed a great deal of overlap, but the differences between most Western metaphysics and Chu Hsi's project are as interesting as the similarities.

THE FOCUS OF THE TRIPARTITE SCHEMA

Before I review and expand the sketch of the tripartite schema of form, dynamics, and unification, I need to explicate what I think is going on in such an analysis. For instance, Neville would probably assert that what I am proposing is a fairly standard form of Whiteheadian cosmology—interesting as far as it goes, but a move that does not address the ontological question of fundamental creativity per se. In Neville's terms, all that I am basically doing is tinkering with some of the terminological aspects of process thought in order to make the schema better fit Chu Hsi and Whitehead within a global comparative perspective. None of this is a surprising move, since Needham noted the structural similarities between Chu Hsi and Whitehead in the 1950s. But does the language of the Western metaphysics do justice to what is going on in the comparison? Is the old trio of metaphysics, ontology, and cosmology adequate? I do not believe any three of these Western terms to be completely serviceable for reasons that will become more clear as the argument unfolds.

As already noted, my alternative terminological description of the fundamental issues involved is derived from Hall and Ames' recent study (1987) of the Confucian project. Hall and Ames point out that the basic Western

distinctions of metaphysics, ontology, and cosmology do not really fit the
Confucian project (see chapters 2, 4, and 5 and the appendix). In general,
Hall and Ames maintain that in the West there are two main streams of
cosmological speculation, *ontologia generalis,* or general ontology, and *scientia
universalis,* or the science of principles. General ontology is often identified
with the question of why there is anything at all rather than nothing. The
science of principles or universal science, on the other hand, seeks "to delin-
eate the principles underlying the character of things and their relationships
to each other" (Hall and Ames 1987, 199). Hall and Ames go on to suggest
that the distinction between these two forms of discourse is not always all
that distinct.

Hall and Ames suggest that the term *ars contextualis* is a better way to
characterize the Confucian "cosmological" project. Although they apply this
reasoning primarily to Confucius, as well as to some of the other classical
Confucian texts of the pre-Han and Han periods, and not to the Neo-Confucian tradition, I believe that their suggestion has merit for the Sung revival of
classical Confucianism.[20]

> The term *ars contextualis* is used here to capture the meaning of Confucius'
> form of "aesthetic" cosmology. In contrast to investigating the general char-
> acter of the being of things (*ontologia generalis*) or to articulating the prin-
> ciples of a universal science (*scientia universalis*), the Confucian sensibility
> may be said to presuppose the activity of contextualization in which any
> element in a context is assessed by the contribution it makes to construing
> the context, and alternatively the contribution made by the context to the
> constitution of that element. (1987, note 7, 358)

It is precisely this kind of attention to the field of creation, to the interplay,
contact, and overlap of whole and parts, that is suggested by the Confucian
and Neo-Confucian project. As we shall see, I believe that the specification
of *ars contextualis* in terms of form, dynamics, and unification can also be
applied to a Whiteheadian understanding of creation.

However, I will avoid characterizing the Neo-Confucian tradition as an
aesthetic expression of an *ars contextualis,* because I believe that this unduly
limits the range of the Neo-Confucian vision.[21] It constrains the Neo-Confucian
contribution to an *ars contextualis* by suggesting a purely aesthetic nature to
the tradition.[22] While it is entirely true that Neo-Confucianism was a tradition
dedicated to the arts, especially those of the literati such as poetry and painting, for instance, it was a tradition of civil engineering, personnel manage-
ment, and penal law as well. It was a world of the judgment of the ugliness
of human misconduct as well as a celebration of the beauties of the created
order. Rather than being only aesthetic in nature, I interpret the Neo-Confucian

project as being profoundly axiological in orientation, with the aesthetic dimension only one aspect of a broader interest in value as a foundational category for reality as it is in this cosmic epoch.

The Neo-Confucian vision also is one of a realistic pluralism, or a world made up of concrete object–events of wonderful complexity, beauty, and even danger. The great Sung-Ming Neo-Confucians never tired of pointing out that they had a doctrine of the "real" or *shih,* as they called it, a teaching of the concrete nature of the object–events of the world. They contrasted this teaching to that of their main rivals, the Taoists and Buddhists. The Neo-Confucians argued that the Taoists and Buddhists taught, respectively, doctrines of nothingness and emptiness. In their more charitable moments, the Neo-Confucians conceded that there was a wonderfully seductive quality to Taoist and Buddhist thought, based on the meditative and artistic skills of the traditions. The Neo-Confucians warned that it was one thing to seek the calm stillness of the mind–heart but another to entirely read into this quasi-psychological state of meditative vacuity for the richness of the whole cosmos.

It also is important to remember that the Neo-Confucian appeal to the buzzing pluralism of the world is not, on the other hand, a bald acceptance of the merely mechanistic or crass elements of reality. The Neo-Confucians remembered the great Legalist tradition that taught of imperial control in a world without ideals, without dreams, of a world of pure power politics where to the victor went the spoils.[23] The Neo-Confucians, like all Confucians, held out, sometimes against the reality of a tyrannical political situation, the dream of a win-win world wherein wisdom and good order would prevail for the mutual benefit of all. The Neo-Confucians never lost sight of the transcendent power of the good as embodied in the teachings of the ancient sages.

There is another aspect of the Neo-Confucian world that resembles Whitehead. This is the characterization of the world in what Neville calls "the language of closure." Neville argues that the secular modern understanding of the world is modeled on the modern mathematical notion of closure.

> People's conception of the sum total or boundaries of the world can be expressed by the mathematical notion of "closure." Closure is the characteristic of a set of things defined by a particular operation or trait; it might be internally infinite but is definite with respect to what falls outside it as not sharing the trait. For instance, the set of even numbers has closure, infinite though it is and distinct from odd numbers. (1993, 143)

One of the present problems with theology, according to Neville, is that it also adopts this modern understanding of the world as defined by closure. At best,

Neville believes that some theological schools, especially the process movement, " . . . have defended a view of God whose being is finite within the closure of determinate things albeit perhaps infinite in other ways" (1993, 148).

This is the crux of the issue for Neville, as it was also for the Neo-Confucians in their confrontation with the Taoists and Buddhists. The problem is, does Neville's definition of closure as a view of the world as lacking in ontological creative potential do justice to the Neo-Confucian vision? Is there some other order of traits beyond the world of the ten thousand things that is the ontological locus of creativity? What if the definite set of traits, albeit truly self-referencing, are not constrained or closed in some finitistic sense but rather are creative, both definitionally and actually? And what if this creative trait or set of traits is infinite in terms of the openness of the future as well as appropriate for the past and appreciation of the immediacy of the present? Does it then make any sense to say that this is a closed system even if, technically speaking, it is a "closure" world as Neville wants to define it?

The world of Chu Hsi and Whitehead is definitely not a closed world if we think of closure as defining something static, a world in which there is nothing new. The very act of creativity is not just some other thing among the ten thousand things as the Neo-Confucians like to say, but is rather always the very nature of the universe as it moves from indeterminateness to determinateness without ceasing. However, it may be closed in that it is resolutely pluralistic: all we can do is speak of the object–events themselves. Creativity is not some thing, but every thing, that is, every object–event is an instance of creativity as the supreme Mandate of Heaven, *t'ien-ming*, as Chu Hsi would say. It is only through the ceaseless creativity of the object–events that the universe is made ever new. The comprehensive nature of the decisions made by the object–events as they become definite creates and embodies creativity per se.

Cheng Chung-ying, in his study of the relationship of principle and matter–energy, throws more light on the characteristic Neo-Confucian sense of creativity.

> The creative activity of *ch'i* is continuous as well as purposive. It is purported to preserve life and to continue life by making the creative activities of life the constant activity of reality. . . . The importance of *sheng* (life-generation) lies in the fact that the process of change is not merely a circular interchange of *yin* and *yang* in repetition, but one of interchange without repetition. (1991, 510)

Cheng carries out some of his analysis in a study of creativity in Whitehead and Neo-Confucianism. His conclusion is that Neo-Confucianism has an even more radical version of creativity than Whitehead because ". . . the internal dynamics and immanent nature of creativity are not stressed by Whitehead as in Neo-Confucian *t'ai-chi*" (1991, 554). The Supreme Ultimate is able to play this role because it contains all potentiality and is the basis for all actual differentiation and spontaneous novelty, according to Cheng. Hence, "Multiplicity or many are not to be regarded as given, as derived from the Primordial Nature of God, but simply considered as a mode of actualization of the Primal One—the *t'ai-chi*" (1991, 554). There are sections of *AI* that allow for an even more congruence or intercultural mirroring of themes between the normative Neo-Confucian view of creativity and Whitehead, as we shall see.

However, before I carry out the task of showing how Chu Hsi and Whitehead can be interpreted as exponents of a process *ars contextualis*, an elaboration of the tripartite schema is in order.

FORM, DYNAMICS AND UNIFICATION

Form

Form (or forms) define the normative, objective, or essential characteristic or pattern of anything that is—concrete, literary, fantastic, imaginary as embedded in the mind—in any sense at all; the formal traits function to distinguish object-events from each other as elements of definiteness. For Whitehead, the eternal objects are the formal traits of any actual entity, occasion, or society of natural complexes—what I now call generically object–events in order to indicate both Whitehead's actual entities and Chu Hsi's *wu* or concrete things or events.[24] For Chu Hsi, *li,* or principle, plays the role of formal traits, the defining characteristics of one thing over against some other thing. However, the defining trait/s of any actual entity/object–event is more than a rational or an essential description of the object–event in question, for the formal traits of the cosmos also index the configurations of moral value, the delight of artistic harmonies, or the shock and revulsion at the recognition of depravity. For instance, these formal traits describe what a thing or person should be and indicate the profoundly axiological nature of everything that is. In fact, these formal traits are the axiological characteristics of any object–event or societies of entities, or any kind or pattern of activity whatsoever.

The obvious Western analogies to my revised process formal traits are notions such as Platonic ideas, Aristotelian forms, or Whitehead's eternal objects. While this is a reasonable comparison, it is not precisely the range of concepts I am trying to define, especially when we factor in comparative material from the Neo-Confucian tradition of Chu Hsi. For instance, Chu Hsi suggests that one way to understand the formal traits of object–events is to think in terms of a boundary as a form of definiteness. He points out that most things have boundaries that serve to define the thing for us, and that these boundaries can be axiological as well as physical, for instance (Berthrong 1979, 62–63). A good act, according to Chu Hsi, has a boundary of propriety, excellence, civility, kindness, or deference that distinguishes it from a bad act, just as the unique shape of a human being is different from the classical Chinese writing brush. It is here that many scholars also have suggested a Confucian affinity with Aristotle. In religion, we recognize good and bad faith; in art, we distinguish one genre of poetry from another and one painter's style from another's set of mannerisms.

Another important dimension of the formal side of reality has to do with the norms, the sources of values. This is of particular importance for the Neo-Confucians who were preoccupied with the cultivation of humane social values, arts, and virtues. For instance, form can be discussed in terms of the beauty of a painting or poem. It also can refer to the rightness or fitness experienced when interpersonal relationships such as friendships are evident. Form carries with it axiological aspects of value in terms of art, religion, morality, and politics. Whitehead, remembering his mathematical training, often but not exclusively writes that formal mathematical relationships can express form, often the form of spare rigor or elegance. Chu Hsi, with the persistent Confucian commitment to community, often but not exclusively notes the ethical and communal side of form in terms of human social conduct and personal virtues. Whitehead also notes the impact of colors as forms, and Chu Hsi tried in his poetry to demonstrate the graceful nature of Confucian formal social life.

In terms of archic variables, the formal trait corresponds or matches the essential vision of reality. As Dilworth points out, the essentialist thinker "sees ideal forms and general, continuous, or enduring traits of nature and experience in the form of graded patterns, functions, and values" (1989, 28–29). This description of essential traits describes many of the characteristics of form as derived from both Chu Hsi's and Whitehead's reflections on the patterning aspects of object–events. What is important to note is the axiological character of this way of defining form. Ethical, emotional, and artistic values can be just as important in defining form as mathematical relationships.

Dynamics

Dynamics is even harder to define than form because it is not a pattern, boundary, or any other kind of particular definiteness. This observation holds true for both the Western and the Chinese side of the equation. The dynamic side of reality gives little purchase for description in terms of the other two fundamental traits. It is the protean power of transformation that has so fascinated thinkers as diverse in time and culture as Chu Hsi and Whitehead. It is the vital, impulsive side of reality that becomes configured into something only through form and unification. This also is the abysmal side of the divine reality that is beyond the forms of goodness, rightness, or beauty. Job and Arjuna, in their confrontations with God, would recognize this powerful aspect of reality. In Neo-Confucian discourse, it is often called *ch'i,* or matter-energy, and it is one of the most difficult of all Chinese philosophic concepts to translate into English because it carries so many rich connotations in the pan-Chinese philosophic vocabulary. Hence, *ch'i* is often called matter–energy, vital force, or some other neologism that tries to get at the dynamic side of all that is.[25]

Whitehead's fundamental notion of creativity as part of the Category of the Ultimate is yet another attempt to thematize the dynamic side of reality.[26] The dynamic side of reality is doubly hard to articulate because (1) it is a true metasystemic concept within any process philosophy, never taking a holiday from conceptualization, and (2) it is essentially and unceasingly the protean, the mobile, the uncanny, the simply new or transformed side of everything that is. Hence, Whitehead called it creativity and Chu Hsi likened it to the unceasing productivity (*sheng sheng pu-hsi*) that lies at the heart of the Tao as the Mandate of Heaven. Chu Hsi, following Chang Tasi as the great Sung theorist of creativity, often defined the dynamic trait in terms of *ch'i,* or matter–energy.[27] You cannot call it any one formal name because it is, as Lao Tzu might have said if he had wanted even to speak of it, the mother of all names and no one name in particular. It is the fertile matrix of all generativity.

Here again, archic analysis proves helpful. As we have seen in the discussion of the formal trait, Dilworth observes that most Neo-Confucians share an essential variable with Whitehead (1989, 29). This form of formlessness also obtains for something as protean as *ch'i* for Chu Hsi or the abysmal, primordial, and creative nature of God for Whitehead, with his emphasis on creativity as such an important aspect of his system. Here the notion of continuous activity with infinite potential forms as always and everywhere present in the concrete object–events is key without the distinctive trait of specifying a particular form or principle beyond the admittedly nebulous notion of creativity. And while it is always dynamic, ever changing, it is as uniformly liable to take on form as to lose form in the formless generativity of becoming. Hence we cannot even begin to comment upon the dynamic side until it does take on form. We anticipate dynamics more than we define or name it. We only know something by means of difference, and creativity is never different in the same sense that one object–event is different from other object–events.

Because the dynamic trait is so protean and creative, it also is important to note that it can be described as a principle in terms of archic analysis, although Chu Hsi, for instance, would not call it principle in the technical Neo-Confucian sense of principle as *li*. The dynamic trait is as difficult to define in terms of archic analysis as it is to translate the Neo-Confucian notion of *ch'i* into English. As a principle, it is always described as potentially being creative but without the norming characteristic of the formal side of reality, or the decisive or harmonious trait defined by the process of unification. On the one hand, it is ceaseless activity first and foremost, although it does take on form in order to become some definite object–event. But on the other hand, it also is a comprehensive principle in that it is necessary for any discussion of the universal causation of the cosmos (Dilworth 1989, 30).

Unification

Unification, or the trait of unity, describes how the formal and dynamic side of reality comes together to be some thing, object, or event. Mere form and dynamic energy would be chaotic without the unifying trait, without any purposive act to hold the two together. Without a final unity, for Whitehead concrescence would fail to achieve satisfaction and for Chu there would be no place for the mind–heart to be fully cultivated. According to Hartshorne, this is actuality per se as creative synthesis. However, nothing can be truly actual until it is unified, determinate. Neville's extended discussions of the nature of the person as a fusion of essential and conditional features points toward the role of unification as a fundamental notion in his anthropology.

Furthermore, there is the generation or creation of new values through the unifying process, which demonstrates the axiological character of this version of process thought. Referring again to Chu Hsi and Whitehead, we can see how this works itself out in philosophic practice in the Western tradition and in Neo-Confucianism. Chu Hsi's notion of *hsin*, or the mind–heart, is a good Neo-Confucian example of how form and dynamics find unity in the human person. Mou Tsung-san calls this the point of experiential unity of the Mandate of Heaven and human nature. In Whitehead's mature thought, the whole theory of concrescence is yet another way to define the unity of actual entities. For Whitehead, the satisfaction of the actual entities in the perpetual perishing of object–events defines how the actual entities unify all of their constituent elements into something actual, definite.

In a universal sense, God's consequent nature also expresses something of the divine process of synthesis. Whitehead, especially in *AI*, speculated on the role of divine eros as the creative advance into novelty. There was always an advance into a novel creation, a moment of unified fact expressing the values of the new object–event. In terms of the archic variables we have been using, Dilworth posits a creative principle for Whitehead and a comprehensive principle for Chu Hsi and the Neo-Confucians. There is something both creative and comprehensive to be found in the unification of each creature. For Chu Hsi, we have noted that the mind–heart functions to unify the human person. On a more systematic level, Chu Hsi also indicates that the Supreme Ultimate (*t'ai-chi*) and even the Will of Heaven (*T'ien-ming*) bring unity to principle and *ch'i* in the formation of the ten thousand things. This is to be expected in philosophic systems that place such a high premium on organic and relational themes.

As a principle, the trait of unification is not easy to categorize in terms of the variables of archic analysis, as presently proposed by Watson and Dilworth. On the surface, unification suggests some variation of the dialectical or sublational method. As Dilworth defines it, dialectic as sublation "observes a logic of higher agreement, which presupposes and accomplishes a synthetic unity of opposites, contrasts, or multiplicities" (Dilworth 1989, 29). Dilworth himself believes that this is the method of both Chu Hsi and Whitehead. I am not so sure. For instance, Chu Hsi always vigorously resisted any talk about principle or *ch'i* being superior or inferior to each other; nor would it make any sense to say that the creation of a new creature moved to some phase below, beyond, or above the ceaseless interaction of form and dynamics.[28] My interpretation of unification as a method is more like Dilworth's synoptic or problematic method.

> This method converts a problem or subject matter into an analysis of generic and specific, relevant and irrelevant features. The whole and parts are seen together (hence synoptically) and treated as form and matter of the same holistic function (Dilworth 1989, 30).

As we have seen, Chu Hsi (and most Chinese philosophers) do tend to see reality in terms of whole and parts forming a pattern "seen together."

Another way of looking at the trait of unification is to borrow the language of Stephen C. Pepper in *Concept and Quality* (1966). Pepper is well known for his theory of root metaphors, and in this later work he suggests an addition to his previous list of root metaphors specifically designed to take into account a close reading of organic philosophies such as Whitehead's.[29] Pepper suggests the metaphor of a "purposive act" as a model for his revisioning of some key Whiteheadian categories (1966, 5–6). He came to believe that Whitehead's notion of an actual occasion as a form of the purposive act is yet another major philosophic root metaphor. Such a notion fits well with the idea of unification when we also consider Chu Hsi's ways of talking about the unification of reality. A purposive act, a root metaphor for Pepper, also demonstrates the axiological character of reality that is so important to Whitehead and Chu Hsi.

Returning to Whitehead, we also register that unification is closely related to the notion of harmony, as expressed in *AI*, or of concern in *MT*. Interestingly enough, no one within the broad sweep of process thought has written more eloquently about the role of harmony in the constitution of actual entities than Neville. For Neville, the whatness of any object–event is more than a mere togetherness or a melange of unassociated parts. This togetherness of an object–event expresses the harmony it achieves through its dynamic unification of its settled past. This is the basis for the axiological bias in both Chu Hsi and Whitehead. Without the note of harmony as the unification of process and reality, there would be no meaning for either the Cambridge don or the Sung literatus.

The last question about unification is, where in the tripartite schema do we find creativity defined by the Whiteheadian sense of the primal eros of the universe? Does creativity find a special affinity with form, dynamics, or unification in some particular, definitive fashion? One way to answer this question leads again to the tool of archic analysis and specifically the boundary between Whitehead's creative principle and Chu Hsi's comprehensive principle. One of the great differences between the Whiteheadian and Neo-Confucian versions of organic/process thought appears to reside in the two different archic principles embraced by Whitehead and Chu Hsi. What does this difference tell us about the role of creativity in organic/process thought?

ARCHIC PROFILE OF THE REFORMED PROCESS PHILOSOPHY

For reasons both internal to the Western process tradition and comparative concerns, I have chosen to refer to my version of Whitehead's philosophy as a revised process philosophy or as an organic, processive *ars contextualis*. My terminology remains clunky to say the least. The more one learns about philosophic and religious traditions beyond one's natal culture, the more one learns that concepts from one culture simply do not always fit the professional usage of other cultures. Elegance and simplicity must, as we work in comparative thought, often be sacrificed because of the need for a decent regard for telling the truth about the various traditions as we compare them. This is a good example of what the primal relation of overlap does when comparing two philosophers.

It is helpful to remember that Whitehead himself called his mature system a philosophy of organism. In the preface to *PR*, he stated that "These lectures are based upon a recurrence to that phase of philosophic thought which began with Descartes and ended with Hume. The philosophic scheme which they endeavour to explain is termed the 'Philosophy of Organism.' " (*PR,* xi). Leaving aside the question of whether or not Descartes, Locke, or Hume would have agreed with Whitehead's bold rhetoric about the actual content of their diverse philosophies, he does consistently use the terms *organism* and *organic* to describe his philosophy. Whereas it is true that process is a key element of the philosophy, and the element that has most fascinated his followers and critics, there still is a persistent element of organic unity and even axiological normativity to be found in the system. We must never forget that Whitehead's title for his Gifford lectures affirms the connection of process *and* reality—with reality always expressing the values created by the ceaseless advance into novelty. Reality is relational, or relative, as he puts it, and hence is always organic in its pluralistic realism.

To better understand and contrast this revised process philosophy with Neville's revised Platonic enterprise, archic analysis again provides a method of highlighting some pertinent contrasts. I acknowledge that archic analysis is a limited heuristic and exegetical tool. It is basically a taxonomy, useful in showing some of the deep structural levels of a text. What it is not capable of demonstrating as a method is the precise nature of what the specific content of the text in question will become; the question of specific content of a text depends on its particular cultural and intellectual context. No texts are context free. The reasons for this are not hard to discern. As far as written records go, it is a trivial though an important axiom that every philosopher or theologian lives in a specific lifeworld, a special time, place, and culture.[30]

The content of all philosophy is specified by the ongoing trajectories of discourse internal to the tradition in question. Confucians ask Confucian questions; Western rationalists, empiricists, and analytic language philosophers debate about principle, facts, language, and interpretation; deconstructionists deconstruct; feminists tell us that all of this is an illusion because we are dealing with nothing more than different versions of a common post–Neolithic patriarchal global culture, a unified worship of male power. Yet each of these forms of discourse appeals to its sensibility as pointing to the way the world really is.

The specific content of my project relies on two very different cultural traditions of discourse. The first is Whitehead's own post–Enlightenment Western tradition; the second is Chu Hsi's Southern Sung *tao-hsüeh.* Is this connection viable? Or is it just another farrago of syncretistic politically correct multiculturalism?

I hope I am not unmindful of the potential problems involved due to the temporally and culturally mixed nature of my synthesis. Anyone who has worked seriously with texts cross-culturally is alert to the problems of comparative misunderstanding. Even philosophers and theologians within one cultural area demonstrate an amazing ability to miss each others' points with gusto. Yet the reality of the contemporary world, I believe, militates against any sustained, isolated, and purely monocultural effort in speculative philosophy.[31] As with all such efforts at cross-cultural interpretation and understanding, the difficulties are immense. But the rewards are equally enticing, as I have tried to demonstrate in chapter 5. For instance, the history of the rise of East Asian Buddhism alerts us to the potential for cross-cultural thinking. In this regard, the justly famous Kyoto School indicates how supple Buddhism can be in confronting and interpreting other cultural artifacts. And last, but not least, the new migration of peoples from Asia and Africa to Europe and the Americas demands new paradigms of scholarly interaction.

The specific archic profile of the proposed revised process system has (1) a disciplinary perspective, (2) an essentialist affirmation of reality, (3) a problematic method, and (4) a creative principle. The first question to address is, how does this profile relate to the parent traditions? To answer this question, we must to review the archic profiles of Chu Hsi and Whitehead. First, Chu Hsi has (1) a disciplinary perspective, (2) an essentialist reality, (3) a dialectical method, and (4) a comprehensive principle. Second, Whitehead's profile is (1) a disciplinary perspective, (2) an essentialist reality, (3) a dialectical method, and (4) a creative principle. The revised organic archic profile is mixed compared to its foundational schools in that it shares two variables with Chu Hsi and three with Whitehead.

One initial caveat about the distribution of variables is important. While I am convinced, at least in part, that Dilworth is correct in assigning a comprehensive principle to Chu Hsi and a creative principle to Whitehead, I am not sure how rigorously to take this difference when we examine the specifics of the two schools of thought. It has always struck me that Chu Hsi has a very creative, comprehensive notion of principle. The whole thrust of the Chu Hsi's synthesis of his Northern Sung Neo-Confucian masters was to make the notion of *li* (principle) and *t'ai-chi* (The Supreme Ultimate) supremely creative as well as comprehensive in scope. Hence it could well be the case, if we read Chu Hsi as embodying a very creative version of comprehensive principle, that I share, more or less, three variables with each of my parent traditions.

Where I definitely diverge is in having a problematic method instead of the dialectical method common to both Chu Hsi and Whitehead. Here I share the problematic method with Aristotle. That is not really surprising because both Aristotle and I (with great modesty on my part) manifest an interest in the history of world philosophy as we know it as an important part of the philosophic enterprise. It just so happens that my world is larger if not more complex in terms of different cultural variables than Aristotle's, although I am sure Aristotle would have been delighted with all of the new information. Watson and Dilworth note as well that the problematic method is preferred by the American pragmatic tradition. There also is a problematic strain in the Confucian tradition concerned with historical and social analysis and the need for the Confucian worthy to take part in civil administration.

Another reason for this problematic archic variable has to do with the influence of Chu Hsi's Neo-Confucian thought as *ars contextualis*.[32] Within such an organic form of life, the relationships of parts and wholes are very important. The parts and wholes are dynamically related in terms of the analysis of specific traits. Hence the use of the problematic method arises out of the specific Chinese proclivity to deal with the world in terms of the analysis of wholes and parts. If one likes, this is a genetic trait of the revised organic system inherited from the Chinese parent. Neville (1993) also has argued that the Confucian tradition, through the notion of the all-encompassing Tao, is a very fecund source for comprehensive principles.

It has always struck me that Chu Hsi's understanding of the Tao, as a technical term, is where the comprehensive and the creative principles join. In this I agree completely with Neville's reading of these Neo-Confucian texts. A brief examination of Ch'en Ch'un's explanation of Chu's notion of the Tao confirms this as a reliable reading of the Neo-Confucian understanding for the Tao.[33] Ch'en's glossary is composed of two chapters or sections, and the second chapter contains the exposition of terms such as *Tao, principle, virtue*, the *Supreme Ultimate*, and others that are identified with the more abstract side of Chu's philosophy. Ch'en begins chapter 2 with Tao and helps confirm the comprehensive nature of principle as well as its creative features. In Ch'en's account, Tao is always linked to principle and the Supreme Ultimate as an expression of the creative traits of this cosmic epoch. In Neville's terms, whatever else Tao is for Chu and Ch'en, two of its essential features are its comprehensiveness and creativity.

In the introductory section on Tao, Ch'en makes it clear that "Tao is the way" (1986, 105). While the image is indeed of a way or a road that all people can walk, the Tao is not some common, mundane thing. "Its source must be traced to Heaven." Slightly later, Ch'en states that "Heaven is principle." All of the links of Tao to the way of human conduct, principle as the normativeness of human conduct, and the creative power of heaven are expressed in Ch'en's opening remarks.

> Obviously principle is not something dead just lying there. As the material force of the One Origin spread out, it produces man and things. There are thus lines and veins, as it were. They are the way followed by man and

things. This is what it is when once traces the source of the creative process. (1986, 106)

Ch'en takes pains to contrast this Neo-Confucian understanding of principle with the Buddhist notion of emptiness and the Taoist idea of nothingness. According to Ch'en (and all of the other Neo-Confucians agreed on this point, regardless of their other difference,) this Tao is a solid principle, the principle of a pluralistic and real world.

Probably the most succinct account of the comprehensive and creative nature of Tao is found in Ch'en's supplemental remarks on the Supreme Ultimate, principle, and matter–energy.

(242) Speaking from the point of view of the process of creation, in the production and formation of the ten thousand things in the universe there is nothing from the past to the present that is not true. They are scattered above and below. They exist in the past and they also exist in the present. It is not that they existed in the past and no longer exist in the present. All this is the work of true principle. (1986, 189)

(244) Originally there was only one material force. It is divided into yin and yang and further divided into the Five Agents. The two and five separate and combine in their own way as they operate, producing and reproducing throughout time without cease. There is not only material force; there must be its master, namely, principle. Principle is the pivot in the operation of material force. Therefore in the operation of the Great Transformation, production and reproduction have never ceased. Has there ever been anything outside of nature and not controlled by the principle of one's mind? Whatever principle may be, its reach is unlimited and penetrating, its smallness enters into everything and goes through all, and it endures throughout the generations and pervades all things. (1986, 190)

All of this is part of the unceasing, comprehensive, and creative aspect of Heaven as the Way, the principle of the Supreme Ultimate. All are woven together in Chu's and Ch'en's vision of the unceasing productivity of the Way.

THE ACTUAL, THE POTENTIAL, AND THE COMPOSED

As we have noted earlier in this chapter, in his *AI* discussion of adventure, Whitehead submits that there are three metaphysical principles necessary for an adequate description of reality. It is important for our revisionist project to notice how Whitehead is always tinkering with his philosophic vocabulary, always willing to admit that any verbal formulation of complex matters can be improved. Obviously there is a basal continuity in the search for a process philosophy that ties *SMW, RM, PR, AI,* and *MT* together; but there are subtle shifts of language signaling new emphases of the interpretation of experience or revised thoughts about what he has written before. Beyond the twists and turns of language, Whitehead was seeking to express a new vision of reality.

Chu Hsi was likewise concerned with stating his vision with as much terminological accuracy as possible. It is recorded that just three days before his death he was still working to revise and correct his famous commentary on the *Great Learning.* His great student, Ch'en Ch'un, was faithful to his master's intent by writing a philosophical dictionary that enshrined Chu Hsi's unique understanding of the Confucian philosophic lexicon for the East Asian Confucian world. What is clear in the study of the development of Chu Hsi's thought is that he struggled throughout his entire life to find the best way to express the unity of the vision of the Tao he sought to commend to humankind.

I argue that by the time Whitehead came to publish *AI* and *MT,* all of the elements for my revised organic philosophy had been articulated in various parts of his mature canon. This is a distinctly limited claim. It is not a claim that this is the only way to parse the Whiteheadian vision. Whitehead himself changed his opinions often enough to show that different interpretations are possible at many points. This does not mean that Whitehead proposed such an organization, but I believe we can make the case that such a revised system is warranted on internal Whiteheadian grounds. Further, the revisions I am offering also connect Chu Hsi's Neo-Confucian synthesis with these Western notions to suggest a cross-cultural model for process thought. While neither Chu or Whitehead actually proposed such a model, it is a design that rests on their work.

In the development of the organic/process school after Whitehead I can cite the examples of Hartshorne, Cobb, Neville, and Hall as thinkers who have appropriated and modified Whitehead's philosophy in search of their own speculative philosophy. In East Asia, one can think of the great Korean thinker Yi T'oegye (1501–1570) as reconstructing key elements of Chu's thought in order to explore the notion of principle as a creative element of process speculative philosophy. With a realistic understanding the actuality of the past and the organic connections of object–events, including philosophic texts, there is even an internal warrant for such reconstruction. In fact, anything less would be odd from the perspective of the Neo-Confucians.

One of the key notions for this is an analysis of the elements of composition. I will make use of Chu Hsi's understanding of the role of harmonious composition, Whitehead's notion of concrescence, and Neville's own reflections on essential and conditional features in the generation of any object–event. The actual, creative unity of divine matters resides in the activity of composition. Chinese notions of the complementary nature of the creative process offer needed contrasts to Western vacillations between ontological and cosmological creativity. The actual and the potential are composed into something new, something comprehensive of what went before, what is now, and what is yet to be.

NOTES

1. This story has come down to me from friends who studied with Mr. McKeon at the University of Chicago, as well as through a personal conversation with him in Toronto at a conference on Chinese philosophy in the summer of 1983. Although this is clearly my paraphrase from the memory of his memorable table conversation, I believe it captures his point. Earlier, Leibniz made much the same point about philosophers being much more interesting in stating their positive views than in their criticism of other thinkers. For a study of the development of McKeon's thought, see Plochmann (1990).

2. McKeon is famous for, among other things, championing the cause of pluralism in philosophy. McKeon is important here because one could hardly argue that he was a sloppy or an emotional thinker. McKeon demonstrates that one can be rigorous and pluralist at the same time. He, and his students such as Walter Watson, have argued that there are many legitimate forms of philosophy.

3. Neville has defended just such a view of the place of theory in philosophy on numerous occasions. *Normative Cultures* (1995) has an extended defense of the role of theory as a map for interpretation of various norms in culture.

4. For a fascinating counterexample to this general observation, see Ching's and Oxtoby's (1992a) study of Leibniz and Wolff on Chinese philosophy. At least at the beginning of the German Enlightenment these two great thinkers were interested in Chinese thought, both for its intrinsic humanistic value and its confirmation of some of their own philosophic positions. No great European philosopher has matched Leibniz's interest in classical and Neo-Confucian thought to this day.

5. I believe Hartshorne can defend himself against Neville if he so desires. While it is clear that I deeply appreciate some aspects of Hartshorne's natural theology (see Berthrong 1994), I am not convinced that we need to abandon Whitehead's notion of God as an actual entity for Hartshorne's revision, that is, that God is social in nature.

6. For an outline or a summary of Neville's fourfold analysis, see *HAM*, pp. 268–73. He also calls these a "primary cosmology." They include (1) the Limit, (2) the Unlimited, (3) Mixture, and (4) the Cause of Mixture.

7. This is an exaggeration for some aspects of the analytic philosophic tradition. For instance, although Searle (1993) and Nagel (1987) do not attempt to construct grand metaphysical structures, they both are committed to a view of reason that is

coherent, adequate, and logical from a Whiteheadian perspective. Both definitely appeal to a sense of tradition, the grand tradition of Western rationalism.

8. What makes the argument seductive is, who can be against clarity, logical argumentation, even the philosophic virtue of humility before the facts of natural science and common language and culture? One problem is the very brilliance of the technique. All such technical virtuosity is embedded in the particularity of specific cultural and philosophic traditions. Comparative philosophy must ask a prior question, namely the shape and configuration of the entire enterprise and not just selected topics from within the larger matrix. Comparative philosophy seeks to move from the examination of the parts to the whole in order to see what the parts of each whole are and how they might possibly be compared and contrasted.

9. Just what to call form, dynamics, and unification (are they elements, notions, concepts, or postulates?) is a difficult question. Some care is necessary here to not prejudice the discussion by prior linguistic commitments to the specialized nomenclature of certain well-defined philosophic schools. I will generally call form, dynamics, and unification "traits." My use of traits is inspired by Justus Buchler, who wrote that "The term 'trait' is the most satisfactory of the terms that can serve to identify a constituent of a natural complex" (1966, 12–13). In Buchler's own metaphysics, a natural complex designates anything at all that exists in any sense whatsoever. The term *trait,* Buchler believes, allows the discussion to proceed without invoking the habit of calling one trait more real than another.

The main terminological inspiration for the triad of form, dynamics, and unification comes from W. Widick Schroeder, the Whiteheadian sociologist of religion. His analysis (1976) of the role of religious institutions in terms of form, dynamics, and unification demonstrates the range of the triad as a heuristic tool.

10. I am acutely aware of how dangerous it is to give labels that suggest affinities or analogies between Chinese and Western thought. I agree with Chad Hansen's (1992) strictures on this matter to the extent that, minimally, we must be alert to the great differences that exist between Indo-European systems of philosophy and characteristic Chinese modes of expression. However, by choosing to focus on the comparatively late, mature, and sophisticated work of Chu Hsi as a representative of Sung Neo-Confucianism, some of these problems are less acute than they would be in proposing such a comparison based on texts from the Chinese classical period. We need to remember that Sung Neo-Confucianism, among other things, was a self-conscious Chinese Confucian response to Chinese Buddhist thought, a world of concepts derived from a core of Indo-European systems of thought. Sung Neo-Confucianism was already more of a global philosophy than its classical progenitors.

11. The original discussion of metaphors is found in Lakoff and Johnson (1980). The argument is massively extended in terms of contemporary philosophy and linguistics in Lakoff (1987). Mark Johnson has shown the power of the metaphor in two recent works on the philosophy of body, mind, and ethics (1987, 1993).

12. Given Whitehead's own love of neologism, I am certainly on solid ground here. I will also argue that, although not of Whitehead's scholastic provenance, form, dynamics, and unification point to central traits of Whitehead's and Chu Hsi's thought.

13. In his most recent work, *Normative Cultures*, Neville introduces a set of terms that come close to my triad of form, dynamics, and unification. Neville's triad is importance, unity, and diversity. Both Neville and I owe the notion of importance to Whitehead's *Modes of Thought*.

14. Peter Berger (1992) has ventured the hypothesis that all humanity shares in what he calls the "mythic matrix." According to Berger, if we push far enough back into the origins of human consciousness we can discover this mythic matrix—such that ideas of relationality and the living quality of reality emerge with great clarity. One should to hesitate to call this a natural theology, because such a designation would constrict such a vision to those traditions with some kind of notion of a divine agent. One must always construct these typologies with the most austere Theravadin Buddhist in mind. Perhaps it would be better to call this a natural philosophy of religion.

15. As we have seen, however, MacIntyre has argued that St. Thomas, the architect of many Western of theological and philosophic cathedrals of thought, believed that he was surveying all of the best of human thought available to him. St. Thomas was certainly aware of the classical Greco-Roman world and of the continuing challenge of Jewish and Islamic thought.

16. For an account of Mou Tsung-san's position, see Berthrong, chapter 4 (1994). This argument is part of Mou's confrontation with Chu Hsi. I have chosen to cite Mou rather than scholars more favorable to Chu Hsi because I believe that we often learn more from our critics than from our friends.

17. In a previous work on Confucian-Christian dialogue, I have tried to provide an outline of Mou's insightful criticism of Chu Hsi (1994). As I noted in this book, it is unfortunate that so little of Mou's work has been translated into English. In many respects, Mou is as interesting as the justly famous Kyoto School thinkers in terms of his penetrating synthesis of Western, Buddhist, and Chinese thought.

18. I must be careful to note that Neville much prefers to order these elements in a fourfold manner derived from his exegesis of Plato's *Philebus*. From within Neville's framework, another reading would be conditional = form, essential = dynamics, and harmony = unification. Neville has pointed out to me that for him essential features are what make the dynamic transformation of reality. His diagnosis is that the difference in interpretation comes from the fact that Whitehead and I think that dynamics are temporal, whereas he holds that time is the result of dynamics. Neville, even when he proposes triads such as outlined here, almost always returns to his more characteristic way of phrasing in terms of fourfold categories. Hence, in chapter 3 of *NC*, he adds the notion of singularity to his list of importance, unity, and diversity.

19. Scholars of Asian Confucian thought will notice that I am just dealing with the Chinese part of the tradition. The reasons for this are essentially pragmatic. This

is not a study in comparative thought. It is very true that Confucian thought played a vital role in Korean, Japanese, and Vietnamese intellectual history. In some cases, such as the great scholastic debates between T'oegye and Yulgok in Yi dynasty Korea and the great Japanese thinkers such as Ekkan in Tokugawa, Japan, the tradition was advanced with true genius. However, the metasystemic case can be made on the basis of the Chinese sources, so I will stay, I confess, with the material that I know best. Most specifically, I will focus my attention on the strain of thought identified both in China and the West as the Chu Hsi school.

In an earlier study of Chu Hsi and Ch'en Ch'un (1159–1223), I used a modified version of these three traits designed to fit more specifically the Chu Hsi school. The terms for the three traits were normative, configurational, and relational. I believed that at that time this way of stating the issue would better match some of Chu Hsi's and Ch'en Ch'un's concerns such as how to describe the relationship of mind/*hsin*, human nature/*hsing,* and feeling/*ching*. I have come to believe that an even less culturally specific designation of the traits are form, dynamics, and unification.

20. I need to note that Ames and Hall do not make this claim. One of the main features of their work is criticism of the Neo-Confucians for misreading the classical Chinese tradition. One of the aims of their project is to rescue Confucius from the Confucians. Ames and Hall argue that the transcendent element found in the Neo-Confucians is not present in the ur-text of Confucius. However, I still believe that they have described a persistent trait of the speculative side of the Confucian tradition, whatever our scholarly disagreements on the origin of Neo-Confucian speculation on the transcendent elements of reality. So while this is not the authorial intent, I believe their term is serviceable in teasing out some special features of the Confucian project.

21. The notion of Chinese philosophy being aesthetic in nature is linked to the early comparative work of one of Whitehead's students, F.S.C. Northrop. This claim has often been disputed, but because of the essentially axiological nature of the Confucian project, there is a kernel of truth to what Northrop noticed, even if the doctrine of an entirely aesthetic worldview is overstated.

22. However, if Yi Fu Tuan is correct, this may be too narrow an approach to the notion of the aesthetic. Tuan wants to expand the notion of aesthetic to much, much more than what would be recognized as the fine arts in the West and China (1982, 1990, 1993).

23. I realize that I have given a standard and flawed interpretation of the Legalist tradition here. In my defense, this is the way Neo-Confucians read the Legalists. On the other hand, we now know that some of the great Legalists thinkers, especially the greatest of them, Han Fei Tzu, while having a harsh view of human nature and civil society, also had hopes for the creation of a just if not a utopian world. Han Fei Tzu, if confronted by someone like Chu Hsi, would probably argue that even though his measures were harsh, they were designed to create law and order and hence a form of decent civil society.

24. I borrow my terms for the creatures of this or any other world from Whitehead and Buchler. From Whitehead, I take the term *actual entity* and from Buchler the notion of a "natural complex." Whitehead also uses the term *actual occasion*, along with *actual entity,* to describe the creatures of the cosmos.

25. Recently the Chinese scholar Yang Ru-pin (1993) has collected a range of detailed papers written by Chinese, Korean, Japanese, and North American scholars dealing with the study of classical *ch'i* theory. The various essays in the book give an excellent overview of the scope of the notion of matter–energy in East Asian thought.

26. One could also make the case for the primordial nature of God, except that unless creativity or eros is found as part of this primordial nature, then the dynamic element is diminished. Of course, the burden of my argument is to prove that creativity and God are united in a revised Whiteheadian vision.

27. Chu Hsi also tried to deal with dynamics by embracing Chou Tun-i's notion of *wu-chi* as the Uncontrived Ultimate always and everywhere linked to the Supreme Ultimate.

28. One must be cautious when discussing the relationship of principle and matter–energy in the world of Neo-Confucian discourse. This is one of the most contested topics of debate in the whole history of that tradition. There are, for instance, a number of very important Neo-Confucians who felt that Chu Hsi did just this, namely created a dualism out of principle and matter–energy. If this were the case, the argument continued, then Chu Hsi was wrong. Whatever the interpretive viewpoint, the Neo-Confucians resolutely resisted the creation of an ontological or a cosmological dualism in regard to these two fundamental notions.

29. In his earlier work, *World Hypotheses: A Study in Evidence* (1942), Pepper suggests that there are, at least in the history of Western thought, four relatively adequate root metaphors in philosophy. Pepper labels these "formism," "mechanism," "contextualism," and "organicism." In this earlier work, Pepper argued that Whitehead had an eclectic philosophy that did not fit into any one of the four pure types. But in 1966, Pepper had come to believe that the notion of a purposive act was indeed Whitehead's true metaphor and that this was really another root metaphor to add to the other four. Pepper noted that the actual occasion for Whitehead " . . . does act as a selective system and as a purposive structure. It is an intrinsically qualitative feeling and yet can be conceptually analyzed in retrospect" (Pepper 1966, 6).

30. This is very much the case for oral traditions as well, even if they are sometimes freer with their material than textually based traditions. Anyone who takes the time to speak to Native American Elders knows the scholastic richness of the various oral traditions of Native peoples. There is a rigor to the worldview and consistency of expositions, even if there is no appeal to written texts.

31. Perhaps one reason modern North Atlantic linguistic philosophy is so little interested in comparative issues comes from the fact that it limits its analysis to one language, English, and a very narrow tradition of English language philosophy at that.

However, there are indications that analytic or linguistic philosophy can be applied to comparative materials. The recent work of Chad Hansen illustrates that this is an exciting possibility.

32. Actually, Hall and Ames want to argue that all of Chinese philosophy, in its fundamental modes, can be characterized as *ars contextualis*. They are presently collaborating on the exposition of this thesis. Their argument is certainly plausible when considering philosophic Taoism and high T'ang Buddhist schools such as T'ien-t'ai and Hua-yen.

33. There are good reasons to use Ch'en Ch'un's analysis of philosophic terminology. First, Ch'en has always been recognized as Chu's philosophically reliable student. Ch'en was a genius at outlining the complex teachings of Chu Hsi. Second, to recognize Ch'en's contribution is to recognize the disciplinary nature of the Neo-Confucian tradition.

7

The Unity of Divine Things

THE TRINITARIAN RESPONSE

In this concluding chapter, we return to the tangled, ambiguous question of the God–creativity–world relationship from the perspective of a revised Whiteheadian philosophy and natural theology—with added insights gained from a comparison with Chu Hsi's and Ch'en Ch'un's Neo-Confucian understanding of principle, matter–energy, and the cultivation of the mind–heart. In terms of the emerging discourse of Pacific Rim cultural exchange, this comparative philosophy represents a purposive, relational, and process model of philosophy as creative synthesis, a comparative *ars contextualis* qua creative synthesis seeking the goals of peace and harmony. The themes of relationship and process are natural links to the expansion and reformation of Christian theology beyond its traditional North Atlantic world. None of this should come as a surprise because Christian philosophic theology has a natural inclination toward Trinitarian formulations interpreted from both its internal historical development and dogmatic structures of philosophic discourse.

The reasons for such proclivities are obvious, given the crucial role that speculation on the Trinity has played in orthodox Christian theology. The Holy Trinity, within the complex matrix of West Asian religion, has been a key concept distinguishing Christianity from Judaism and Islam. Furthermore, the Trinity has also been something of a *betê noire* for Christian theology in terms of philosophic coherence, moral anthropology, and religious generality.[1] It also is often the concept that serves to differentiate Christian philosophic speculation from other great world religions and worldviews, because it has given rise to the distinctive Western fusion of philosophic speculation and the interpretation of religious symbols as a mode of religious intellectual discipline.

However important philosophic speculation on the Trinity is, we need to remember that the Trinity, at least for the living faith of Christians, is first and foremost a religious icon, symbol, and metaphor of a crucial Christian religious insight. Initially, reflection on trinitarian structure makes sense formulated as an important element of philosophy, only within Christian or Christian-influenced circles. However, I believe that we can show, at least by analogy, how such Trinitarian thought relates to other world texts. By expanding the range of the concept of the Trinity beyond its point of Christian origin, I believe that the tripartite schema presented in this essay does make sense out of a number of systematically related classics in process thought.[2]

According to Whitehead, in *PR*, *AI*, and *MT*, trinitarian speculation, at its best, is an attempt to see the whole of reality in the complex pattern of the integral relationship of things divine with things mundane, things eternal with things temporal, things trivial with things inspiring, and things silly with things of ultimate awe. In many respects, the Eastern Christian theologians have done a better job, through their cultivation of apophatic theology, in reminding Christians that this organic trinitarian vision is ultimately a mystical insight into the nature of reality.[3] Part of the mystery is that apophatic theology asks us to open our angle of vision beyond the merely propositional, definitional, and to try to sense the wholeness of things within the processive life of the Holy Trinity. Eastern apophatic theology reminds us that we are dealing with a religiously cultivated sense of awe before divine things that cannot be encapsulated in precise or absolute labels. Christians live by the metaphor of the Holy Trinity as an expression of the power of God's creative love for the world.

Having proposed a revised Whiteheadian schema of form, dynamics, and unification as a tool of analysis, it is now time to direct our attention to the question of comparative natural theology, a meditation on the nature of divine things. The essential question for any Whiteheadian theology is: How do we understand the intricate and foundational relationships of God–creativity–world? How can the hypothetical understanding of God and creativity relate to the rest of Whitehead's thought as well as to the body of the Christian cumulative tradition? And does this revised natural theology function effectively in the comparative context of modern religious diversity? The analogous question for Chu Hsi focuses on the relationship of principle and matter–energy as well as on Chu's place in the formation of the contemporary phase of Neo-Confucianism, the New Confucianism of thinkers such as Mou Tsung-san, Tu Wei-ming, Liu Shu-hsien, Ts'ai Jen-hou, and Cheng Chung-ying. This also is a problem for critical Western scholars such as Wm. Theodore de Bary, Peter Bol, Hoyt Tillman, Thomas Wilson, and Lionel Jensen.

The problem of the separation of creativity and God's primordial nature is crucial for a coherent, adequate Whiteheadian natural theology because, if left unresolved, it threatens the harmony of the system. Much the same holds for any Neo-Confucian thinker following Chu Hsi's lead in the interpretation of the creative synthesis of principle and matter–energy in the cultivated mind–heart of the profound person. While strict logical coherence is not always the end of a philosophic or theological system, Whitehead believed that any adequate system should be as logical, coherent, and adequate as possible. One of the real benefits of process theology is that it attempts to avoid any arbitrary diremption of first principles. The most glaring exception to this was the separation of creativity and God found in *PR*. Much the same could be said about Chu's analysis of the relationship of principle and matter–energy.

In one respect, the experiment of these essays in comparative philosophy and theology is an attempt to add a Neo-Confucian voice to the interaction of Western process thought and Asian philosophy. This has been done before. For instance, David Hall's *The Uncertain Phoenix* seeks the same end for the Chinese Taoist and Buddhist tradition that I am attempting for Chu Hsi. Hall argues, much as I have done, that it is time to open the windows of Western speculative philosophy to certain forms of Eastern thought to reinvigorate modern Western thought. One of Hall's key concepts for the creation of such a new philosophic sensibility is the notion of creative synthesis.[4] In some respects, Hall believes that the ideas embedded in the analysis of the notion of a creative synthesis as derived especially from the classical Taoist tradition can reorient the Western mind away from its inordinate captivity to the philosophy of substance.

While Hall is not particularly wedded to any one verbal formulation of the new vision of a mixed-process philosophy, his notion of a philosophy of creative synthesis supplements, from the Western perspective, his suggestion made with Roger Ames, that early Confucian thought should be characterized as an *ars contextualis*. I suggest that yet another way to thematize my version of this comparative vision is to call it an *ars contextualis* as creative synthesis.[5] At least for the Neo-Confucians, there is a role for principle in creative synthesis. If there is not, then Chu Hsi and his disciples wasted an immense amount of time and energy over the centuries trying to balance the mutual interlocking concerns of principle and matter–energy into some coherent balance.

Because I also agree with Hall's call for the reformation of Western thought by means of an opening to Chinese thought, I want to include the Neo-Confucians for all of the reasons I have outlined in the last six chapters. Although the Taoist voice is, as we are discovering through modern Chinese, Japanese and Western scholarship, never to be neglected in the articulation of the overall structure of Chinese and East Asian thought, we must not forget the dominant, vital role the Neo-Confucians played in East Asia since the Sung revival.

My task is more modest than Hall's pioneering study of Eastern and Western speculative philosophy in a process mode based on certain Taoist themes. I am focusing on different schools of Chinese thought, albeit the major post–Sung school founded by Chu Hsi, in order to suggest a way forward in comparative philosophy and theology. But in another respect, I am trying something more ambitious with Chu Hsi's school of principle (*li-hsüeh*) than Hall does with his general interest in Taoist and Buddhist thought. I am seeking a way to make use of Chu's thought in order to continue Whitehead's project, both in terms of suggesting new terminology and in trying to extend the sense of relationship between process thought East and West. To do this, I have proposed the tripartite schema of form, dynamics, and unification.

Time and time again I have indicated that I am aware of how much this comparative reconstruction runs against the grain of modern academic philosophy as well as general cultural criticism. From the perspective of modern analytic philosophy, all of this is rather vague and smacks of the sloppy banalities of "Eastern mysticism" or the romantic view that the Chinese grass is greener than "real" philosophy, as practiced on Monday morning after the first cup of rational coffee. On the other hand, my search for a schema is equally offensive to the deconstructionist wing of modern cultural critics who believe that structures of any kind are part of the problem, not part of the solution. Oddly enough, Chu Hsi faced the same kind of problem. On the one hand, there were those Taoist and Ch'an Buddhist colleagues, as well as fellow Confucians such as Lu Hsiang-shan (1139–1193), who believed that Chu's search for an integral vision was mistaken because one should never mistake system for the experience of reality or emptiness. On the other hand, there were other Neo-Confucians, especially in the Ch'ing, who rejected Chu's philosophic project for more empirical, textual, bureaucratic, historical, or artistic pursuits.

The very language I am using suggests to one crucial problematique. To the analytic philosopher of language, what I have been doing must appear slippery, ill-defined, and much too vague. I have studiously avoided trying to bring too much linguistic precision or ever too much internal consistency to the present discourse. Along with Aristotle, I believe one can bring only as much precision to a project as the project itself will bear.[6] We are at the very early stages of comparative philosophy and theology and must to be cautious in our claims for precision or even accurate translation. We need to be cautious—even tentative—and always open to revision, because we are still groping for helpful ways to frame the comparative discourse.

In Chu Hsi's terms, however, this has not been a terminological conversation without its principle. For instance, I have used Buchler's term *traits* and Lakoff's and Johnson's notion of "metaphor" so as not to commit myself prematurely to some Western analogy for labeling the elements of the tripartite schema; I want to be somewhat vague in framing the schema to allow for appeals to more specialized cross-cultural material. As Hall has correctly argued, we are much too early in the game of comparative thought to make too many one-to-one correlations of terminology. Besides, as Neville has shown, correctly I believe, vagueness has its own virtues in philosophic construction.[7]

One of the virtues of imprecision in the service of precision is that it allows the aesthetic, metaphorical side of thought to play a role. What good teacher does not discover that sometimes a story, a picture, or even some musical analogy makes a "principle" clearer than a logical outline of the issues at hand? Along with Hall and Neville, I believe that process thought provides a bridge to certain forms of Asian thought. The bridge must be spacious enough to allow a lot of traffic to flow across it in both directions. As more and more comparative work is done, the different lanes can be defined and the speed limit can be raised, but at the beginning, more leisurely strolling is the order of the day. New flavors must be tasted, new sights allowed to delight, new sounds heard, and new configurations of ideas enjoyed.

CREATIVE SYNTHESIS

One of the characteristic themes of Whiteheadian process thought qua purposive creative synthesis is its analysis of causality. Cheng Chung-ying (1991, 98ff) presents the dominant Chinese model of causality in terms of three principles. He argues that these three principles work just as well for the Neo-Confucian synthesis as they do for Taoist thought and, in fact, are a pan-Chinese model for causality. "A fundamental assertion in Chinese metaphysical thinking is that all things arise from one source in a natural and spontaneous way" (1991, 93). The first principle is that of holistic unity. All things are linked together in the Tao. "They all share the same nature and quality of reality" (1991, 98). According to Cheng, there is a unity, oneness, or harmony of the Tao as the matrix of all orders and things determinate that indicates a common origin.

Second, Cheng defines the principle of life-movement as an important element in the Chinese understanding of causality. Each thing moves of itself in a manner that is not the result of action being "imposed by other things or God but is derived from the inexhaustible source of the energy of life, which is the Way" (1991, 98). This source of movement or creativity (dynamics, in my terminology) is infinite in its scope, complexity, and fecundity. Cheng also calls this principle the "principle of intrinsic life-growth." Insofar as it relates to the internal sui generis nature of the concrescence of any object–event, it is like a "principle of internality."

For Cheng, the third element of classical Chinese causal theory is the "principle of organic balance." It is not surprising that a modern Confucian philosopher, ever mindful of the *Doctrine of the Mean*, is going to have an important place for balance, timeliness, and so on, in his or her philosophy. "By this I mean that all things and processes in the world are related in processes which proceed toward a balance and a harmony" (1991, 99). I take this to be Cheng's way of defining what I call one aspect of the trait of unity and those elements that Neville rubricizes as the harmony of essential and conditional features. In terms of the methodological evaluation of object–events, this is a "principle of organicity."

> Although one may regard the three principles to be methodological illustrations of a Chinese dialectic of thinking, in the sense that any thinking about things must simultaneously conform to these principles in order to correctly represent reality, as Confucian and Taoist metaphysics depict it. (1991, 99)

Cheng further characterizes the specific Confucian worldview in terms of the relationship of a whole–part paradigm. "Life is not a single part of a whole, a whole of parts; nor is it an isolated phenomenon which is externally related to external things" (1991, 94). The notion of relationship is key to unpacking the Confucian worldview. Without an analysis of the whole–part matrix, we cannot understand the emergence of object–events. "In this sense, parts and whole are defined in the relationships in which they find themselves" (1991, 95). This correlates well with Whitehead's own speculation on the nature of parts–whole as one aspect of metaphysical analysis, as we have already seen.

It is significant that Charles Birch and John Cobb, Jr., in *The Liberation of Life* (1981) define the meaning of life in terms that resonate with Cheng's definition of the Confucian sense of causality. In determining what it means to be a living organism from a perspective informed by process thought, Birch and Cobb assert that two features dominate the discussion, namely "the ability to replicate themselves faithfully and the ability, sometimes, to change during replication" (1981, 14). Later in their argument about the nature of the second law of thermodynamics, they note that "Life is a special sort of organisation of atoms and molecules that decreases entropy. . . . Life is characterised by the capacity for self-reproduction. It thus constitutes a spreading centre of order in a less well-ordered universe" (1981, 42). Whitehead made this point about entropy not being the final metaphysical word, though without reference to the biological sciences central to Birch and Cobb, in his study of the function of reason. For Whitehead, reason is something more than merely the technical manipulation of logical forms. Reason expresses

the eros of order needed for the complexification of the cosmos. While neither Whitehead, Birch, nor Cobb want to underplay the notion of the entropy
of matter, they do point to other aspects of the emergence of object–events,
which indicates that the general rundown of the present universe is not the
whole answer to the question of being.

Along with a call for a new ecological sensibility based on process
thought, Birch and Cobb ultimately see life as the creative advance into novelty,
a feature of process cosmology typical of both Whitehead and Chu Hsi.

> Life is purposeful. Indeed, it is defined by its purpose. It is not the sheer
> blind 'ongoingness' of things, but the cosmic aim of value. Life aims at the
> realisation of value, that is rich experience or aliveness. It is life that intro-
> duces into the midst of the sheer giveness of the physical world the attrac-
> tive vision of unrealised possibility. (1981, 197)

Chu Hsi, following the teaching of Ch'eng Hao (1032–1085) about the true
meaning of humanity, likened life to not being numbed or becoming insen-
sitive by means of some medicinal drug, but rather to being sensible to the
values found in human interaction and to the endless interplay of yin–yang.
Perhaps even more so, if we accept Cheng's description of a pan-Chinese
sense of causality for Taoism and Confucianism (1991), Chu stresses the
immanent nature of creativity even more strongly than does the Western wing
of the process movement.

If the language of the immanent nature of creativity does not seem quite
right for describing Chu Hsi's notion, then we can switch to the image of *ars
contextualis* as a wonderfully fecund matrix of creative synthesis. Yet there is
no getting around one of the perennial points of the characteristic Western
dispute between and among cosmologically oriented and ontologically driven
thinkers. The cosmologists ask: What and where? The ontologists ask: Why?
Both groups are vehemently defending the position that their question is the
fundamental one, even though the two questions must be coordinated to give
an account for all which is, is not, not yet, or maybe never will be, except in
fantasy or reflection. This leads to a third question, namely: How do object–
events come to be? Joseph Needham pointed out that this how question was
a favorite of the Neo-Confucians in that it initiates their favorite strategy of
asking about the relationship of the components of object–events because
the how of any object–event is connected to its constituting relationships
(1954–, 2:455 ff). This of course brings us back to Whitehead's severely
abstract notion of metaphysical principles as a catalog of part–whole connections, identities, overlaps, and disconnections.

Still, the question of where is crucial for a creative synthesis process account of divine things. Chu Hsi and Whitehead are clear about this—or as clear as anyone can be in dealing with such fuzzy matters. For Chu, the where is the Tao that serves as the symbol for the infinite where creativity is to be found. For Whitehead, it is the primordial nature of God that locates the infinite font of creativity. In another sense, Neville also has an answer to the where question. For Neville, creativity, in a strictly ontological sense, is literally nowhere insofar as we only deal with the abstract notion of creation. Neville is careful to point out that God has created this world so that we know at least some of the determining traits of the God who creates this cosmic epoch. While Neville does not make extensive use of the Eastern Christian apophatic tradition in theology, such a Christian response is warranted in terms of avoiding the idolatry of identifying some created good with the divine good as well as demonstrating a sense of epistemological humility before the ultimate source of creativity.

Along with the where and how question, Neville also wants to ask the what question. For him this question is intimately linked to the how and where question in terms of the *sui generis* features of the object–events as they constitute themselves in any particular cosmic epoch. It is here, in the fusion of the essential and conditional features, in the mutuality of eternity and time, that the mystery of creativity exists. Something new has emerged in the world that was not there before. In this sense, the generation of any object–event is a replication of the divine creation *ex nihilo*. One of Neville's persistent complaints against the process school is that they cannot answer the question of "what goes on" in the creativity of the emerging object–event because there is no "what" prior to the where and the how of the ontological act of primal creativity. Neville has grave doubts that even as complicated a set of "what goes on" mechanics as Whitehead describes in Part III of *PR* will do the trick.

Tu Wei-ming (1989), in talking about the Chinese concept of nature, also agrees with Needham's, Cheng's, Neville's, and Hall's characterization of Chinese thought as organic/processive in nature. Along with the features of the continuity of being and the wholeness of the cosmos, Tu notes that there is a third motif, "dynamism, lest the idea of organismic unity imply a closed system" (1989, 70). I find it revealing that Tu argues for the open nature of the Chinese cosmos against any notion of closure. "The Chinese world view is neither cyclic nor spiral. It is transformational" (1989, 71). One reason for this openness comes from the fact that "As there is no temporal beginning to specify, no closure is ever contemplated. The cosmos is forever expanding; the great transformation is unceasing" (1989, 71). Tu is quick to add that this does not imply some form of melioristic progress in the nineteenth-century sense of the inevitability of progress toward some beatific end of history. There are simply too many possible forms of the great transformation for there to be any fixed destination for history, according to Tu.

I have cited Cheng Chung-ying and Tu Wei-ming to make some points about the nature of Chinese thought. First, they are two of the most articulate members of the movement called New Confucianism writing in English and both are familiar with the Western philosophic scene. As spokesmen for the modern New Confucianism of the Chinese Diaspora, they are eager to present traditional Chinese thought in terms that are faithful to its integrity as a series of interconnected traditions and to communicate this cultural and intellectual sensibility to a Western audience. They are both accomplished comparative thinkers, as at home in Western thought as they are in the Chinese world. Second, they are both well versed in the Western process tradition and recognize the valid points of comparison and difference from the perspective of the Chinese traditions of philosophic Taoism and Confucianism. Third, they are also Confucian partners in dialogue with Neville in the search for the creation of a truly global speculative philosophy, alert to the diversities of different cultural traditions.

THE EROS OF THE TRINITY

To deal with my ever-growing catalog of problems with creativity, I am going to borrow a number of hints drawn from *AI* and *MT* to seek a way out of these difficulties. The first suggestion has to do with what Whitehead calls importance and the second with concern, concepts highlighted in *MT*. In *MT*, he writes that "The doctrine that I am maintaining is that neither physical nature nor life can be understood unless we fuse them together as essential factors in the composition of 'really real' things whose inter-connections and individual characters constitute the universe" (*MT*, 205). In this universe, things matter in terms of their importance. "Thus one characteristic of importance is that it is that aspect of feeling whereby a perspective is imposed upon the universe of things felt" (*MT*, 15). This notion of importance is not some kind of raw appeal to a forceful will or dramatic urgency that is to be judged without recourse to what Whitehead calls "worth." "At the base of our existence is the sense of 'worth.' . . . It is the sense of existence for its own sake, of existence which is its own justification, of existence with its own character" (*MT*, 149). As always, the profoundly axiological nature of Whitehead's thought is obvious.

The notion of concern, which Whitehead draws from the English Quaker tradition as another specification of importance, brings us yet again to the Confucian connection. Mou Tsung-san, building on the work of his New

Confucian friend Hsü Fu-kuan, made the following observation about the three great cultural areas of the Eurasian world. While Mou is extremely careful to point out that these are gross overgeneralizations about whole civilizations, he still believes that there is a point to his tripartite division of cultural sensibilities. For instance, according to this typology, the typical genius of the Greek experience is the feeling of wonder before nature. On the other hand, the more typical West Asian and South Asian theistic response is awe in the face of the mystery of the power of divine things. In contradistinction to the Greek or European sense of wonder and the West and South Asian sense of awe, the typical Chinese fundamental sensibility is one of concern. In many places, Mou argues that one of the quintessential features of all Chinese thought is that it is what he calls "concern-consciousness."[8] This is why Western students of Chinese thought are always noting that Confucianism, for instance, is axiological, ethically determined, and aesthetic in nature. According to Mou, all of this is derived from the primordial insight generated by concern-consciousness.

Toward the end of *MT*, Whitehead gives his distinctive interpretation of what Mou calls concern-consciousness (*yu-huan i-shih*).

> Each occasion is an activity of concern, in the Quaker sense of the term. It is the conjunction of transcendence and immanence. The occasion is concerned, in the way of feeling and aim, with things that in their essence lie beyond it; although these things in their present functions are factors in the concern of that occasion. Thus each occasion, although engaged in its own immediate self-realization, is concerned with the universe. (*MT*, 229–30)

This is Whitehead at his most Confucian; Mou Tsung-san could not have given a better definition of the fundamental Confucian axiology of a process *ars contextualis* or purposive creative synthesis. The moral note of concern for the future is an essential ingredient to both the Chinese and North Atlantic sub-schools of the process movement.

Furthermore, something else is found in Whitehead's linked notions of concern and importance. This is eros. As he notes in a more general discussion of the nature of beauty that there is in God's nature an "ultimate concern" for the cosmos, " . . . the doctrine of the valuations involved in the Primordial Nature of God, here also termed the Eros of the Universe" (*AI*, 326). It is likewise fascinating to note that in the crowning discourse on Peace in *AI*, Whitehead joins his concept of concern as eros to the primordial family ties that a New Confucian such as Tu Wei-ming hold to be constitutive of morality and all social solidarity. The paragraph is worth quoting in its entirety.

> But some closeness of status, such as the relation of parent to child or the
> relation of marriage, can produce the love of self-devotion where the poten-
> tialities of the loved object are felt passionately as a claim that it find itself
> in a friendly Universe. Such love is really an intense feeling as to how the
> harmony of the world should be realized in particular objects. It is the
> feeling of what would happen if right could triumph in a beautiful world,
> with discord routed. It is the passionate desire for the beautiful result, in this
> instance. Such love is distracting, nerve-racking. But, unless darkened by
> utter despair, it involves deep feeling of an aim in the Universe, winning
> such triumph as is possible to it. It is the sense of Eros, hovering between
> Peace as the crown of Youth and Peace as the issue of Tragedy. (*AI*, 373)

Such is the scope of Whitehead's erotic hope for the universe. It is crucial to
remember that this is a hope, not a construal of the way things are. As
Whitehead noted in *PR*, Christ is crucified in a cruel world where things do
not always turn out for the best. That is why he calls God, in a memorable
metaphor, the fellow sufferer who understands. The fellow sufferer does not
make all things right. The pain is still there, but always with the resounding
theme of hope and the eros of hovering between anticipation and tragedy.

I find it instructive that neither the Neo-Confucians nor Christian theologians have a great deal to say about the erotic element of the universe as
a positive aspect of God's primordial nature. There are a number of obvious
reasons for this reticence. The first is surely the reality that both Neo-
Confucians and Christian theologians have normally been guardians of traditional social morality.[9] In neither case has the erotic been highly regarded as
a crucial moral value, even if there is always a place for such mundane
affections—in due balance and under the constraints of probity. Of course,
there were always the odd mystics and nonconformists who reminded the
more orthodox of the passionate, erotic, concerned side of reality that is only
ignored to the detriment of the true discernment of the way things are.

The second reason is even more complex, at least in philosophic terms.
This has to do with what I call the order of recognition and the order of
organic unity. The reality behind the distinction is a problem both for Chu Hsi
and Whitehead. To explicate their thought, they devised strategies of presentation—one has to start somewhere with some kind of coherent narrative.
Whitehead begins with the Category of the Ultimate and Chu Hsi commences
with the differentiation of principle and matter–energy. Chu often referred to
this complex set of problems by the tag of *li-i fen-shu*/principle is one but its
manifestations are many. In the Category of the Ultimate, Whitehead has
been interpreted as postulating creativity as somehow separate from even
God's primordial nature. Let me be clear. There are sound reasons that every

Whiteheadian scholar can quote pro and con on the question of the relationship of God, creativity, and the world in the Category of the Ultimate.[10] For
instance, Whitehead is capable of speaking of God being as much in the grasp
of creativity as the merest puff of subatomic activity in the farthest reaches
of the cosmos.

On the other side of the world, Chi Hsi was repeatedly asked by his
students about the relationship of principle and matter–energy. While Chu
was always careful to teach the ultimate unity or harmony of *li* and *ch'i*, he
does confess that it is often principle that we recognize first and hence give
some kind of priority to it, at least in terms of the dawning recognition of the
structure of reality. There began, as we have already seen, an ongoing hermeneutic struggle about what Chu Hsi really meant about the relationship of
matter–energy and principle. The chief question was: Is Chu some kind of
quasi-dualist in terms of the origins of object–events? And if he is a dualist,
does one of the poles have priority over the other? Whatever the answer to
these questions, Chu himself never tired of telling his students that this was
the wrong way to put the question. In my terminology, it confused the order
of recognition with the order of organic unity. The organic unity of the Tao
was always utmost for Chu, even if he consistently acknowledged the importance of epistemological concerns, the domain of the order of recognition.

I have come to believe that Whitehead and Chu had good reasons for
their divergent strategies. On the one hand, Whitehead was struggling with a
philosophic tradition in the modern West that prized, on his reading of it,
substance over process. He wanted to emphasize process and hence took
every opportunity to stress the role of creativity as being crucial to understanding the nature of process.[11] On the other hand, Chu had to deal with a
tradition that needed to respond to the Buddhist and Taoist challenge. Both
Taoism and Buddhism, at least in Chu's time, had a place for process in their
metasystems but did not pay enough attention to the role of principle as
articulated by the Northern Sung philosophic masters according to the Confucians. Hence Chu felt the need to indicate the crucial role of principle in
the cosmos. In Chu's case, principle helped him defend the realistic and
pluralistic nature of the Neo-Confucian creative synthesis.

Nonetheless, certain features of process thought as a creative synthesis
preclude the reading of Whitehead and Chu Hsi as dualists. For Whitehead,
this rejection of cosmological dualism is enshrined in the Ontological Principle and in his further elucidations of this principle as the basis of the
persistent pluralism of the cosmos. For Chu, this finds its expression in the
proper reading of the fusion of the Supreme Ultimate and the Uncontrived
Ultimate as the ceaseless generativity of the Tao. In Justus Buchler's metaphysical terms, Whitehead and Chu practiced ontological parity for their

philosophic systems, at least at the fundamental level of the order of organic unity.[12] It is crucial to remember that it is this level that is of paramount importance to them, even as they gave careful consideration to the order of recognition.

There is an epistemological reason for the nature of this kind of endemic conceptual bind for process discourse. As Whitehead pointed out, we learn by the method of difference. We detect elephants by "prehending"—to use Whitehead's technical term for the various modes of perception—the facts and appearances of elephants when we see them, then contrasting the moments when elephants are present to us when they are not. Contrast is essential to any kind of knowledge. The problem, then, is one of the presentation of the items of discourse. We have to start somewhere, even if the vision of process thought teaches that all things are interconnected and share a rough ontological parity even in their plurality. We lift specific object–events of importance out of our general experience in order to talk about them individually. This sometimes gives the impression that they are individual in a special ontic sense of being independent of the context in which they are found and from the whole extensive continuum of the present cosmic epoch. For in intellectual analysis we have the capacity to isolate discrete items for discussion, but this should not blind us to the more fundamental reality of the organic nature of the cosmos. Hence there is always a problem when we move between the order of recognition and the order of organic unity.

It is for these reasons that I do not believe we can label Chu and Whitehead dualists, at least as this is understood in the history of Western philosophy.[13] They do not hold that the world is composed of two different and unrelated substances or modes of being. The problem arises in both cases because Chu and Whitehead were convinced of the complexity of the cosmos as cosmological process. Neither were satisfied by an analysis of the world as some eternal binary opposition of dualistic philosophies. While they shared an integral vision that included a profound understanding of the interconnections of object–events, this did not blind them to the realistic nature of pluralism and the need for a nuanced description of reality that was not dualistic. Because of the axiological nature of these object–events, and here I agree with Neville's description of the essential and conditional features of these object–events in their harmony of creative synthesis, we need specific modes of narration in order to describe them. What Chu and Whitehead were eager to avoid was a simplistic reductionism that pretended that the world is amenable to some kind of simple description in terms of a limited set of discrimanda.

One of the defining characteristics of the type of process thought illustrated by Chu and Whitehead is a commitment to the pluralism of the cosmos.

For instance, even in the definition of God's primordial nature, Whitehead makes this clear. "The primordial created fact is the unconditioned conceptual valuation of the entire multiplicity of eternal objects. This is the 'primordial nature' of God" (*PR*, 31). He goes on to point out that "This divine ordering is itself matter of fact, thereby conditioning creativity" (*PR*, 31). This is a very tricky business for Whitehead. The descriptive twist has to do with the fact that

> Creativity is without a character of its own in exactly the same sense in which Aristotelian 'matter' is without a character of its own. It is that ultimate notion of the highest generality at the base of actuality. It cannot be characterized, because all characters are more special than itself. (*PR*, 31)

Because we can only know by the method of difference, we cannot know "creativity" until and unless we prehend "created" object–events. In this sense, to know something of the divine things means that we know something more specific about the divine reality than the mere fact of creativity itself.

One thing we know is the "concern-consciousness" of the divine eros. We comprehend this fact of concern or divine eros in a number of ways.

> The "superjective nature" of God is the character of the pragamatic value of his specific satisfaction qualifying the transcendent creativity in the various temporal instances. This is the conception of God, according to which he is considered as the outcome of creativity, as the foundation of order, and as the goad towards novelty. (*PR*, 88)

As the goad of novelty, God, in all of the divine richness, is concerned for creation. Or that "The true metaphysical position is that God is the aboriginal instance of this creativity, and is therefore the aboriginal condition that qualifies its action" (*PR*, 225). All of these decisions and actions, creatures and God, are part of a vast social effort. "Each task of creation is a social effort, employing the whole universe" (*PR*, 223). This is why Whitehead affirms that "The universe is a creative advance into novelty" (*PR*, 222).

Chu Hsi, in terms of his explication of Chou Tun-i's *Diagram of the Supreme Ultimate*, was working with a similar kind of fundamental expression of concern-consciousness.[14] I find it fascinating that Chu also had to resort to the ambiguous language of the Supreme Ultimate and the Uncontrived Ultimate, the famous *t'ai-chi erh wu-chi*, in order to tease out the fact that the unconditioned is always and everywhere known by means of the conditioned. The frustration is that we cannot describe either pole of the relationship without the other, except that Chu was convinced that at the base of this relationship was the urge for the creative advance into novelty, or as he put it, the Tao of unceasing generativity (*sheng sheng pu-hsi*).

In the supplemental material traditionally appended to Ch'en Ch'un's glossary, there is a wonderful little section that captures the Neo-Confucian sense of the relationship. "The Supreme Ultimate is the wondrous undifferentiated functioning. From nothing into something, and from something into nothing again. It is only the undifferentiated Supreme Ultimate"[15] (Ch'en 1986, 188, Supplement 1a). If you like, the Supreme Ultimate represents the primordial nature of God in its valuation and creativity, in terms of the uncontrived nature prior to the generation of specific object–events. While we "know" only the created order, we know that this created order rests on an undifferentiated creativity, which we cannot name because it is nameless. Many later Confucian commentators were very nervous about Chu's use of the notion of the Uncontrived Ultimate because it appeared to be a concession to the Taoist tradition. But then, when we need to speak of undifferentiated chaos, who better to quote than the philosophic Taoists?

Lewis Ford, in his meticulous 1984 study of the emergence of Whitehead's mature metaphysics, makes the point that Whitehead only settled on his definitive pluralist position fairly late in the game. In fact Whitehead only developed his fully pluralistic perspective by the end of the composition of *PR*. In terms of the development of a pluralistic vision, *AI* and *MT* continue the elaboration of cosmological diversity in their exposition of history and social issues. As Whitehead wrote in *PR*, he rarely addressed any important topic only once. One can argue that he introduced the technical philosophic system of his mature pluralism in *PR* and then demonstrated its intellectual history in *AI* and *MT*. In almost all of his works, Whitehead circles around his topic, examining and rediscussing it from various perspectives in terms of different themes. In this regard, Whitehead is quite Confucian.

I see nothing mysterious in such an expository style. Whitehead was a pluralist and realist; in this regard, history was the drama of the concrescence of new object–events in the ever-changing patterns of realized value. History is in many ways the realm of the particular par excellence. Sometimes history works out the way we might expect, and sometimes there are dramatic paradigm shifts away from the causal past. Put more accurately, our vision of the relevant causal past is enlarged and we prehend a different chain of events that impacts a person, a culture, a whole civilization. For instance, the growing interest in all forms of Asian thought will surely have unanticipated effects on the internal development of Western thought in the decades to come. Only time will tell whether the influx of Asian modes of thought will have as great an impact on modern Western thought as did, for instance, the rediscovery of classical Greek thought, via the Islamic world, on the medieval synthesis. One cannot imagine Aquinas without Aristotle; can we think about Neville without Chu Hsi and Wang Yang-ming? In one sense, Whitehead's turn to history in *AI* and *MT* is an affirmation of the pluralism of his vision of philosophy.

Even in the midst of Whitehead's more historical narratives in *AI* and *MT*, he always returns to some of his favorite philosophic themes. For instance, in his discussion of activity in *MT*, he makes the following comment after some observations about the mode of existence that should be attached to form. "Again everything (i.e., form) is something, which in its own way is real" (*MT*, 95). In defining what he takes to be the real as disclosed in human experience he notes two fundamental modes of awareness from which all other kinds of experience are derived. "The two types in question can be named, respectively, The Type of Actuality, and The Type of pure Potentiality" (*MT*, 96). For Whitehead, these are two extreme types that always demand some kind of interconnection, some mode of unity or harmony. "Some blessed word, such as the word 'composition' itself, covers up all the perplexities that reflection discloses" (*MT*, 96). Here again we can see the pattern of form, dynamics, and unification with little verbal modification of Whitehead's own prose. In terms of Neville's project, as with much of Neo-Confucian discourse, the idea of harmony becomes a sign for the process of composition that Whitehead believes always accompanies the contextualization of actuality and potentiality.

Continuing his analysis, Whitehead connects the ideas of actuality, potentiality, and composition with other aspects of human experience, especially the valuation of the experience in terms of our sheer enjoyment of the moment. "What is our primary experience which lies below and gives its meaning to our conscious analysis of qualitative detail? In our analysis of detail we are presupposing a background which supplies a meaning" (*MT*, 158). It is just this sort of statement that makes it plausible to use the notion of *ars contextualis* as a cross-cultural comparative term to describe the intersection of Whitehead's and Chu's thought. In many ways, Whitehead is as interested in the part-whole relationship as he is in the context of meaning as Chu ever was.

But Whitehead does not stop with a "formal" analysis of common human experience.

> Our enjoyment of actuality is a realization of worth, good or bad. It is a value-experience. Its basic expression is—Have a care, here is something that matters! Yes—that is the best phrase—the primary glimmering of consciousness reveals, Something that matters. (*MT*, 159)

In his ongoing analysis of this "something that matters" he restates the three-fold typology of concern. He calls these three primary traits "Totality, Externality, and Internality" (*MT*, 159). Why is Whitehead shifting between various verbalizations, a conflation of narrative focal perspectives, to make his point? I believe he is doing so because he is trying to stimulate us to think about a reality that only dimly emerges in the beginnings of the conscious sensorium, if conscious at all. "There is the totality of actual fact; there is the externality of many facts; there is the internality of this experiencing which lies within the totality" (*MT*, 159). The trick of human consciousness is that it holds these levels of awareness together in the lived world of human knowing, willing, and doing. The unity is real, but the analytic distinctions are likewise real.

This returns the discussion to the previous question of what Buchler calls ontological parity, the equality of all that can be discriminated, imagined, or dreamed. By this I take Buchler to mean that what is or can be discriminated in any way whatsoever is as real, actual, definite, and so forth, as anything else.[16] For instance, according to Buchler's notion of parity, there is no ontological gap between a Platonic idea and a materialist's stone. Both are as fully real as the other. I believe another reason Whitehead is forever mixing his language is linked not only to the heuristic function of a skillful teacher but also to the question of ontological parity.

Interestingly enough, Buchler holds that Whitehead's philosophy does not express ontological parity. For Buchler, Whitehead's actual entities are the only fully real constituents of Whitehead's world; everything else is only real as it relates to the actual entities. Buchler is correct at one level of interpretation. However, the problem may be clarified by recourse to the notion of an *ars contextualis* rather than an appeal to either ontology or cosmology per se. If Chu and Whitehead are really working out of a paradigm dominated by creative synthesis *ars contextualis*, then it is much easier to see that they are both defending ontological parity, even when they are at their most analytic and discriminating. As I mentioned before, in the order of recognition, we make distinctions, and they are often good distinctions that make sure we navigate the complex traffic patterns of a Boston traffic roundabout—as fine an example I can think of as representing something that mixes order and chaos, often at the same time.[17]

Thinkers who make use of an *ars contextualis* qua creative synthesis as a fundamental mode of analysis are forever shifting back and forth between part and whole, focal point and background, the actual and potential, the formal and the concrete. Their ur-question as intellectuals is to ask the how of connecting part to whole and relationship between object–events, the process whereby things are organically generated rather than the question of the primal ontological query about why there is something rather than nothing or the immediate causal chain of cosmological connection. What is frustrating to colleagues embracing other worldviews, the Western paradigm of ontology as creation *ex nihilo* in Neville's case being a classic example, is that this focus on the how of object–events seems either slippery or muddled or both. But from within the contextual paradigm of an *ars contextualis*, it seems merely necessary.

Contrariwise, from the perspective of *ars contextualis*, the whole paradigm embedded in the ontological question of ultimate whys will always be deemed reductionist because it privileges one level of being over some other level of being, or non-being if Taoist, as primary or creative. If it does not privilege one level, then it becomes a form of contextualism and no longer asks the classical ontological question. On the other hand, what is not part of the context, any context, simply is not a matter of concern for *ars contextualis*.[18] This does not mean that only concrete things like stones and tables are really real. An idea motivating a great revolution is surely as real as the stones used to overthrow the old regime. However, the process thinker, in expressing a contextualist sensibility, is perfectly willing to concede that the stone and the rock are, indeed, different and that this difference makes a difference, depending on the situation. This characteristic move is always disputed by thinkers with other paradigms who will want to know either more or less about the ultimately real. Simply being told that it depends on the context is not taken to be a very helpful answer.[19]

However, I do believe that an analysis of the philosophic commitments of *ars contextualis*, and especially in a process mode, shows that Chu and Whitehead embrace a form of ontological parity, although this issue is not the decisive internal question that drove them to articulate their worldviews. Like Neville, they were more concerned to ask the question of the creation of object–events and of values in the cosmos. Likewise, Whitehead was aware that he was proposing a novel way of organizing the Western tradition. Both were more interested in the *sui generis* nature of pluralism than in figuring out whether or not there was an ontological locus to creation. The question is there a beginning of everything is not the one that excites Chu and Whitehead. Rather, they are more fascinated by what Whitehead calls "concrescence" and Chu calls *sheng sheng pu-hsi*, or the ceaseless productivity of the Tao. Whatever actually or potentially is, or is to be believed, dreamed, feared, or hoped for, comes out of the act of concrescence or unification. This holds as much for God as it does for the most insignificant element of far-off empty space.

Yet in the case of God, there is a concern for the novelty of the cosmos. This concern is the basis for Whitehead's memorable affirmation of the creative advance into novelty that characterizes the world. The nature of Whitehead's supposition that civilization is the victory of persuasion over force also speaks to the divine eros of reality. In the concluding sections of *AI*, he weaves together the notion of adventure, beauty, and eros with the supreme virtue of peace as the final justification for the creative synthesis of the cosmos. The penultimate paragraph of *AI* deserves quotation and exegesis at this point.

> The incompleteness of the concept (i.e., namely civilization in its fullest sense) relates to the notion of Transcendence, the feeling essential for Adventure, Zest, and Peace. This feeling requires for its understanding that we supplement the notion of Eros by including in it the concept of an Adventure in the Universe as One. This Adventure embraces all particular occasions but as an actual fact stands beyond any one of them. It is, as it were, the complement to Plato's Receptacle, its exact opposite, yet equally required for the unity of all things. In every way, it is contrary to the Receptacle. The Receptacle is bare of all forms: the Unity of Adventure includes the Eros which is the living urge towards all possibilities, claiming the goodness of their realization. The Platonic Receptacle is void, abstract from all individual occasions: The Unity of Adventure includes among its components all individual realities, each with the importance of the personal or social fact to which it belongs. Such individual importance in the components belongs to the essence of Beauty. In this Supreme Adventure, the Reality which Adventure transmutes into its Unity of Appearance, requires the real occasions of the advancing world each claiming its due share of attention. This Appearance, thus enjoyed, is the final Beauty with which the Universe achieves its justification. This Beauty has always within it the renewal derived from the Advance of the Temporal World. It is the immanence of the Great Fact including this initial Eros and this final Beauty which constitutes the zest of self-forgetful transcendence belonging to Civilization at its height. (*AI*, 380–81)

We are a long, long way from the disinterested, mere conceptual valuation of eternal forms found in *SMW* in this declaration of faith in the creative advance into novelty. This Whiteheadian appeal reminds me of Confucius' assertion that if you can hear the Tao in the morning, you can die happy at night. To hear the Tao, to realize the divine eros of the cosmos, is to discover the nature of divine things for Whitehead. Nor does it seem that creativity, thematized as beauty, adventure, and zest, is somehow outside of the matrix of creative synthesis. Both Whitehead and Confucius posit a level of concern as the foundation of the cosmos that justifies Mou Tsung-san's root metaphor of concern-consciousness for the Confucian vision.

However, this is not quite the end of the story. In the next and final paragraph, Whitehead writes that "The Adventure of the Universe starts with the dream (i.e., the dream of youthful adventure and beauty) and reaps tragic

Beauty. This is the secret of the union of Zest with Peace—That the suffering attains its end in a Harmony of Harmonies" (*AI*, 381). In his discussion of adventure, he notes that eros, here as a function of the psyche, is the reason we find process at the basis of the universe. In the psyche as the living soul, eros "is the urge towards the realization of ideal perfection" (*AI*, 354). He speaks of eros as indwelling in the soul without which we would only have a static world. In *AI*, this is the way Whitehead reinforces the definition of his thought as based on process. "One principle is that the very essence of real actuality—that is, of the completely real—is *process*" (*AI*, 354). As we have noted before, this is the first of Whitehead's rephrasing of his basic metaphysical principles in *AI*.

Whitehead believed that his doctrine of eros helped him be the heir of both Plato and Aristotle. He conjectured that he could make this claim because of the linkage of actuality with process. This connects, in his mind, the Aristotelian notion "that all agency is confined to actuality . . . ," and the Platonic rule "that the very meaning of existence is 'to be a factor in agency,' or in other words 'to make a difference' " (*AI*, 253–54). In most respects, this is a restatement of the Ontological Principle, or that reality is "a factor in the analysis of some actuality" (*AI*, 254). He continues with an aside about the difference between the real and the actual. "Thus though everything is real, it is not necessarily realized in some particular set of actual occasions. But it is necessary it be discoverable somewhere, realized in some actual entity" (*AI*, 254). From this insight he builds out from the real, the actual to a unity, to a nexus, regions, persons, events—to all of the various levels of complexity of the object–events of the cosmic epoch.

The ground for freedom in such a vision is found in "The causal independence of contemporary occasions is the ground for the freedom of the Universe" (*AI*, 255). It is here that Whitehead denies that the past alone creates or totally conditions the emergence of the present object–events in the process of concrescence. Some factors are accepted into the new synthesis, some are rejected. There is always the freedom of the emerging entity in the moment of its creation to achieve a new synthesis.

> The running stream purifies itself, or perhaps loses some virtue which in happier circumstances might have been retained. The initial phase of each fresh occasion represents the issue of a struggle within the past for objective existence beyond itself. The determination of the struggle is the supreme Eros incarnating itself as the first phase of the individual subjective aim in the new process of actuality. Thus in any two occasions of the Universe there are elements in either one which are irrelevant to the constitution of the other. (*AI*, 256)

My main point here is the exegetical act of reading the mature Whitehead by means of holding to the hypothesis that the Ontological Principle is the primary factor in controlling the interpretation of the text. I take this to be plausible on the basis of the various quotes I have assembled, although no mere exercise in proof texting ever makes a philosophic point. However, it is clear that Whitehead always returned to the scene of the crime, and so I believe that at least one fiduciary reading of the text is generated by this means. As Whitehead might say, the elements of my reconstruction are irrelevant to other reconstructions. Yet like Plato, Whitehead is always capable of revising his own thought. In my revision there is a way to find a place for creativity in the divine nature if we take eros and adventure seriously as elements of unification. Besides, exegesis is a preferred Neo-Confucian form of philosophic discourse. To be creative is fine, but to be unconnected to history and custom, unrelated to the world, is to mistake the nature of creative synthesis within *ars contextualis*.

In *Eros and Irony*, David Hall proposed an interpretation of the relationship of God and creativity based on comparative Chinese materials quite different from either Whitehead or Neville. "By grounding novelty and harmony in a hierarchical ordering of atemporal forms, Whitehead provided an alternative to the conception of the world as dependent upon a unilateral exercise of volition" (1982a, 245). In terms of Hall's own Taoistic reading of Western philosophy, such an urge for the ordering of creativity is linked to Whitehead's persistent desire to embrace the theorial vision of reality governed by reason.[20] In this exegesis of the world, "The theorial intuition, upon which the most direct understanding of creativity may be based, is the sense of a primordial harmony illustrating the self-creative activities of each item of the totality in accordance with its insistent particularity" (1982a, 245). Hall argues that the real interpretive problem for Whitehead and Chu is not to explain the order of the universe but " . . . rather why things sometimes fall apart" (1982a, 245), According to Hall, creativity in such a system "is always reflexive and polar" (1982a, 249). The real question is not to seek a single, ontological source of order as Neville requires, because order is immanent in the context and relationships of the object–events, divine and mundane, of the cosmos. For Hall, the really primal question is to query why there is disorder rather than order at all, which is what one would expect from someone fascinated by the classical Chinese Taoists such as Lao Tzu and Chuang Tzu.

Likewise, Hall's analysis of the positive role of chaos makes a great deal of sense to anyone who has spent time reading the long Neo-Confucian accounts of the fall into disorder that marks history after the great sages. We need to remember that one of the primal Confucian myths is that of the perfect social order achieved by the first sages, subsequently lost but always available again if human beings can cultivate sage wisdom. The Confucian project does not begin with chaos or the void, but rather with the hard work, wisdom, and social compassion of the early sages. It is true that the sages have to order the world, but they are able to do so because they already have the means to bring order to the world, namely their sagely wisdom and willingness to engage in social reconstruction. The task of the later Confucians has always been to restore this primal order rather than to overcome some kind of primal disorder or epic fall from the garden. Here again we can see the mark of a distinctive philosophic sensibility. The Neo-Confucian problem of evil is framed: Why, for instance, if the Supreme Ultimate is such a wonderful principle of order, is there so little real ordering principle for the common social good in the world? The great Neo-Confucian riddle of the problem of evil springs out of the notion of creativity found in such organic/ process thought.

COMPREHENSIVE PRINCIPLE AND CREATIVITY

One way to address the problem of creativity, God, and the Tao from the perspective of *ars contextualis* is to compare and contrast the archic profiles of Chu Hsi and Whitehead. This will help us step back from the historical context, content, and details of the two systems in order to view some of the questions of deep structure that inform both and allow us to specify them as belonging to the realm of *ars contextualis* and as a specification of a process approach to reality. One move caveat. This is an approach that works, if it works at all, because archic analysis and Neville's philosophy are examples of modern Western comparative philosophy. If I were trying to explicate problems derived from Chu's Sung Neo-Confucian synthesis, I would have to approach the taxonomy and comparative issues from a different, that is to say, East Asian comparative perspective. I fully agree with the growing chorus of comparative philosophers and theologians who argue that you can not solve problems in one culture by simply importing the categoreal system and methods from an alien cultural milieu. Notwithstanding the comparative caveat, because the presenting problem for creativity for Whitehead, as well as Neville's challenge to Whitehead's solution, arose from within the hermeneutic circle of modern Western speculative discourse, the appeal to a Western taxonomy and comparative methodology is legitimate insofar as we constantly remind ourselves about the nature of this restricted comparative process. Further, I believe this is a helpful strategy for dealing with Neville's criticism and serves to show how the critique can be answered without recourse to capitulating to Neville's position or offering yet another form of ontology in its place.

My archic profile for Chu is:

1. Disciplinary perspective[21]
2. Essentialist reality
3. Dialectical method
4. Comprehensive principle.

My archic profile for Whitehead is:

1. Disciplinary perspective
2. Essentialist reality
3. Dialectical method
4. Creative principle.

In another context I have asked, if a principle becomes truly comprehensive can it overlap with the creative variable as defined by the Watson–Dilworth method of archic analysis (Berthrong 1994)? When principle becomes as comprehensive as Chu's notion of Tao or the Supreme Ultimate, and especially when its content is specified as a principle of creativity per se, does it become a creative principle according to the definition of archic analysis?

In terms of archic analysis, Chu Hsi faithfully followed Confucius' comprehensive principle. The other two classical Confucian alternatives for defining principle in the Chinese classical period were Mencius, with an elemental principle, and Hsün-tzu, with a creative principle. My preliminary suggestion is to assign Chu a comprehensive principle but to stipulate that one key metaphor of the comprehensive principle for Chu is creativity itself. The justification of this addition of the creativity as a stipulated metaphor for comprehensive principle begs for additional justification.

To begin, in no fashion can we identify Chu's notion of creative, comprehensive principle with Dilworth's interpretation of Mencius' elemental principle. Mou Tsung-san would agree with the divergence of Chu and Mencius on this point as well. The other reading of a major Confucian figure in the classical age of Chinese philosophy, namely Hsün Tzu's use of a creative principle, is much more intriguing in light of Mou Tsung-san's criticism of Chu. One of Mou's provocative interpretations of Chu is that although he subscribed verbally to the Mencian orthodoxy, Chu really had much more philosophically in common with Hsün Tzu. Dilworth writes of Hsün Tzu that, "Creative in principle and essentialist in sense of reality, the *Hsün Tzu* ranks with the philosophical program of John Dewey in envisioning the transformation of human life through melioristic institutions and agencies" (1989, 73–74). Dilworth argues for a creative principle in Hsün Tzu because it is the sage who actually creates social order through education and ritual activity. It has always struck me as ironic that Hsün Tzu, who so strongly believed in the possible transformation of the human person, should be almost completely identified with the doctrine that human nature is evil.[22]

Likewise, the suggested link with Dewey and the larger pragmatic tradition makes sense both for Hsün Tzu and Chu Hsi if we remember that all of the Confucians really do believe that sage wisdom can improve human life. While Hsün Tzu may have held a speculative meliorism, it is certainly not the case that he had an overly optimistic view of the real potential for the victory of the good in the immediate circumstances of late Warring State China. Like Chu after him, Hsün Tzu had a robust understanding of the evil that men do. It was not enough for either Hsün Tzu or Chu to merely note the possibility of human transformation for the good. Any such transformation takes a great deal of effort, and not everyone will be successful either, even if there is almost always hope for the transformative moment to occur if one can find the teachings of the sages and study and apply them earnestly. The need for informed, realistic effort to achieve the good marks the Confucianism of Hsün Tzu and Chu, as well as the pragmatism of Dewey.

We do not need to buy into all of Mou Tsung-san's analysis and critique of Chu's Neo-Confucian synthesis to accept the insight into the connection of archic first principles between Hsün Tzu and Chu Hsi. Although this is not the place to argue the case, I believe that Mou does have a good point about the creative nature of Hsün Tzu's understanding of the sage and its affinity with Chu's understanding of the necessity for rigorous effort and the examination of things as the basis for self-transformation. According to Mou, such a notion of creativity can be predicated of the entire tradition, including Mencius. It is certainly the case that neither Hsün Tzu nor Chu would have believed in ultimate self-transformation merely by the cultivation of the individual mind–heart. The world was too complicated for such a simplistic epistemological and transformative praxis.

Once we begin to explore the question of principle for the Neo-Confucians, we need to consider the fourth set of variables in Watson's and Dilworth's archic analysis, the reflexive principle. In terms of the Greeks, it is Aristotle who defines the reflexive principle most characteristically. As Watson points out, "Reflexive principles differ from creative principles because they do not determine consequences arbitrarily, but in accordance with what they themselves already are" (1985, 136). However, Watson traces the origin of this principle not to Aristotle per se but to Xenophanes' notion of mind as the reflexive principle. He notes that Anaxagoras had a notion of mind as self-ruling that is reflexive in its ordering of the cosmos. Of course, it is Aristotle who puts an indelible stamp on the reflexive principle by means of his ruminations on the nature, method, and order of the sciences.

Again, it is interesting to note that Chu Hsi's notion of mind has some suggestive affinities with the reflexive principle of the classical Greeks. The only problem is that we have now seen how forbidding it is, without forcing the issue drastically, to offer a comprehensive, creative, and then reflexive reading of Chu's principle qua principle. What is the basic meaning of *li* in terms of archic analysis if it can be read in such a complex, dare we say ambiguous, fashion? What if there is no easy or satisfactory answer to this question of the mixed nature of Chu's principle? There are three ways to respond to the second question. First, it could be that Chu was either confused in the presentation or consciously provided different answers corresponding to comprehensive, creative, and reflexive traits. Chu would not be the first great philosopher to be confused. As Whitehead noted, Plato was capable of refuting his own philosophy from time to time.

Second, it could be that the Watson–Dilworth archic analysis itself is flawed and incapable of providing an adequate taxonomy to deal with the richness of Chu Hsi's thought. Third, and related to the second choice, it could be that Neo-Confucian thought simply does not lend itself to easy categorization by what is essentially a Western analytic method.

The first choice makes sense if we remember that Chu Hsi wrote an extraordinary amount of material over a number of decades. We know from the recent and exhaustive studies of the development of his thought by scholars such as Ch'ien Mu, Mou Tsung-san, Liu Shu-hsien, Zhang Liwen, Donald Munro, Thomas Wilson, and Hoyt Tillman that Chu occasionally changed his mind about important issues. Furthermore, some of Chu's most important philosophic statements were made in the context of dialogue with his friends and students. Chu responded to specific questions to try to make clear the Confucian Way as he had come to understand it himself. For Chu, the Confucian Way was comprehensive, creative, and even reflexive in different moments. Nor was Chu's exposition, as we also have seen, without moments of ambiguity regarding first principles. The persistent argument in the tradition about the role of principle and its relationship to matter–energy proves that all was not as clear as Chu would have liked it to be. Like Whitehead, Chu was constantly trying to refine and revise his philosophic perspective. In the sense that his philosophy was a hermeneutical enterprise of restoring the teaching of the sages as well as creatively adapting the sage teachings to the new conditions of the Southern Sung, it was always a creative act. However, it was also comprehensive if only one could really appropriate correctly the sage teachings and apply them intelligently to the present situation. Chu assumed it was a comprehensive Way in that it provided a complete outline for the reformation of society. Further, it was reflexive in that it did not refer to any agency beyond the world of object–events for everyone to prehend it.

The second and third possibilities are interrelated. As I have continually noted in this essay, we are just beginning the serious construction of comparative methodologies for philosophy and theology. We should expect a modest amount of overlap of basic categories. Besides, as both Watson and Dilworth have indicated, archic analysis is not a value-neutral schema. It too has its own archic profile. My reading of the Watson–Dilworth text is that it has a disciplinary perspective, an essentialist reality, a synoptic method, and a reflexive principle. However, one of the strengths of the pluralistic bias of the architectonic of meaning is that it expects other systems to differ and to differ radically from its own archic profile. Even though harsh comparative philosophic critics such as Hall and Ames (1995) hammer the point that archic analysis is a modern Western taxonomy with limited categoreal flexibility for making major comparisons with Confucian cultural sensibilities, at least the method is pluralistic and does try to take into account South and East Asian texts. Archic analysis anticipates and welcomes dialogue with other culturally defined comparative methods.

Watson and Dilworth provide an illuminating snapshot of texts from an irenic Western perspective that honors and anticipates the pluralism of the worldviews of major world philosophers. However, this does not mean that material from other great world traditions, such as Chinese Neo-Confucianism, will always fit comfortably in the Western architectonic grid. In some cases the question of assigning an archic variable depends on the kind of historically Western philosophic question that is being asked. I believe that this is the case with the archic analysis of principle, and, by extension, of Whitehead as well, as he sought to make process rather than substance the key to his philosophy. We must remember that Neville's challenge to Whitehead is made on the most hallowed of Western philosophic playing fields, that of metaphysics, ontology, and cosmology. If Chu Hsi put the ball into play from a different angle than is normal, this is to be expected, because Chu is playing with different rules, and such a divergence should soon be acknowledged as a possible outcome of the comparison.

When Neville asks his fundamental ontological question about the origin of being and the beings, the proper archic reading of Chu's response is reflexive. This is so because Chu has little place for any elaborate process such as Neville claims for *creatio ex nihilo* to sustain his analysis of the flourishing of being. Alternatively, from the perspective of Dilworth's analysis of Neo-Confucian thought, principle qua the Supreme Ultimate is comprehensive in scope. From the perspective of Whitehead's interest in process, creativity, and concrescence, Chu's Supreme Ultimate is creative. Yet all of these are viable readings because Chu's Neo-Confucian principle is a principle of order and pattern as opposed to other philosophic Taoist or Buddhist readings of principle as emptiness or nothingness. It is this Neo-Confucian sense of order that makes *li* as form a principle in terms of the architectonic of meaning. All three readings work because none of them alone is adequate to the range of Chu's Neo-Confucian preoccupations.

From a Neo-Confucian perspective, Whitehead's principle of creativity can also be read in this tripartite fashion. It is most definitely a comprehensive principle. There is nothing beyond or outside of creativity as the divine eros of the universe. There is nothing the divine eros does not constitute, because it inclusively comprehends all that is. Furthermore, it is creative in intent. To be is to be creative for Whitehead. While it is true that things are conditioned by the past object–events of their cosmic epoch, there is always a moment of *sui generis* generativity beyond what went before, even if the creativity is mostly repetition of past forms. Last, if we see the primordial nature as including the divine eros, then the principle is reflexive in terms of the model of the architectonic of meaning sketched here. This last point is one that agrees strongly with Chu's mature philosophic synthesis.

Does any of this answer Neville's question about creativity and God? I believe that it does in part and that it is consistent with the general thrust of Whitehead's work from *RM*, *PR*, and *SMW* to *MT*. Everyone begins the interpretive quest from somewhere within the hermeneutic circle in dealing with specific authors or philosophic schools. I have argued that we can interpret the essential nature of God for Whitehead by means of recognizing the centrality of the Ontological Principle; this is a reading that demands that we find a place for creativity as a primal element of the process of the formation of this or any world within God's nature qua the ultimate divine referent as eros understood as ultimate concern-consciousness. The warrants for such a reading are suggested by an interpretive stance that takes some suggestive aspects of *AI* and *MT* as being systematically more important than they have been taken before in support of the centrality of the Ontological Principle. One of the benefits of such a reading is that it allows for a response to Neville's challenge that is internal to the Anglo-American process tradition as a whole. It concedes that there is a problem with the separation of God and creativity in *PR*, but it denies that we have to abandon the Ontological Principle to respond to Neville. The key to such a response is to see creativity as the divine eros of God, the ultimate concern of the God for all the creatures of the world. Support for such an interpretation comes from *AI* and *MT*.

If we accept the plausibility of such a reading then we no longer need to define creativity as something beyond even God's nature. Creativity in its most primal sense is the divine eros that always seeks to create. In that sense, God and creativity are not exceptions to the general metaphysical rules of the game; they become supreme exemplifications of the highest patterns or principles of object–events. I have always suspected that this is one reason why Chu Hsi loved to speak of the highest principle as the Supreme Ultimate. This was the Neo-Confucian way to indicate the supremely reflexive and creative nature of the fundamental principle of the universe. What I have done in making use of Chu Hsi in this fashion is to read Whitehead as a Western version of a Neo-Confucian *ars contextualis*. The proper answer to the ontological question is always: It is so of itself, and that this self-so-ness is ceaselessly creative. This answer, at least in the Chinese case, has been given consistently by the philosophic Taoists and the Neo-Confucians throughout the whole development of their distinctive intellectual histories. For the Taoists, the focus is on the freedom of creativity per se for the object–events. Compared to the Confucians, the philosophic Taoists believe that too much reflection on social organization will stifle the creativity of the Tao.[23] Hall has styled this as a truly anarchic philosophic position in that it refuses to privilege one principle over any other—hence, it really is self-referencing in a chaotic mode of infinite generativity.

Just as with the Taoists, Neo-Confucians are equally interested in the creative act, but they are much more concerned to set the creative act of any one object–event within the context of all of the other object–events of a realistic universe. Things matter not only as they are creative of themselves but also for all of the other object–events that they influence. Things unfold responsively but with definite orders and implications, as the world moves forward in the ceaseless creativity of the Tao. I believe that Whitehead would agree; there is both process and reality in the world. To ask for the ultimate nature of things is to ask to see what and how they become in the context of what Mead called sociality.

Such a move will never satisfy someone like Neville, who takes his creativity, like a good drink, neat. If we live in a pluralistic world, I doubt that we should expect that fundamental ontologists like Neville, always looking for the unity behind the many, will ever consent to the final philosophic viability of such a reply. It is neither dialectical nor ontological enough to be accepted as a response for someone like Neville, who seeks the source of the mixture of the limited and the unlimited. But then, why should it? One of the things archic analysis, itself a species of pluralistic philosophy, suggests is that there are various, diverse, and persistent patterns of philosophic explanation that disagree about the fundamental disposition of thought, action, and passion. Because of these different paradigms of ultimate meaning, no one with such a purely creative principle as Neville's advocacy for *creatio ex nihilo* will accept Chu's Supreme Ultimate or Whitehead's divine eros as the principle of principles. From the perspective of an ontologist seeking final reasons, such as Neville assuredly is, Chu and Whitehead will be seen as being too limited in their explanatory scope, too willing to accept the cosmological closure of the world. Of course, the very cogency of the organic/process response as *ars contextualis* is predicated on the internal dynamics of the global organic/process tradition that accepts just such an ultimate self-referencing of all object–events.

Furthermore, such a re-reading of Whitehead's text helps make more religious sense of his ultimate vision of the way things really are—ultimately together in what he calls God's consequent nature with as much harmony as the pluralism of reality allows. The magisterial paired antitheses of Part V of *PR* were his way of trying to show that things really are connected to each other, and that finally we really are left with these things as coordinated and preserved in the eternal care of God's love. These things are generated from each other, and although the divine reality, called God in the Western theistic traditions, is the supreme example of all that we can name, know, or do in this cosmic epoch, God functions as one among the many, even if the divine reality is a supremely creative and sensitive agent of the creative advance into novelty. God is an exemplar of creativity, and creativity is reflexive within God. Or as Chu Hsi taught, principle is one and many.

Perhaps one of the real benefits to be derived from increasing attention to the philosophic aspects of comparative thought is that it may well teach all of us to speak intelligibly across the boundaries of alternative worldviews. For instance, if we remember Mou Tsung-san's notion of concern-consciousness and its resonance with Whitehead's suggestion in *MT* of concern as defined best in the Western tradition by the Quakers, we are in a good position to try to suggest a reason why Chu and Whitehead will never completely agree with Neville. Since Neville, Chu, and Whitehead are all concerned with the issues of speculative philosophy as adumbrated by Whitehead, it is easy for them to speak to each other in one sense, the sense of trying to make sense out of the world; since their understanding of principle, God, and creativity is so diverse, agreement is not possible.

The reason they cannot agree on the procedures to follow to explore the question or the warrants that apply to the analysis of the common world of experience lies in the very nature of Confucian concern-consciousness, Whiteheadian divine eros, and the contrasting Nevillian search for the ultimate dialectical harmony of harmonies. Do we seek harmony or concern—a pointed but suggestive way to contrast the search for speculative answers to metasystemic questions. It strikes me that concern-consciousness will always be a principle of movement, of at least mild anxiety about the contrast of what is with what could or should be that will never let itself become part of just another neatly resolved dialectical synthesis.

The point need not be overstated as some kind of ultimate philosophic dualism, a battle between concerned or harmonious philosophers. While it is true that Chu and Mou, about as different a pair of Confucians as one can imagine within the tradition, seek harmony through the appropriation of ritual practice for each person and culture, the search for an ultimate, final, and dialectical harmony does not take pride of place in their pursuit of sage wisdom. Rather, Chu and Mou are concerned about concern and the harmony appropriate to the interweaving of all of the particular object–events of the cosmic epoch as *sui generis* axiological entities. I hold that a concern-based speculative system tends more toward reflections on the imperfect and ever–shifting balances and rhythms of love and eros as the final characteristics of God rather than on a search for a perfected ontological harmony and the dialectical resolution of the many into the one and one back into the many. In this regard, a process sensibility, understood as *ars contextualis* qua creative synthesis, defines principle as comprehensive, creative, and reflexive through the ceaseless generation of new values embodied in the concrescence of object–events. Or in a revised Whiteheadian vision, creativity is embodied in the divine reality as a loving, even erotic, concern for the creatures. While Chu might be, good Sung Neo-Confucian that he was, not concerned about extolling the power of the erotic, he was aware that the very root of humanity was human generativity between husband and wife. Creativity cannot be understood as something beyond God's true nature but as a supreme characteristic of it as an embodied and eternal concern for any cosmic epoch whatsoever.

Even if we do not agree about the nature of the contrast of concern-consciousness and the search for harmony, and find the warrants, arguments, analogies, and metaphors of the other inadequate, we can now better see the other paradigm in a more refracted light because more facets of its structure are revealed in alternative cultural settings. Reading Whitehead by means of Chu's and Mou's pan-Confucian text helps us understand that we can find an integral place for creativity both in the Tao and in God. It also frames a revised Whiteheadian response to Neville's profound challenge. A better form of insight we must leave to the sages.

NOTES

1. This is especially the case for the complex web of dialogue and violence that links Judaism, Christianity, and Islam. For different reasons, it is precisely the Holy Trinity that bothers Jews and Muslims about the monotheistic claims of the Christian tradition.

2. Part of the philosophic justification for such an approach rests upon the pluralist position adopted in this essay. I fully realize how controversial such a position is, especially when it is linked to the contemporary debate in philosophy concerning "systematic pluralism." As Walter Watson had defined the issue, systematic pluralism defends the thesis " . . . that the truth admits of more than one valid formulation. . . . " (1985, ix). However, formal validity does not always mean that one formulation is not better, more noble, more exciting, or even more useful than another. Philosophic pluralism does not automatically mean what the Roman Catholic Church has called indifferentism, the (false) belief that no pattern of thought is better or more true than another. For a discussion of the nature of this debate, see Reck (1990), James Ford (1990), and Watson (1990). Of course, the patron saint and founder of this school is Richard McKeon, even though he probably would not have liked my labels. Nonetheless, McKeon's turn to rhetoric late in his career, a move caused by his desire to do justice to the various forms of philosophic discourse, demonstrates the need for an informed pluralism in the study of the history of philosophy.

Although not often highlighted, we need to remember that McKeon was concerned enough with world philosophy to undertake a joint translation with A. N. Nikam of the famous edicts of the Buddhist emperor Asoka. This was published in 1957 by The University of Chicago Press as *The Edicts of Asoka*.

3. For an example of this kind of Eastern Orthodox contemporary discourse, see Dumitru Staniloae (1994). Staniloae is ecumenically recognized as one of the most important Orthodox systematic theologians of the twentieth century. He carries on his work with a careful eye on his Western Christian co-religionists.

4. David Hall notes that Charles Hartshorne wrote a major work in 1970 with the term *creative synthesis* in its title (1982b, 224, n. 23). Hall wants to acknowledge his debt to Hartshorne in *The Uncertain Phoenix* as well as show wherein he diverges from Hartshorne. The point that Hall keeps returning to is the basically anarchic nature of his vision of the world without principles. Among other things, this means that self-creativity is stressed rather than any notion of external creation. Hall is quite taken with the sensibility of the Taoist notion of *tzu-jan*, or spontaneity. He acknowledges that this is his version of a modern Taoist reading of the history of Chinese philosophy; I will be offering a Neo-Confucian reading of the texts that makes a place for principle, albeit in a manner divergent from the dominant Western traditions outlined in Hall's work.

In Hall's later collaborative work with Roger Ames, he has come to call this distinctive sensibility an *ars contextualis*.

5. Stephen Pepper also develops a similar theory in *Concept and Quality: A World Hypothesis*. Adding to his repertoire of root metaphors, Pepper proposes the notion of the purposive act as another way to construe the world. Part of the reason for this additional root metaphor came from Pepper's continued re-reading of Whitehead.

6. For a characteristic statement of the philosopher on this point following W. D. Ross' translation (McKeon 1941), see the *Nicomachean Ethics*, Book I, Chapter 3,

wherein Ross writes " . . . for it is the mark of an educated man to look for precision in each class of things just so far as the nature of the subject admits; it is evidently equally foolish to accept probable reasoning from a mathematician and to demand from a rhetorician scientific proofs."

7. The positive role vagueness plays in the formation of philosophic systems has been a recurring theme in Neville's work. For a recent defense of vagueness, see *HAM*, 146–47. For instance, Neville notes that, "Philosophical categories and propositions in system should not be general but, rather, vague. A vague proposition is one that requires a further assertion to identify its object and give it a truth value" (*HAM*, 146). Here Neville is relying on the work of Peirce.

8. It would be wonderful to be able to refer the reader to some English translations of Mou's work at this point, but, alas, hardly anything of his extensive corpus has yet been translated into English. For a discussion of Mou's thought, see Berthrong (1994).

9. For a fascinating study of and contrast between the notions of desire and the erotic in France and China, see Tonglin Lu's *Rose and Lotus* (1991). Lu points out how all societies have a place, however repressed, for the erotic. Dorothy Ko's wonderful study of educated Confucian women at the end of the Ming dynasty reveals that they tried to convince their male audience of the importance of emotion and even of the value of companionate marriage (1994). While not highly erotic, these ladies of the Way stoutly defended emotion, even the emotion of passionate love as appropriate topics of Confucian reflection. If we ever doubted this fact, Camille Paglia's sometimes outrageous, provocative, but always stimulating research demonstrates the point in terms of narrative in Western fiction and art (1991). Even the mystical traditions of Christian spirituality often have a place for love, even a love tinged with the erotic. See Zagano (1993) for some accounts of the classical Western women mystics, as well as for some fascinating modern examples, such as the poetry of Jessica Powers.

10. Everyone from Christian (1959) to the more recent studies of Ford (1984) and Nobo (1986) address this question in detail. For instance, Hartshorne has concluded that Whitehead was just plain incorrect or incoherent in his portrait of God, hence Hartshorne devised an entirely different account of God's nature. The possibilities for internal Whitehead scholarship on this question seem almost endless.

11. McKeon has pointed out how the idea of creativity itself can become a rather vague commonplace in the rhetoric of modern philosophy in his article "Creativity and Commonplace" (1987). But, as Neville has also shown, there is a place for the vague, the unspecified, in the development of complex systems of thought.

12. Buchler, in his study of the metaphysics of natural complexes (1966), would not have agreed with my position. He argued that Whitehead did not have a proper notion of ontological parity because the actual entities were the really real objects of Whitehead's system and that all other things, forms, and so on, were somehow less ontologically real for Whitehead.

13. The classic study of dualism in Western philosophy is Arthur Lovejoy's (1930) study of what he calls the revolt against dualism. Lovejoy devotes a chapter to Whitehead's critique of "simple location" as one sign of twentieth-century conflict with the great thinkers of the seventeenth century. The term *dualism* also is current in the modern history of Chinese philosophy, as written by Marxists in the People's Republic of China. In the PRC, it often is linked with the notion of realism as opposed to idealism, or the contrast of the Chu Hsi school to that of Wang Yang-ming.

The cross-cultural geographer, Yi Fu Tuan, has pointed out how the human senses tend toward certain fundamental dualistic interpretations of reality or fundamental binary oppositions, such as we find in various color schemata (1990, 16–18). Tuan also goes on to note that these dyads are then almost always synthesized into more complicated patterns.

14. For Chou's original text, see Wing-tsit Chan's translation and commentary (1963, 463–65). The debate about what this short text really signifies is as complicated as the debate about what Whitehead took to be the relationship of God, creativity, and the world.

15. I have relied on the fine translation of Wing-tsit Chan but have modified the passage to illustrate my point. Ch'en's classical Chinese is wonderfully terse and evocative. A great deal of the difficulty of translating the passage resides in the contrasted verbal pair of *yu/wu*. A. C. Graham, in numerous articles, has demonstrated that the Chinese understanding of "being" and "non-being" is not the same as the classical Western interpretation—if there is one.

16. Buchler's key text for the notion of ontological parity is *The Metaphysics of Natural Complexes* (1966).

17. It is interesting to note that, at least in terms of vehicular traffic patterns, a Cambridge, England, and a Cambridge, Massachusetts, roundabout demonstrate rather nicely—unless you are in the American version—the contrast of order and chaos.

18. Whitehead argues that this is the fate of God in much Western theology. "The worst of a gulf is that it is very difficult to know what is happening on the further side of it. . . . It is only by drawing the long bow of mysticism that evidences for his existence can be collected from our temporal World" (*AI*, 217). Of course, more orthodox theologians argue that we know about God through revelation of the Word. Another position is Neville's, who holds that we know something about God, namely that God is the creator of this kind of order. God is hence the ontological ground of all that is created.

19. David Hall outlines a similar reason for the difficulty in pinning Whitehead down if we have recourse to traditional Western philosophic labels. Hall notes that while Whitehead wants to be comprehensive in his synthesis, he is not attempting to be systematic in the traditional sense of the term. "His insistence upon system is grounded in a recognition of the bifocality of theory which directs it toward the sphere of theoria as well as that of praxis. For Whitehead, in precisely the same manner as

for Plato, system ensures not only practical relevance, but provides the ground for self-transcendence" (1982a, 104). Or, "What makes Whitehead's thinking so difficult to characterize is that he has explicitly appealed to the broadest possible sources of evidence in the construction of his philosophic system" (1982a, 105).

In his later work, especially in his collaborative comparative work with Roger Ames, Hall gives the name *ars contextualis* to this philosophic sensibility. Hall and Ames have made use of their work in defense of the viability of the Taoist tradition. Although they have not been so kind to the Neo-Confucians, I believe that their insights can be applied with equal benefit to the Neo-Confucians as well.

20. In writing about Hall's interpretation of Chinese thought, I need to be cautious. Since the publication of *Eros and Irony* in 1982, Hall has begun a fruitful collaboration with Roger Ames (1987, 1995). Therefore, Hall's opinions about Chinese philosophy are in a state of constant revision due to his work with Ames.

21. This is a modification of the profile as developed by Watson (1985) and Dilworth (1989). Dilworth has argued for a diaphanic perspective; Watson follows this reading too. While I can understand why they read Chu's text in this fashion, I have been persuaded by the careful work of Hoyt Tillman (1992) that Chu's perspective is disciplinary. I have argued this case in an article (Berthrong 1993) on Chu's use of *ch'eng*, or self-realization. It is true that what the disciplinary method will ultimately reveal is a transcendent understanding of the cultivated mind congruent with the mind of the Tao. Nonetheless, the community of scholars is crucial for Chu; there would be no enlightened mind without study within a community of teachers and scholars. It is true that the goal of the scholar must be a very special form of Neo-Confucian illumination of the mind of the Tao, but the perspective on the illumination is disciplinary. The truth that shines forth, however, is still diaphanic in that it reveals the mind of the Tao.

22. Of course, the precise nature of Hsün Tzu's claim that human nature is evil has been a source of constant debate ever since it was first proposed. For a summary of the debate and for a sound interpretation of the original, see Knoblock's complete scholarly translation of the texts in question (1988–1994). Knoblock has not only finally translated all of Hsün Tzu, but he has carefully summarized the debates about this convoluted debate.

23. This is a debate that has gone on since the beginning of Chinese philosophy. One can think of the debates between Mencius, Chuang Tzu, and Hsün Tzu. For some excellent modern discussions of these issues, see Graham (1985, 1989, 1992), Hansen (1992), Chan (1991), Nivison (1996), Ivanhoe (1996), and Kjellberg (1996). Chan's work is especially useful in that it shows how this debate was conducted by some of the later Neo-Taoist exegetes and philosophers.

Appendix

The Structure of Archic Analysis

The method of archic analysis was introduced by Walter Watson in *The Architectonics of Meaning: Foundations of the New Pluralism* (1985; revised edition with new preface, 1992) as a comparative hermeneutic for analyzing the diversity of the world's philosophic texts. David Dilworth adopted archic analysis in *Philosophy in World Perspective: A Comparative Hermeneutics of the Major Theories* (1989) and broadened the scope of inquiry to include more Asian religious and philosophic systems of thought. In both cases, Chinese philosophic texts played important roles in illustrating the cross-cultural possibilities of the method.

It is crucial to recognize the limitations of archic analysis. It is not the golden bullet of comparative philosophy and theology. It is simply one taxonomy among others. Hall and Ames (1995) have argued at length that it is also a taxonomy that distorts the evidence of Chinese thought because it, holus bolos, forces on Chinese thinkers a form of categoreal organization inappropriate to Chinese intellectual concerns. The long and short of Hall's and Ames's complaint is that, especially in Dilworth's version, archic analysis privileges Aristotle and the whole Western appeal to the cosmic organizing power of technical rationalism and principles in order to interpret texts in its own image. This is not just seeing through a glass darkly, it is like looking into a distorting mirror that mocks any honest engagement with the spirit of the text. On the contrary, Hall and Ames argue that the genius of Chinese thought resides not in appeals to reasons and principles, but rather in correlative thinking, aesthetic judgments, and the metaphoric examinations of the world and human conduct. Hall and Ames assume that it is unrealistic to assume that a very Western taxonomy such as archic analysis will help interpret early Chinese thought to the modern Western reader. This holds even when the Western taxonomy is dedicated to a critical, pluralistic vision of philosophic and religious discourse.

There is a great deal of merit to Hall's and Ames's critique. We must be vigilant in applying categoreal schemes across cultural divides because of the possibility and temptation of misinterpretation. However, as Paul Feyerabend

(1988), an arch relativist if there ever was one, has noted, we have to start somewhere, and we inevitably begin where we are; that is all we have as human beings. Feyerabend asserts that, therefore, we are, as individual human beings, pluralistic and relativistic if we are honest with ourselves. The location of modern Western intellectuals is their specific history of ancient, medieval, and modern European thought and the broader world of global philosophy and theology. As long as we recognize that we are using categoreal taxonomies from one tradition, in this case the modern West, we are at least being honest about what we are doing.

Further, and here I disagree with some of Dilworth's more unguarded enthusiasms in assuming that archic analysis is the perfect way to examine all forms of thought because of its pluralistic Aristotelian roots, students of classical Chinese thought could make a similar argument for Chuang Tzu being the root of a method of philosophic taxonomy because he had pluralistic tendencies and lived during a richly variegated philosophic period. One of Chuang Tzu's later followers even wrote one of the first philosophic analyses of the history of Chinese thought and appended it to the other essays of the master and his disciples. Archic analysis is a hermeneutic artifact constructed out of the philosophic resources of classical, medieval, and modern Western philosophy. It is not an objective embodiment of all truth and reason for all times, even though it recognizes the inherent pluralism of philosophic discourse.

What is pertinent is that both Watson and Dilworth understand that modern philosophers and theologians are now dealing with world or global philosophy, a vision of philosophy that includes ancient, medieval, and modern Western thinkers, as well as Asian, African, and primal authors and texts—philosophy and theology are viewed as being truly ecumenical disciplines. Watson's and Dilworth's hermeneutical and historical hypothesis is that the diversity of fundamental philosophic worldviews is a permanent and welcomed feature of all critical human thought. Therefore, the basic approach of archic analysis is contextual, hermeneutical, and historical in nature.

Watson contends that the history of philosophy, at least in the West, goes through a characteristic cycle of styles, moving

> . . . from an ontic epoch concerned with that which is, or being, to an epistemic epoch concerned with how we know that which is, or knowing, to a semantic epoch concerned with the expression of what we know about that which is, or meaning, and back again to an ontic epoch concerned with being. (1985, 5)

Watson avers that we are now living in a semantic or hermeneutic age. Contemporary North Atlantic thinkers often argue that the world is constituted by its "intertextuality," the self-referencing of text and reader in dialogue with each other. "The word *text* is here used in a broad sense to include any expression of thought, not merely expressions of thought in words" (Watson 1985, 13). For instance, the shout of a Zen master in medieval Japan is as much a text as is the whole modern Taisho Tripitaka, the largest single collection of scriptures for any tradition. A Shang dynasty bronze ritual vessel is as expressive of the world of the form and function of bronze technology and artistic and religious style as are the collected works of Confucius, Mencius, Hsün Tzu, Han Yü, Chu Hsi, Wang Yang-ming, or Tai Chen.

Following Justus Buchler, Dilworth further expands the meaning of a text when he states, "All texts convey meaning in an assertive (prepositional), active (morally and politically agential), and exhibitive (aesthetic, performative) modes of expression or judgment" (1989, 18). However, both Watson and Dilworth argue that the world itself is never a text per se because it is always viewed through a particular perspective of an archic profile. Any view of the world as a whole is an interpretation of the world, the expression of its own architectonic analysis, even if it is not self-consciously articulated as such. For instance, there is something brilliantly cohesive about Chuang Tzu's vision of spontaneity, although it is self-consciously the least systematic of all of the great classical Chinese philosophies.

One reason for the appeal of Chuang Tzu is the potent strength of the metaphors devised by this classical Chinese Taoist thinker. H. G. Creel observed that Plato and Chuang Tzu, along with being two of the most important thinkers in the history of the world, also were artistic geniuses of the highest order. In Chuang Tzu's case, this artistic brilliance found expression in the wonderful, strange, and sometimes even bizarre world of images and metaphors Chuang Tzu piles upon us until we blink in the beauty of it all, even if we are not able to state in strictly propositional terms what we have learned. But no one who has pondered Chuang Tzu's story of the dreaming butterfly will ever look at the world, the mind, or the self in quite the same way. The power of Chuang Tzu resides in the metaphors he suggests we use in order to live in difficult times. A strong case could be made, following the work of George Lakoff and Mark Johnson on metaphor and prototype theory (1980, 1987, 1993), that Chuang Tzu is an example of a philosopher working in the exhibitive and metaphoric mode of discourse rather than in an assertive mode. And if Lakoff and Johnson are correct, the metaphor is the mother of all propositions.

As we examine the history of global thought, modern English philosophic and theological categoreal vocabulary works well enough when used to describe and analyze the religions and philosophies of West Asia and Europe. At least in their theoretical moments, all of these traditions made extensive use of the assertive and active modes of discourse as defined by Buchler (1966). It was out of this matrix of Judaism, Christianity, Greco-Roman civilization, and Islam that the modern categories of the history of Western thought arose, even if their modern venue is the post–Enlightenment secular academy. The terminological precision and usefulness of the West Asian and European vocabulary begins to wane when we reach India. The language continues to work fairly well with the theistic portions of what is now called Hinduism, but creaks when applied to the nontheistic sections of the great family of Indian traditions. Scholars really start to notice problems when the terminology is applied to the Buddhist tradition wherever it is found in Asia. Once East Asia is reached, there is real confusion. For instance, in the early study of Confucianism, no one was ever sure whether Confucianism was a religion, a philosophy, or something else altogether.

THE METHOD OF ARCHIC ANALYSIS

Fundamentally, archic analysis is a simple method based on the use of Aristotle's four questions about the nature and causes of the cosmos.[1] It is a typology constructed around the analysis of texts using four archic variables of textual signification. The claim is that every text has: (1) an authorial perspective or standpoint on the world; (2) a vision of reality of the world embedded in the text; this expresses what the text takes to be the ultimately real, and this vision of ultimate reality, in turn, is governed by; (3) a method that entails the text's logical or discursive format or the method of articulation the text uses to order or combine its concepts; and finally, (4) every text has a unique principle of organization, its root metaphor; this is the text's ultimate integrating intention. Because he deals extensively with Asian texts, we will follow Dilworth's definition of terms (1989, 173–74).

The first assumption of archic analysis depends on defining what Watson and Dilworth call the four archic variables, followed by specifying the particular archic values for each text. These four variables define the "archic profile" of each text. As Watson says, "In order to have a name for what we are seeking, I will call the internal variable essential to any text, whose values are causes of its functioning, and are reciprocally prior to one another, *archic variables*" (Watson 1985, 13). Watson also claims that "All texts that are not fragmentary will have their archic elements. . . . The archic elements of a text may be reasonably obscure and confused, however, and it will be best to seek them in texts in which they are clearest" (1985, 13).

Nor does it matter how long or short the text is. The text could be the whole of a tradition, as is the case when we commonly talk about religions in terms of being specific entities such as Christianity, Islam, Judaism, Hinduism, Taoism, Shintoism, Confucianism, and so forth. A text can be as short, as Dilworth notes, as the Ho! shout of a Zen master. For instance, within the rhetorical context of Zen Buddhism, such a shout speaks volumes about the nature of philosophic discourse and the ultimate nature of reality, or in this case, nothingness; it also points to the realization of no-mind and enlightenment. Or the notion of concern-consciousness shines through Chang Tsai's "Western Inscription," demonstrating the profound nature of the Sung Neo-Confucian commitment to and importance of the world and its humane values.

A second methodological assumption is that the world has many philosophic texts. In fact, the world, can be described in terms of the intertextuality of its multiple texts. With its own philosophic commitments, archic analysis is part of the new pluralism in North American philosophy.[2] Archic analysis, because of the nature of its variables, acknowledges pluralism as an irreducible part of the world we confront. It seeks to explain pluralism and offer a way to organize the texts we find expressing major worldviews. It recognizes that its method of organization is predicated on its own archic variables and hence will be contested by other philosophic schools that do not share a pluralist reading of philosophy, history, or the cosmos.[3] Hence, archic analysis presents only one version of hermeneutical interpretation.[4] Of course, Watson and Dilworth recognize the ideal nature of their description; actual philosophers and theologians, just like all other human beings, do not always organize their thoughts into neat little patterns. People change their minds and are disorganized. However, most great philosophers do have some systematic way of reading the world and this is what archic analysis tries to tease out of their texts. In fact, we recognize philosophers as being "great" because they have the ability to organize thought in cohesive and persuasive ways that others lack; great philosophers make us see the world through the lens of their theories. While great philosophers may not claim to be systematic thinkers—Confucius, Chuang Tzu, and Plato are examples of philosophers not noted for the perfect organization of their thoughts—other intellectuals perceive their ability to present ideas via inviting patterns of thought, action, and passion.

In summary, the four variables or factors of semantic control include the following:

1. *Perspective*: the text's voice, as self-validating epistemic warrant
2. *Reality*: the text's reference to what is ultimately real, not just apparent
3. *Method*: the text's logical or conceptual form
4. *Principle*: the text's motivating and integrating intention (Dilworth 1989, 173–74)

Watson and Dilworth further stipulate that each of these fundamental archic variables can be additionally specified in terms of four more values for each variable.

Perspectives

1. Personal: subjective, idiocentric, the self-presentation of the author, often as a first person singular voice.
2. Objective: impersonal, normal, unexceptional, often the voice of the author as narrator or spectator of the given world and its objects.
3. Diaphanic: religious, revelatory of a higher view, often a prophetic form of discourse that bears witness to a greater illumination.
4. Disciplinary: schooled, expert, competent, universally referenced, often the 'we' voice of the community of scholars who share a theoretical perspective or a group of scientists working within one paradigm.

Realities

1. Existential: immediately lived, contingently experiential, often the world of immediate acts.
2. Substrative: material, underlying, recondite, cryptic, suppressed, that which underlies all reality, that which must be traced back to its true and perhaps hidden source or force or matter.
3. Noumenal: supersensibly general and ideal, that which transcends the surface of reality, that which exists as transphenomenal or eternal.
4. Essential: historically general and ideal, the world as recurring or normative forms, self-defining structures or values.

Methods

1. Agonistic: paradoxical, texts of contending forces, or good or evil without any possibility of compromise or conciliation.
2. Logistic: computational, texts that present simple units or measures, such as atoms, ideas, essences, ideas, or computer bytes.
3. Dialectical: sublational, the logic of higher integration, the text of synthesis wherein everything is subsumed into a new reality.
4. Synoptic: problematic, the textual analysis of problems by means of general and specific, the analysis of the relationship of wholes and parts.

Principles

1. Creative: volitional, making a difference, the text makes a difference in that the new replaces the old and the world is transformed through creativity.
2. Elemental: simple, self-same, repetitious, recycling; that all is the same, the absolute identity or indifference of things, of conservation, of repetition, of oneness, of things without parts.
3. Comprehensive: totalistic, hierarchically encompassing, Plato's Idea of the Good, the multiplicity of forms, norms, or values.
4. Reflexive: autonomously active and self-completing, Aristotle's recognition of the diversity of functions, the autonomy or telos of things, that each thing has its specific nature.

Because of their Aristotelian foundations, Watson and Dilworth provide lists of what they call "pure modes" or complete semiotic profiles based on the history of Greek thought as interpreted by Aristotle. The four profiles are named after the most representative Greek philosopher presenting these "pure" types. Any other order of the variables is called "mixed modes."[5] While there may be some merit to this procedure in the West, where most philosophers are, as Whitehead noted, footnotes to Plato (often as interpreted by Aristotle), to call this a "pure" profile in terms of global thought makes less than perfect sense when applied to Islamic, Indic, or East Asian materials. For comparative purposes, I have included the archic profiles of Chu Hsi, A. N. Whitehead, R. C. Neville, and Watson and Dilworth. It will be noted that archic profiles of Chu, Whitehead, and Neville are affine, save for Chu's comprehensive principle. At least in terms of archic analysis, Neville is more like Chu and Whitehead than it might appear on the surface. I also have included an even more extensive list of the archic profiles of major Chinese philosophers interspersed with other Indian and European thinkers for comparative purposes.

THE ARCHIC ANALYSIS OF CHU HSI

Archic analysis is especially useful in discovering how thinkers using a common philosophic vocabulary, such as in the case for the Confucian tradition, often use the same inherited concepts with dramatically different shades of meaning. Archic analysis allows us to dig deeper, to use computer jargon, into the operating systems of the philosophy, the controlling insights of the tradition, below even the particular software of the individual thinker. For instance, both Chu Hsi and Wang Yang-ming (1472–1529) are famous for their fascination with the notion of *hsin*/mind–heart. But Chu's and Wang's root metaphors for the mind–heart are different. For Wang, the mind–heart expresses an elemental Mencian simplicity of fundamental goodness, whereas for Chu Hsi, *hsin* represents a comprehensive principle of potential universal good as would be the case for Confucius and the *Book of Changes* (and perhaps Hsün Tzu as well). For Wang, one must have the basic insight into the mind–heart on the basis of self-cultivation, whereas for Chu Hsi, one must carry out the arduous process of the investigation of things and events before the mind–heart can become the organ of pellucid insight.[6] Archic analysis helps us get behind the mask of verbal similarities to discover what is going on at a more schematic level.

According to my interpretation of Chu Hsi, I propose the following archic profile:

1. Disciplinary Perspective
2. Essentialist Ontological Focus
3. Dialectical Method
4. Comprehensive Principle

I differ with Dilworth (1989, 97–102; 219) in that I believe Chu Hsi developed a disciplinary rather than a diaphanic perspective. While it is true that Chu Hsi, along with the other major Northern and Southern Sung philosophic Neo-Confucians, postulated that they were exploring and expounding the truth, they did so as a community of scholars first and foremost. As Peter Bol (1992) and Hoyt Tillman (1992) have demonstrated so conclusively, the Sung philosophers elaborated their work as a fellowship of thinkers. The Sung philosophers shared a common research project and were willing to undergo mutual correction and criticism. The path seeking discernment was almost as important, because it was open to critical correction, as the final goal of comprehensive understanding. Besides, according to Chu's process view of reality, there was never really any final goal because of the generative nature of the comos.

In fact, the maturation and completion of Chu Hsi's own thought is the outcome of just this sort of interchange.[7] He began the reformulation of the tradition that he learned from his teacher Li T'ung (1093–1163) through a series of exchanges with his friend Chang Shih (1138–1180) on the nature of the mind. This exchange of ideas with Chang, who was a partisan of the Hu school, commenced when Chu Hsi was about thirty-seven and continued, at least in terms of Chu Hsi's maturation, into his early forties. Chu Hsi's "great turn" toward his own mature position took place between his forty-first and forty-third year, the year when he composed his definitive "new" treatise of

Chung-ho (Mou 1968–1969, 3:176–228). In the history of Chinese thought, this awakening was as important as Kant's reading of Hume. The outcome of Chu's philosophic awakening was the complete transformation of the Neo-Confucian tradition.

My archic profile of Whitehead agrees with Dilworth and Watson.

1. Disciplinary Perspective
2. Essentialist Ontological Focus
3. Dialectical Method
4. Creative Principle

As can be seen, Chu Hsi and Whitehead are affined except for the fourth variable, principle—with the contrast between the creative and comprehensive modalities of their thought. Here Whitehead, as do most philosophers influenced by the Western Christian tradition, has a creative principle. As the *Book of Revelation* teaches about divine creativity, lo, behold, all things are made new. "Look, I am making the whole of creation new" (*Revelation* 21: 5; New Jerusalem Bible). Archic analysis helps confirm, on different grounds, Needham's insight into the striking "family" relationship of these two forms of process and relational philosophy in terms of certain deep and governing functions of their thought.

EXTENDING THE ANALYSIS

It is interesting to speculate, given the importance of creativity in both Chu and Whitehead, about how archic analysis might be further refined in light of these family similarities, differences, and shared metaphors. Dilworth argues, in terms of his Aristotelian reading of archic principles, that Whitehead has a creative principle whereas Chu has a typically Confucian comprehensive principle. I have no quarrel with Dilworth as far as the initial analysis goes. Perhaps even more illuminating would be to ask, from within the perspective of a global vision of process thought, whether Chu Hsi's comprehensive principle has become so vast that it verges on becoming a principle of creativity. For instance, the role of yin–yang forces within the dynamic *ch'i* gives one pause about whether one can ever assign too much generativity to Chu Hsi's notion of principle.

I have made the argument for creativity in exposition and substance for Chu Hsi's thought in other studies (Berthrong 1979, 1994). Furthermore, Mou Tsung-san, Tu Wei-ming, Liu Shu-hsien, and Cheng Chung-ying have all declared creativity an essential feature of Confucian moral metaphysics in all of its characteristic Sung, Yüan, Ming, and Ch'ing formulations. And what

Pure Forms of Greek Archic Profiles

	Perspective	Reality	Method	Principle
Sophistic	personal	existential	agonistic	creative
Democritean	objective	material	logistic	elemental
Platonic	diaphanic	noumenal	dialectical	comprehensive
Aristotelian	disciplinary	essential	synoptic	reflexive

Profiles of Chu Hsi, Whitehead, and Neville

Chu Hsi	disciplinary	essentialist	dialectical	comprehensive
Whitehead	disciplinary	essentialist	dialectical	creative
Neville	disciplinary	essentialist	dialectical	creative

about Whitehead? Does his cosmology become so encompassing that the category of creativity becomes a creative *and* comprehensive principle in archic analysis? Questions like this will drive the practitioners of archic analysis into deeper and more sustained meditations on the specifics of each tradition. In our case, the resolution of such a question may help with the question of creativity in Whitehead's thought.

Until a much more comprehensive cross-cultural list is compiled, the following three sets of archic profiles will outline the "pure" modes based on the classical Greek tradition, the profiles of Chu, Whitehead, and Neville, and a general list of profiles with a special focus on the Confucian tradition. Because the Watson–Dilworth method itself is a text, its archic profile is (1) disciplinary in authorial perspective, (2) essential in worldview, (3) synoptic in method, and (4) reflexive in principle. Watson and Dilworth faithfully follow Aristotle.

CONFUCIAN AND GENERAL PROFILES

Hermeneutic typologies such as archic analysis are always "ideal" types in the Weberian sense that they are composites drawn from the actual practice of philosophy and theology. Archic analysis can never replace the careful reading of outstanding individual texts, because these seminal texts of world philosophy and religion always contain unexpected new possibilities for interpretation. Only a careful reading of specific texts will discover if the differences that appear in a typological analysis are real or illusory when one examines the details of the particular historical development and richness of content that every world-constituting text provides.

For instance, according to Dilworth, both Hsün Tzu and St. Paul have creative principles, but no one would mistake one for the other. Life is in the details. Beyond taxonomies there is the fecundity and genius of individual thought that must be honored in any coductive and dialogical exchange. However, taxonomies are wonderful maps, and it does help to have a common understanding of where we begin. If archic analysis helps in the beginning, it will have made its contribution to comparative thought.

GLOBAL COMPARATIVE ARCHIC PROFILES

Confucius	*Hsün-tzu*	*Mencius*	(Archic Profile)
diaphanic	objective	diaphanic	perspective
essentialist	essentialist	essentialist	reality
agonistic	agonistic	agonistic	method
comprehensive	creative	elemental	principle

Mo Tzu	*Chuang Tzu*	*Lao Tzu*	(Archic Profile)
personal	diaphanic	diaphanic	perspective
substrative	substrative	substrative	reality
logistic	agonistic	dialectical	method
comprehensive	elemental	elemental	principle

Yang Chu	*Kung-sun Lung*	*I Ching*	(Archic Profile)
personal	objective	diaphanic	perspective
substrative	essentialist	essentialist	reality
logistic	logistic	dialectical	method
elemental	comprehensive	comprehensive	principle

Tsou Yen	*Han Fei Tzu*	*Tung Chung-shu*	(Archic Profile)
objective	objective	diaphanic	perspective
essentialist	substrative	essentialist	reality
dialectical	agonistic	dialectical	method
comprehensive	creative	comprehensive	principle

Wang Ch'ung	*Shao Yung*	*Chang Tsai*	(Archic Profile)
objective	diaphanic	diaphanic	perspective
substrative	substrative	substrative	reality
agonistic	dialectical	dialectical	method
elemental	elemental	elemental	principle

Chou Tun-i	Ch'eng Hao	Ch'eng I	(Archic Profile)
diaphanic	diaphanic	diaphanic	perspective
essential	essentialist	essentialist	reality
dialectical	dialectical	dialectical	method
comprehensive	comprehensive	comprehensive	principle

Lu Hsiang-shan	Lo Ch'in-shun	Wang Fu-chih	(Archic Profile)
diaphanic	diaphanic	objective	perspective
essentialist	essentialist	substrative	reality
agonistic	dialectical	logistic	method
elemental	comprehensive	creative	principle

Yen Yüan	Tai Chen	Hindu	(Archic Profile)
objective	objective	diaphanic	perspective
substrative	existentialist	noumenal	reality
logistic	logistic	dialectical	method
creative	elemental	elemental	elemental

Chu Hsi	Wang Yang-ming	Augustine	(Archic Profile)
disciplinary	diaphanic	diaphanic	perspective
essentialist	essentialist	noumenal	reality
dialectical	dialectical	dialectical	method
comprehensive	elemental	creative	principle

Aristotle	Ch'an/Zen	Buddhism	(Archic Profile)
disciplinary	diaphanic	diaphanic	perspective
essentialist	existential	existential	reality
synoptic	dialectical	agonistic	method
reflexive	elemental	elemental	principle

Islam	Judaism	Christianity	(Archic Profile)
diaphanic	diaphanic	diaphanic	perspective
noumenal	noumenal	noumenal	reality
agonistic	dialectical	dialectical	method
creative	creative	creative	principle

Christian Mystic	Whitehead	Taoist	(Archic Profile)
diaphanic	disciplinary	diaphanic	perspective
noumenal	essentialist	substrative	reality
dialectical	dialectical	dialectical	method
elemental	creative	elemental	principle

Watson–Dilworth	Neville	Plato	(Archic Profile)
disciplinary	disciplinary	diaphanic	perspective
essentialist	essentialist	noumenal	reality
synoptic	dialectical	dialectical	method
reflexive	creative	comprehensive	principle

Berthrong			(Archic Profile)
disciplinary			perspective
essentialist			reality
synoptic			method
creative			principle

NOTES

1. The modern stimulus for Watson's work is found in the philosophy of Richard McKeon of the University of Chicago. For instance, McKeon was a defender of the notion of the inherent pluralism of the philosophic enterprise. For a collection of his classic articles on this and other topics, see McKeon (1990). While McKeon's vocabulary is different, his vision of philosophic pluralism is clearly the direct ancestor of Watson's method.

2. See *The Monist*, Vol. 73, No. 3 (July 1990) for a series of articles discussing the notion of systematic pluralism. Both Watson and Dilworth contribute articles to the issue. Andrew Reck contributes a historical study of pluralism as a recent philosophic option. Corrington (1994) has another analysis of pluralism wherein he notes that there are four different types: (1) descriptive naturalism, (2) honorific naturalism, (3) process naturalism, and (4) ecstatic naturalism. From Corrington's point of view, the naturalism of this essay is a species of process naturalism in that it embraces a radical affirmation of cosmological pluralism.

3. For instance, Neville, because of his commitment to a Platonic dialectic, will never find archic analysis a useful tool because it makes use of a synoptic method. Neville is always seeking a higher dialectical synthesis, whereas archic analysis is more comfortable with a buzzing pluralism of philosophic styles that refuse to be unified by any all-embracing dialectic.

4. For an account of the rise of modern hermeneutic theory, see Grondin (1994).

5. An interesting question for the future development of archic analysis is to ask the broader question of whether one can fashion a list of "pure modes" that does not depend on Aristotle and the Greek tradition. For instance, what would the list look like if based on the classical Chinese tradition beginning with Confucius and ending with the late Legalist and Neo-Mohist texts? Or even more widely based, what would the methodology look like if one tried to find the ur-texts of Eurasia? And of course this does not begin to entertain what the profiles would be like if texts from Africa and the Native American indigenous traditions were included.

I believe Watson and Dilworth would argue, at least in the beginning, that one has to start somewhere. Hence we could begin with European, Islamic, Indic, or East Asian thought and develop more specialized lists of archic variables if we wanted to. But in the end, this would simply serve to make the point about the pluralistic nature of philosophy. Nonetheless, once the benchmark archic profiles have been provided for the Islamic, Indic, and East Asian intellectual worlds, it would be intriguing to contrast and compare these lists with the four "pure modes" of Watson and Dilworth. Would it be possible to develop a transcultural list of characteristic archic profiles? But even if this is done, what would it provide beyond the endless exuberance of the human mind?

6. Again, P. J. Ivanhoe offers an insightful metaphor for Wang's way in moral self-cultivation. If Chu has a recovery model, then Wang has a form of "*moral therapy*, designed to address this pernicious form of self-deception" (1993, 70). Wang is particularly concerned to find ways to overcome the obscurations that cover Mencius's primal good human nature. For Wang, mere recovery is not enough; we must begin with an effective therapy to be able to recover anything of value whatsoever.

7. The best study we have of the development and maturation of Chu Hsi's thought is Liu Shu-hsien (1982). Zhang Liwen (1981) also has provided us with an excellent study of Chu Hsi's thought. In English, we have Donald Munro (1988) and Hoyt Tillman (1992). This revolution in Chu Hsi studies rests on the labor of the previous generation of Chinese scholars such as T'ang Chün-i, Ch'ien Mu, Wing-tsit Chan, and Mou Tsung-san. For instance, Wing-tsit Chan's meticulous studies of all aspects of Chu Hsi's thought over the last three decades have provided invaluable insight into Chu's place in Chinese and world philosophy.

BIBLIOGRAPHY

Ames, Roger. 1993. *Sun-tzu: The Art of Warfare.* New York: Ballantine Books.

Basinger, David. 1988. *Divine Power in Process Theism: A Philosophic Critique.* Albany: State University of New York Press.

Berger, Peter L. 1992. *A Far Glory: The Quest for Faith in an Age of Credulity.* New York: Free Press.

Berger, Peter L., and Thomas Luckmann. 1995. *Modernity, Pluralism and the Crisis of Meaning.* Gütersloh: Bertelsmann Foundation.

Berlin, Isaiah. 1992. *The Crooked Timber of Humanity: Chapters in the History of Ideas.* Edited by Henry Hardy. New York: Vintage Books.

Bernstein, Richard J. 1988. *Beyond Objectivism and Relativism: Science, Hermeneutics, and Praxis.* Philadelphia: University of Pennsylvania Press.

————. 1992. *The New Constellation: The Ethical-Political Horizons of Modernity/Postmodernity.* Cambridge, Mass.: MIT Press.

Berthrong, John. 1979. "Glosses on Reality: Chu Hsi as Interpreted by Ch'en Ch'un." Ph.D. dissertation, University of Chicago.

————. 1993. "Master Chu's Self-Realization: The Role of *Ch'eng.*" *Philosophy East and West* 43 (1).

————. 1994. *All under Heaven: Transforming Paradigms in Confucian-Christian Dialogue.* Albany: State University of New York Press.

————. 1998. *Transformations of the Confucian Way.* Boulder, CO: Westview Press.

Birdwhistell, Anne D. 1989. *Transition to Neo-Confucianism: Shao Yung on Knowledge and Symbols of Reality.* Stanford, Calif.: Stanford University Press.

————. 1996. *Li Yong (1627–1705) and Epistemological Dimensions of Confucian Philosophy.* Stanford, Calif.: Stanford University Press.

Birch, Charles, and John B. Cobb, Jr. 1981. *The Liberation of Life: From the Cell to the Community.* Cambridge, Mass.: Cambridge University Press.

Black, Alison Harley. 1989. *Man and Nature in the Philosophical Thought of Wang Fu-chih.* Seattle: University of Washington Press.

Bloom, Irene, trans. and ed. 1987. *Knowledge Painfully Acquired: The K'un-chih chi by Lo Ch'in-shun.* New York: Columbia University Press.

Bol, Peter K. 1992. *"This Culture of Ours": Intellectual Transitions in T'ang and Sung China.* Stanford, Calif.: Stanford University Press.

Booth, Wayne C. 1988. *The Company We Keep: An Ethics of Fiction.* Berkeley: University of California Press.

Bracken, Jospeh A. 1995. *The Divine Matrix: Creativity as Link between East and West.* Maryknoll, N.Y.: Orbis Books.

Brightman, Edgar Sheffield. 1946. *A Philosophy of Religion.* New York: Prentice-Hall.

Browning, Don S. 1991. *A Fundamental Practical Theology: Descriptive and Strategic Proposals.* Minneapolis, Minn.: Fortress Press.

Bruce, J. Percy. 1923. *Chu Hsi and His Masters: An Introduction to Chu Hsi and the Sung School of Chinese Philosophy.* London: Probsthain; New York: AMS Press, 1973 (reprint).

Buchler, Justus. 1961. *The Concept of Method.* New York: Columbia University Press.

———. 1966. *The Metaphysics of Natural Complexes.* New York: Columbia University Press.

———. 1974. *The Main of Light: On the Concept of Poetry.* New York: Oxford University Press.

Cahoone, Lawrence E. 1995. *The Ends of Philosophy.* Albany: State University of New York Press.

Callicott, J. Baird, and Roger T. Ames, eds. 1989. *Nature in Asian Thought: Essays in Environmental Philosophy.* Albany: State University of New York Press.

Capps, Walter H. 1995. *Religious Studies: The Making of a Discipline.* Minneapolis, Minn.: Fortress Press.

Carman, John B. 1994. *Majesty and Meekness: A Comparative Study of Contrast and Harmony in the Concept of God.* Grand Rapids, Mich.: Eerdmans.

Chan, Alan K. L. 1991. *Two Visions of the Tao: A Study of Wang Pi and the Ho-shang Kung Commentaries on the Lao Tzu.* Albany: State University of New York Press.

Chan Sin-wai. 1984. *An Exposition of Benevolence: The Jen-hsüeh of T'an Ssu-t'ung.* Hong Kong: Chinese University Press.

———. 1985. *Buddhism in Late Ch'ing Political Thought.* Hong Kong: Chinese University Press.

Chan, Wing-tsit. 1963. *A Source Book in Chinese Philosophy.* Princeton, N.J.: Princeton University Press.

———. 1969. *Neo-Confucianism, Etc.: Essays by Wing-tsit Chan.* Hanover, N.H.: Oriental Society.

————. 1987. *Chu Hsi: Life and Thought*. Hong Kong: Chinese University of Hong Kong.

————. 1989. *Chu Hsi: New Studies*. Honolulu: University of Hawaii Press.

Chang, Carsun. 1957–62. *The Development of Neo-Confucian Thought*. 2 vols. New York: Bookman.

Chao, Shun-sun (ca. 1243). 1973. *Ssu-shu tsuan-shu* [Collected Annotations on the *Four Books*]. Kao-shiung, Taiwan: n. p.

Chaves, Jonathan. 1993. *Sing of the Source: Nature and Gospel in the Poetry of the Chinese Painter Wu Li*. Honolulu: University of Hawaii Press, SHAPS Library of Translations.

Ch'en Ch'un (1159–1223). 1986. *Neo-Confucian Terms Explained (The Pei-hsi tzu-i)*. Translated and edited by Wing-tsit Chan. New York: Columbia University Press.

Cheng, Chung-ying. 1991. *New Dimensions of Confucian and Neo-Confucian Philosophy*. Albany: State University of New York Press.

Ch'ien Mu. 1971. *Chu-tzu hsin hsüeh-an* [A New Study of Chu Hsi]. 5 vols. Taipei: San Min shu-chü.

Chin, Ann-ping, and Mansfield Freeman, trans. 1990. *Tai Chen on Mencius: Explorations in Words and Meaning*. New Haven, Conn.: Yale University Press.

Ching, Julia. 1993. *Chinese Religions*. Maryknoll, N.Y.: Orbis Books.

Ching, Julia, and Willard G. Oxtoby. 1992a. *Moral Enlightenment: Leibniz and Wolff on China*. Monumenta Serica Monograph Series XXVI. Nettetal: Steyler Verlag.

Ching, Julia, and Willard G. Oxtoby, eds. 1992b. *Discovering China: European Interpretations in the Enlightenment*. Rochester, NY: Rochester University Press.

Choung Haechung, and Han Hyong-jo, eds. 1996. *Confucian Philosophy in Korea*. Kyonggi-do: Academy of Korean Studies.

Chow, Kai-wing. 1994. *The Rise of Confucian Ritualism in Late Imperial China: Ethics, Classics, and Lineage Discourse*. Stanford, Calif.: Stanford University Press.

Chow, Rey. 1991. *Woman and Chinese Modernity: The Politics of Reading between East and West*. Minneapolis: University of Minnesota Press.

Christian, William A. 1959. *An Interpretation of Whitehead's Metaphysics*. New Haven, Conn.: Yale University Press.

Chu Hsi. 1922. *The Philosophy of Human Nature*. Translated by J. Percy Bruce. London: Probsthain; New York: AMS Press, 1973 (reprint).

————. 1971. *Ssu-shu chi-chu* [Commentaries on the *Four Books*]. Taipei: Chung Hwa Book Company, Ltd.; *Ssu-bu pei-yao* (SPPY) Edition.

————. 1991. *Further Reflections on Things at Hand: A Reader.* Translated by Allen Wittenborn. Lanham, M.D.: University Press of America.

Chu Hsi, and Lü Tsu-ch'ien, eds. 1967. *Reflections on Things at Hand: The Neo-Confucian Anthology.* Translated by Wing-tsit Chan. New York: Columbia University Press.

Chung, Edward Y. J. 1995. *The Korean Neo-Confucianism of Yi T'oegye and Yi Yulgok: A Reappraisal of the "Four-Seven Thesis" and Its Practical Implications for Self-cultivation.* Albany: State University of New York Press.

Clooney, Francis X., S.J. 1993. *Theology after Vedanta: An Experiment in Comparative Theology.* Albany: State University of New York Press.

Cobb, John B., Jr. 1965. *A Christian Natural Theology.* Philadelphia: Westminster Press.

Cobb, John B., Jr., and David Ray Griffin. 1976. *Process Theology: An Introductory Exposition.* Philadelphia: Westminster Press.

Confucius. 1992. *Confucius: The Analects.* Translated by D. C. Lau. Hong Kong: Chinese University Press.

Corrington, Robert S. 1987. *The Community of Interpreters: On the Hermeneutics of Nature and the Bible in the American Philosophic Tradition.* Macon, G.A.: Mercer University Press.

————. 1992. *Nature and Spirit: An Essay in Ecstatic Naturalism.* New York: Fordham University Press.

————. 1994. *Ecstatic Naturalism: Signs of the World.* Bloomington: Indiana University Press.

Cua, A.S. 1978. *Dimensions of Moral Creativity: Paradigms, Principles, and Ideals.* University Park and London: Pennsylvania State University Press.

————. 1982. *The Unity of Knowledge and Action: A Study of Wang Yang-ming's Moral Psychology.* Honolulu: Univeristy of Hawaii Press.

————. 1985. *Ethical Argumentation: A Study in Hsün Tzu's Moral Epistemology.* Honolulu: University of Hawaii Press.

————. 1992. "The Idea of Confucian Tradition." *Review of Metaphysics* 45 (4): 803–40.

Dean, Thomas, ed. 1995. *Religious Pluralism and Truth: Essays on Cross-Cultural Philosophy of Religion.* Albany: State University of New York Press.

Dean, William, and Larry E. Axel, eds. 1985. *The Size of God: The Theology of Bernard Loomer in Context.* Macon, Ga.: Mercer University Press.

De Bary, Wm. Theodore. 1981. *Neo-Confucian Orthodoxy and the Learning of the Mind-and-Heart.* New York: Columbia University Press.

————. 1983. *The Liberal Tradition in China.* Hong Kong and New York: Chinese University Press and Columbia University Press.

————. 1988. *East Asian Civilizations: A Dialogue in Five Stages.* Cambridge, Mass.: Harvard University Press.

————. 1991. *Learning for One's Self: Essays on the Individual in Neo-Confucian Thought.* New York: Columbia University Press.

————. 1993. "The Uses of Neo-Confucianism: A Response to Professor Tillman." *Philosophy East and West*, 43 (3): 541–55.

De Silva, Lynn A. 1979. *The Problem of the Self in Buddhism and Christianity.* London: Macmillan.

Dilworth, David A. 1989. *Philosophy in World Perspective: A Comparative Hermeneutics of the Major Theories.* New Haven, Conn., and London: Yale University Press.

Egan, Ronald C. 1994. *Word, Image, and Deed in the Life of Su Shi.* Cambridge, Mass.: Harvard University Press.

Elman, Benjamin A. 1984. *From Philosophy to Philology: Intellectual and Social Aspects of Change in Late Imperial China.* Cambridge, Mass.: Harvard University Press.

————. 1990. *Classicism, Politics, and Kinship: The Ch'ang-Chou School of New Text Confucianism in Late Imperial China.* Berkeley: University of California Press.

Elvin, Mark. 1996. *Another History: Essays on China from a European Perspective.* Canberra, Australia: Wild Peony.

Ely, Stephen Lee. 1983. *The Religious Availability of Whitehead's God: A Critical Analysis.* In Lewis S. Ford and George L. Kline, eds., *Explorations in Whitehead's Philosophy.* New York: Fordham University Press, pp. 170–211.

Emmet, Dorothy M. 1932. *Whitehead's Philosophy of Organism.* London: Macmillian.

Eno, Robert. 1990. *The Confucian Creation of Heaven: Philosophy and the Defense of Ritual Mastery.* Albany: State University of New York Press.

Farley, Edward. 1983. *Theologia: The Fragmentation and Unity of Theological Education.* Philadelphia: Fortress Press.

Feyerabend, Paul. 1987. *Farewell to Reason.* London: Verso.

————. 1988. *Against Method.* London: Verso.

Fingarette, Herbert. 1972. *Confucius—The Secular as Sacred.* New York: Harper & Row.

Ford, James E. 1990. "Systematic Pluralism: An Introduction to an Issue." *The Monist* 73 (3): 335–49.

Ford, Lewis S., ed. 1973. *Two Process Philosophers: Hartshorne's Encounter with Whitehead.* Tallahassee, Fla.: American Academy of Religion.

———. 1978. *The Lure of God: A Biblical Background for Process Theism.* Philadelphia: Fortress Press.

———. 1984. *The Emergence of Whitehead's Metaphysics: 1925–1929.* Albany: State University of New York Press.

———. 1987. "Creativity in a Future Key." In Robert C. Neville, ed., *New Essays in Metaphysics.* Albany: State Universtiy of New York Press: 179–97.

———. 1991. "Contrasting Conceptions of Creation." *Review of Metaphysics.* 45 (1): 89–109.

Gamwell, Franklin I. 1984. *Beyond Preference: Liberal Theories of Independent Associations.* Chicago: University of Chicago Press.

Gardner, Daniel K. 1986. *Chu Hsi and the Ta-hsüeh: Neo-Confucian Reflection on the Confucian Canon.* Cambridge, Mass.: Harvard University Press.

———, trans. and commentary. 1990. *Chu Hsi: Learning to Be a Sage.* Berkeley: University of California Press.

Gedalecia, David. 1971. "Wu Ch'eng: A Neo-Confucian of the Yüan." Ph.D. dissertation, Harvard University.

Gernet, Jacques. 1985. *China and the Christian Impact: A Conflict of Cultures.* Translated by Janet Lloyd. Cambridge, Mass.: Cambridge University Press.

Goodman, Nelson. 1978. *Ways of Worldmaking.* Indianapolis, Ind.: Hackett.

Goodman, Nelson, and Catherine Z. Elgin. 1988. *Reconceptions in Philosophy and Other Arts & Sciences.* Indianaplois, Ind.: Hackett.

Graham, A. C. 1985. *Reason and Spontaneity: A New Solution the Problem of Fact and Value.* London: Curzon Press.

———. 1989. *Disputers of the Tao: Philosophic Argument in Ancient China.* La Salle, Ill.: Open Court.

———. 1992. *Unreason within Reason: Essays on the Outskirts of Rationality.* La Salle, Ill.: Open Court.

Gray, James R. 1982. *Modern Process Thought: A Brief Ideological History.* Lanham, Md.: University Press of America.

Griffin, David Ray. 1981. "Whitehead, God and the Untroubled Mind: A Review Article." *Encounter* 42 (2): 169–88.

———. 1991. *Evil Revisted: Responses and Reconsiderations.* Albany: State University of New York Press.

Griffiths, Paul J. 1991. *An Apology for Apologetics: A Study in the Logic of Interreligious Dialogue.* Maryknoll, N.Y.: Orbis Books.

Grondin, Jean. 1994. *Introduction to Philosophical Hermeneutics*. Translated by Joel Weinscheimer. New Haven, Conn.: Yale University Press.

Hahn, Lewis Edwin, ed. 1991. *The Philosophy of Charles Hartshorne*. La Salle, Ill.: Open Court.

Halbfass, Wilhelm. 1988. *India and Europe: An Essay in Understanding*. Albany: State University of New York Press.

———. 1991. *Tradition and Reflection: Explorations in Indian Thought*. Albany: State University of New York Press.

———. 1992. *On Being and What There Is: Classical Vaisesika and the History of Indian Ontology*. Albany: State University of New York Press.

Hall, David L. 1973. *The Civilization of Experience: A Whiteheadian Theory of Culture*. New York: Fordham University Press.

———. 1982a. *Eros and Irony: A Prelude to Philosophical Anarchism*. Albany: State University of New York Press.

———. 1982b. *The Uncertain Phoenix: Adventures Toward a Post-Cultural Sensibility*. New York: Fordham University Press.

———. 1987. "Logos, Mythos, Chaos: Metaphysics as the Quest for Diversity." In Robert C. Neville, ed., *New Essays in Metaphysics*. Albany: State University of New York Press: 1–24.

———. 1994. *Richard Rorty: Prophet and Poet of the New Pragmatism*. Albany: State University of New York Press.

Hall, David L., and Roger T. Ames. 1987. *Thinking Through Confucius*. Albany: State University of New York Press.

———. 1995. *Anticipating China: Thinking Through the Narratives of Chinese and Western Culture*. Albany: State University of New York Press.

Hansen, Chad. 1983. *Language and Logic in Ancient China*. Ann Arbor: University of Michigan Press.

———. 1992. *A Daoist Theory of Chinese Thought: A Philosophic Interpretation*. Oxford: Oxford University Press.

Harré, Rom, and Michael Krausz. 1996. *Varieties of Relativism*. Oxford: Blackwell.

Hartshorne, Charles. 1948. *The Divine Relativity: A Social Conception of God*. New Haven, Conn.: Yale University Press.

———. 1965. *Anselm's Discovery: A Re-Examination of the Ontological Proof for God's Existence*. La Salle, Ill.: Open Court.

———. 1967. *A Natural Theology for Our Time*. La Salle, Ill.: Open Court.

———. 1970. *Creative Synthesis and Philosophic Method*. La Salle, Ill.: Open Court.

————. 1972. *Whitehead's Philosophy: Selected Essays, 1935–1970*. Lincoln: University of Nebraska Press.

————. 1973. "Ideas and Theses of Process Philosophers." In Lewis S. Ford, ed., *Two Process Philosophers: Hartshorne's Encounter with Whitehead*. Tallahassee, Fla.: American Academy of Religion.

Hartshorne, Charles, John B. Cobb Jr., and Lewis S. Ford. 1980. "Three Responses to Neville's *Creativity and God*." *Process Studies* 10 (3-4) : 93–109.

Heim, S. Mark. 1995. *Salvations: Truth and Difference in Religion*. Maryknoll, N.Y.: Orbis Books.

Henderson, John B. 1984. *The Development and Decline of Chinese Cosmology*. New York: Columbia University Press.

————. 1991. *Scripture, Canon, and Commentary: A Comparison of Confucian and Western Exegesis*. Princeton, N.J.: Princeton University Press.

Hick, John. 1989. *An Interpretation of Religion: Human Responses to the Transcendent*. New Haven, Conn.: Yale University Press.

Hosinski, Thomas E. 1993. *Stubborn Fact and Creatitve Advance: An Introduction to the Metaphysics of Alfred North Whithead*. Lanham, Md.: Rowman and Littlefield.

Huntington, Samuel P. 1996. *The Clash of Civilizations and the Remaking of the World Order*. New York: Simon & Schuster.

Ivanhoe, Philip J. 1990. *Ethics in the Confucian Tradition: The Thought of Mencius and Wang Yang-ming*. Atlanta, Ga.: Scholars Press.

————. 1993. *Confucian Moral Self Cultivation*. New York: Peter Lang.

————, ed. 1996. *Chinese Language, Thought, and Culture: Nivison and His Critics*. La Salle, Ill.: Open Court.

Jensen, Lionel M. 1997. *Manufacturing Confucianism: Chinese Traditions and Universal Civilization*. Durham, N.C.: Duke University Press.

Johnson, Mark. 1987. *The Body in the Mind: The Bodily Basis of Meaning, Imagination, and Reason*. Chicago: University of Chicago Press.

————. 1993. *Moral Imagination: Implications of Cognitive Science for Ethics*. Chicago: University of Chicago Press.

Kalton, Michael C., trans. 1988. *To Become a Sage: The Ten Diagrams on Sage Learning by Yi T'oegye*. New York: Columbia University Press.

Kalton, Michael C., et al. 1994. *The Four-Seven Debate: An Annotated Translation of the Most Famous Controversy in Korean Neo-Confucian Thought*. Albany: State University of New York Press.

Kaufman, Gordon D. 1993. *In the Face of Mystery: A Constructive Theology.* Cambridge, Mass.: Harvard University Press.

Kekes, John. 1993. *The Morality of Pluralism.* Princeton, N.J.: Princeton University Press.

Kjellberg, Paul, and Philip J. Ivanhoe, eds. 1996. *Essays on Skepticism, Relativism, and Ethics in the Zhuangzi.* Albany: State University of New York Press.

Knoblock, John. 1988–1994. *Xunzi: A Translation and Study of the Complete Works.* 3 vols. Stanford: Stanford University Press.

Ko, Dorthy. 1994. *Teachers of the Inner Chambers: Women and Culture in Seventeenth-Century China.* Stanford, Calif.: Stanford University Press.

Kraus, Elizabeth M. 1979. *The Metaphysics of Experience: A Companion to Whitehead's Process and Reality.* New York: Fordham University Press.

Krausz, Michael, and Jack W. Meiland, eds. 1982. *Relativism: Cognitive and Moral.* Notre Dame, Ind.: University of Notre Dame.

———. 1989. *Relativism: Interpretation and Confrontation.* Notre Dame, Ind.: Notre Dame University Press.

Kreiger, David J. 1991. *The New Universalism: Foundations for a Global Theology.* Maryknoll, N.Y.: Orbis Books.

Küng, Hans. 1991. *Global Responsibility: In Search of a New World Ethic.* Translated by John Bowden. New York: Crossroad.

LaCugna, Catherine Mowry. 1991. *God for Us: The Trinity & Christian Life.* San Francisco: Harper San Francisco.

Lakoff, George. 1987. *Women, Fire and Dangerous Things: What Categories Reveal About the Mind.* Chicago: University of Chicago Press.

Lakoff, George, and Mark Johnson. 1980. *Metaphors We Live By.* Chicago: University of Chicago Press.

Lee, Peter K. H. 1991. *Confucian-Christian Encounters in Historical and Contemporary Perspective.* Lewiston, N.Y.: Edwin Mellen Press.

Leibniz, Gottfried Wilhelm. 1977. *Discourse on the Natural Theology of the Chinese.* Translated by Henry Rosemont Jr. and Daniel J. Cook. Honolulu: University of Hawaii Press.

———. 1994. *Writings on China.* Translated and edited by Daniel J. Cook and Henry Rosemont, Jr., LaSalle, Ill.: Open Court.

Lenk, Hans, and Gregor Paul, eds. 1993. *Epistemological Issues in Classical Chinese Philosophy.* Albany: State University of New York Press.

Leys, Simon, trans. 1997. *The Analects of Confucius*. New York: W. W. Norton & Company.

Li, Ching-te (fl. ca. 1270). 1973. *Chu-tzu yü-lei ta-ch'uan* [The Conversations of Master Chu, Topically Arranged]. 8 vols. Tokyo: 1973 Reprint of Japanese Edition of 1668.

Li, Kuang-ti (1642–1718), ed. 1977. *Chu-tzu ch'üan-shu* [The Complete Works of Master Chu]. 2 vols. Taipei: Kuang Hsüeh She Yin Shu Yuan Yin Hsing.

Liu, James T. C. 1988. *China Turning Inward: Intellectual-Political Changes in the Early Twelfth Century*. Cambridge, Mass.: Harvard University Press.

Liu, Shu-hsien. 1982. *Chu-tzu che-hsüeh ssu-hsiang te fan-chan yü yuan-ch'eng* [The Development and Completion of Chu Hsi's Thought]. Taipei: Student Book.

Lovejoy, Arthur O. 1930. *The Revolt Against Dualism: An Inquiry Concerning the Existence of Ideas*. La Salle, Ill.: Open Court.

Lowe, Victor. 1962. *Understanding Whitehead*. Baltimore, Md.: Johns Hopkins University Press.

———. 1985–1990. *Alfred North Whitehead: The Man and His Work*. 2 vols. Vol. 2 edited by J. B. Schneewind. Baltimore, Md.: Johns Hopkins University Press.

Loy, David. 1988. *Nonduality: A Study in Comparative Philosophy*. New Haven: Yale University Press.

Lu, Tonglin. 1991. *Rose and Lotus: Narrative of Desire in France and China*. Albany: State University of New York.

Lynn, Richard John, trans. 1994. *The Classic of Changes: A New Translation of the I-Ching as Interpreted by Wang Bi*. New York: Columbia University Press.

MacFague, Sallie. 1993. *The Body of God: An Ecological Theology*. Minneapolis, Minn.: Fortress Press.

MacIntyre, Alasdair. 1984. *After Virtue: A Study in Moral Theory*. 2d ed. Notre Dame, Ind.: Notre Dame University Press.

———. 1988. *Whose Justice? Which Rationality?* Notre Dame, Ind.: Notre Dame University Press.

———. 1990. *Three Rival Versions of Moral Enquiry: Encyclopaedia, Genealogy and Tradition*. Notre Dame, Ind.: Notre Dame University Press.

Major, John S. 1991. "Substance, Process, Phase: *Wuxing* in the *Huainantzu*." In *Chinese Texts and Philosophic Contexts: Essays Dedicated to Angus C. Graham*. Edited by Henry Rosemont, Jr. La Salle, Ill.: Open Court.

Margolis, Joseph. 1986. *Pragmatism without Foundations: Reconciling Realism and Relativism*. Oxford: Basil Blackwell.

———. 1991. *The Truth About Relativism.* Oxford: Basil Blackwell.

———. 1996. *Life without Principles.* Oxford: Blackwell.

Mays, Wolf. 1959. *The Philosophy of Whitehead.* London: George Allen & Unwin.

McClendon, James William Jr., and James M. Smith. 1994. *Convictions: Defusing Religious Pluralism.* Valley Forge, Penn.: Trinity Press International.

McHenry, Leemon B. 1993. *Whitehead and Bradley: A Comparative Analysis.* Albany: State University of New York Press.

McKeon, Richard, ed. 1941. *The Basic Works of Aristotle.* New York: Random House.

McKeon, Richard. 1987. *Rhetoric: Essays in Invention and Discovery.* Edited by Mark Backman. Woodbridge, Conn.: Ox Bow Press.

———. 1990. *Freedom and History and Other Essays: An Introduction to the Thought of Richard McKeon.* Edited by Zahava K. McKeon. Chicago: University of Chicago Press.

———. 1994. *On Knowing—The Natural Sciences.* Complied by David B. Owen and edited by David B. Owen and Zahava K. McKeon. Chicago: University of Chicago Press.

McLennan, Gregor. 1995. *Pluralism.* Minneapolis, Minn.: University of Minnesota Press.

Mead, George Herbert. 1938. *The Philosophy of the Act.* Edited by Charles W. Morris. Chicago: University of Chicago Press.

———. 1959. *The Philosophy of the Present.* Edited by Arthur E. Murphy. La Salle, Ill.: Open Court.

———. 1967. *Mind, Self, and Society from the Standpoint of a Social Behaviorist.* Edited by Charles W. Morris. Chicago: University of Chicago Press.

Metzger, Thomas A. 1977. *Escape from Predicament: Neo-Confucianism and China's Evolving Political Culture.* New York: Columbia University Press.

Morris, Randall C. 1991. *Process Philosophy and Political Ideology: The Social and Political Thought of Alfred North Whitehead and Charles Hartshorne.* Albany: State University of New York Press.

Mou Tsung-san. 1968-69. *Hsin-t'i yü Hsing-t'i* [Mind and Nature]. 3 vols. Taipei: Cheng Chung shu-chü.

———. 1974. *Chung-kuo che-hsüeh te t'e-chih* [The Special Characteristics of Chinese Philosophy]. Taipei: Student Book Company.

———. 1983. *Chung-kuo che-hsüeh shih-chiu chiang* [Nineteen Lectures on Chinese Philosophy]. Taipei: Student Book Company.

Mungello, David E. 1977. *Leibniz and Confucianism: The Search for Accord*. Honolulu: University of Hawaii Press.

———. 1985. *Curious Land: Jesuit Accommodation and the Origins of Sinology*. Stuttgart: Franz Steiner Verlag Wiesbaden.

Munro, Donald J. 1988. *Images of Human Nature: A Sung Portrait*. Princeton, N.J.: Princeton University Press.

Nagel, Thomas. 1987. *What Does It All Mean? A Very Short Introduction to Philosophy*. New York: Oxford University Press.

Nasr, Seyyed Hossein. 1996. *Religion and the Order of Nature*. New York: Oxford University Press.

Needham, Joseph. 1954–. *Science and Civilisation in China*. 8 vols. Cambridge: Cambridge University Press.

Neville, Robert C. 1968. *God the Creator: On the Transcendence and Presence of God*. Chicago: University of Chicago Press.

———. 1974. *The Cosmology of Freedom*. New Haven and London: Yale University Press.

———. 1978. *Soldier Sage Saint*. New York: Fordham University Press.

———. 1980. *Creativity and God: A Challenge to Process Theology*. New York: Seabury Press.

———. 1981a. "Concerning *Creativity and God*: A Response." *Process Studies* 11 (1): 1–10.

———. 1981b. *Reconstruction of Thinking*. Albany: State University of New York Press.

———. 1982. *The Tao and the Daimon: Segments of a Religious Inquiry*. Albany: State University of New York Press.

———, ed. 1987a. *New Essays in Metaphysics*. Albany: State University of New York Press.

———. 1987b. *The Purtian Smile: A Look Toward Moral Reflection*. Albany: State University of New York Press.

———. 1989. *Recovering the Measure: Interpretation and Nature*. Albany: State University of New York Press.

———. 1991a. *Behind the Masks of God: An Essay Toward Comparative Theology*. Albany: State University of New York Press.

———. 1991b. *A Theology Primer*. Albany: State University of New York Press.

———. 1992. *The High Road Around Modernism*. Albany: State University of New York Press.

———. 1993. *Eternity and Time's Flow*. Albany: State University of New York Press.

———. 1995. *Normative Cultures*. Albany: State University of New York Press.

Newhouse, Richard John. 1994. "A Voice in the Relativistic Wilderness." *Christianity Today* 38 (2): 33–35.

Nivison, David S. 1996. *The Ways of Confucianism: Investigations in Chinese Philosophy*. Edited by Bryan W. Van Norden. La Salle, Ill.: Open Court.

Nobo, Jorge Luis. 1986. *Whitehead's Metaphysics of Extension and Solidarity*. Albany: State University of New York Press.

Oden, Thomas C. 1987. *The Living God: Systematic Theology: Volume One*. San Francisco: Harper San Francisco.

———. 1992. *The Word of Life: Systematic Theology: Volume Two*. San Francisco: Harper San Francisco.

———. 1994. *Life in the Spirit: Systematic Theology: Volume Three*. San Francisco: Harper San Francisco.

Odin, Steve. 1982. *Process Metaphysics and Hua-yen Buddhism: A Critical Study of Cumulative Penetration vs. Interpenetration*. Albany: State University of New York Press.

———. 1996. *The Social Self in Zen and American Pragmatism*. Albany: State University of New York Press.

Oliver, Harold H. 1993. "A New Whiteheadian Hermeneutic." *Creative Transformation* 2 (4): 3–4.

Paglia, Camille. 1991. *Sexual Personae: Art and Decadence from Nefertiti to Emily Dickenson*. New York: Vintage Books.

Panikkar, Raimon. 1993. *The Cosmotheandric Experience: Emerging Religious Consciousness*. Edited with an Introduction by Scott Eastham. Maryknoll, N.Y.: Orbis Books.

Paul, Ellen Frankel, Fred D. Miller Jr., and Jeffery Paul, eds. 1994. *Cultural Pluralism and Moral Knowledge*. Cambridge: Cambridge University Press.

Peerenboom, R. P. 1993. *Law and Morality in Ancient China: The Silk Manuscripts of Huang Lao*. Albany: State University of New York Press.

Pepper, Stephen C. 1942. *World Hypotheses: A Study in Evidence*. Berkeley: University of California Press.

———. 1966. *Concept and Quality: A World Hypothesis*. La Salle, Ill.: Open Court.

Placher, William C. 1989. *Unapologetic Theology: A Christian Voice in a Pluralistic Conversation*. Louisville, Ky.: Westminster/John Knox Press.

Plochmann, George Kimball. 1990. *Richard McKeon: A Study*. Chicago: University of Chicago Press.

Pols, Edward. 1967. *Whitehead's Metaphysics: A Critical Examination of Process and Reality*. Carbondale, Ill.: Southern Illinois University Press.

Price, Lucien. 1954. *Dialogues of Alfred North Whitehead*. Boston: Little, Brown.

Raz, Joseph. 1986. *The Morality of Freedom*. Oxford: Clarendon Press.

Reck, Andrew J. 1990. "An Historical Sketch of Pluralism." *The Monist* 73 (3): 367–87.

Reese, William I., and Eugene Freeman, eds. 1964. *Process and Divinity: Philosophical Essays Presented to Charles Hartshorne*. La Salle, Ill.: Open Court.

Rescher, Nicholas. 1993. *Pluralism: Against the Demands of Consensus*. Oxford: Clarendon Press Oxford.

———. 1996. *Process Metaphysics: An Introduction to Process Philosophy*. Albany: State University of New York Press.

Roetz, Heiner. 1993. *Confucian Ethics of the Axial Age: A Reconstruction under the Aspect of the Breakthrough Toward Postconventional Thinking*. Albany: State University of New York Press.

Rorty, Richard. 1979. *Philosophy and the Mirror of Nature*. Princeton: Princeton University Press.

———. 1982. *Consequences of Pragmatism (Essays 1972–1980)*. Minneapolis, Minn.: University of Minnesota Press.

———. 1989. *Contingency, Irony, and Solidarity*. Cambridge, Mass.: Cambridge University Press.

Rosen, Stanley. 1989. *The Ancients and the Moderns: Rethinking Modernity*. New Haven, Conn.: Yale Univesity Press.

Rozman, Gilbert, ed. 1991. *The East Asian Region: Confucian Heritage and Its Modern Adaptation*. Princeton, N.J.: Princeton University Press.

Schirokauer, Conrad. 1960. "The Political Thought and Behavior of Chu Hsi." Ph.D. dissertation, Stanford University.

Schroeder, W. Widick. 1976. "Religious Institutions and Human Society: A Normative Inquiry Into the Appropriate Contribution of Religious Institutions to Human Life and to the Divine Life." In Philip Hefner and W. Widick Schroeder, eds., *Belonging and Alienation: Religious Foundations for the Human Future*. Chicago: Center for the Scientific Study of Religion: 181–218.

————. 1988. "Political Economy: A Process Interpretation." In W. Widck Schroeder and Franklin I. Gamwell, *Economic Life: Process Interpretations and Critical Responses*. Chicago, Ill.: Center for the Scientific Study of Religion: 183–211.

Schroeder, W. Widick, and Franklin I. Gamwell. 1988. *Economic Life: Process Interpretations and Critical Responses*. Chicago, Ill.: Center for the Scientific Study of Religion.

Schwartz. Benjamin I. 1985. *The World of Thought in Ancient China*. Cambridge, Mass.: The Belknap Press of Harvard University Press.

Searle, John R. 1993. "Rationality and Realism, What is at Stake?" *Daedalus* 122 (4): 55–83.

Setton, Mark. 1997. *Chong Yagyong: Korea's Challenge to Orthodox Neo-Confucianism.* Albany: State University of New Press.

Sherburne, Donald W., ed. 1966. *A Key to Whitehead's Process and Reality*. Bloomington, Ind.: Indiana University Press.

———— 1971. "Whitehead without God." In Delwin Brown, Ralphe E. James Jr., and Gene Reeves, eds., *Process Philosophy and Christian Theology*. Indianapolis, Ind.: Bobbs Merrill.

Shun Kwong-loi. 1993. "*Jen* and *Li* in the *Analects*." *Philosophy East and West* 43 (3): 457–79.

Smith, Huston. 1970. "Transcendence in Traditional China." In *Traditional China*. Edited by James T. C. Liu and Wei-ming Tu. Englewood Cliffs, N.J.: Prentice-Hall

Smith, Richard J., and D. W. Y. Kwok, eds. 1993. *Cosmology, Ontology, and Human Efficacy: Essays in Chinese Thought*. Honolulu: University of Hawaii Press.

Smith, Wilfred Cantwell. 1981. *Towards a World Theology: Faith and History of Religion*. Philadelphia: Westminster Press.

Soneson, Jerome Paul. 1993. *Pragmatism and Pluralism: John Dewey's Significance for Theology*. Minneapolis, Minn.: Fortress Press.

Standaert, N. 1988. *Yang Tingyun, Confucian and Christian in late Ming China*. Leiden: E. J. Brill.

Staniloae, Dumitru. 1994. *The Experience of God*. Translated by Ioan Ionita and Robert Barringer. Brookline, Mass.: Holy Cross Orthodox Press.

Suchocki, Marjorie Hewitt. 1988. *The End of Evil: Process Eschatology in Historical Context*. Albany: State University of New York Press.

————. 1992. *God Christ Church: A Practical Guide to Process Theology*. New revised edition. New York: Crossroad.

Taylor, Charles. 1989. *Sources of the Self: The Making of the Modern Identity*. Cambridge, Mass.: Harvard University Press.

Thangaraj, M. Thomas. 1994. *The Crucified Guru: An Experiment in Cross-Cultural Christology*. Nashville: Abingdon Press.

Tillich, Paul. 1951–63. *Systematic Theology*. 3 vols. Chicago: University of Chicago Press.

———, 1963. *Christianity and the Encounter of World Religions*. New York: Columbia University Press.

Tillman, Hoyt Cleveland. 1992. *Confucian Discourse and Chu Hsi's Ascendancy*. Honolulu: University of Hawaii Press.

Toulmin, Stephen. 1988. "The Recovery of Practical Philosophy." *The American Scholar* 57 (Summer 1988): 337–52.

———. 1990. *Cosmopolis: The Hidden Agenda of Modernity*. Chicago: University of Chicago Press.

Tracy, David. 1978. *Blessed Rage for Order: The New Pluralism in Theology*. New York: Seabury Press.

———. 1981. *The Analogical Imagination: Christian Theology and the Culture of Pluralism*. New York: Crossroad.

———. 1987. *Plurality and Ambiguity: Hermeneutics, Religion, Hope*. San Francisco: Harper & Row.

———. 1990. *Dialogue with the Other: The Inter-Religious Dialogue*. Louvain: Peeters Press.

Tu, Wei-ming. 1979. *Humanity and Self-Cultivation: Essays in Confucian Thought*. Berkeley, Calif.: Asian Humanities Press.

———. 1985. *Confucian Thought: Selfhood as Creative Transformation*. Albany: State University of New York Press.

———. 1989. *Centrality and Commonality: An Essay on Confucian Religiousness*. Albany: State University of New York Press.

———. 1993. *Way, Learning, and Politics: Essays on the Confucian Intellectual*. Albany: State University of New York Press.

Tuan, Yi Fu. 1982. *Segmented Worlds and Self: Group Life and Individual Consciousness*. Minneapolis, Minn.: University of Minnesota Press.

———. 1989. *Morality and Imagination: Paradoxes of Progress*. Madison: University of Wisconsin Press.

———. 1990. *Topophila: A Study of Environmental Perceptions, Attitudes, and Values*. New York: Columbia University Press.

———. 1993. *Passing Strange and Wonderful: Aesthetics, Nature, and Culture.* Washington, D.C.: Island Press.

Van Zoeren, Steven. 1991. *Poetry and Personality: Reading, Exegesis, and Hermeneutics in Traditional China.* Stanford, Calif.: Stanford University Press.

Watson, Walter. 1985. *The Architectonics of Meaning: Foundations of the New Pluralism.* Albany: State University of New York Press.

———. 1990. "Types of Pluralism." *The Monist* 73, (3): 350–66.

West, Cornel. 1989. *The American Evasion of Philosophy: A Genealogy of Pragmatism.* Madison: University of Wisconsin Press.

Whitehead, Alfred North. 1926. *Science and the Modern World.* Cambridge, Mass.: Cambridge University Press.

———. 1928. *Symbolism, Its Meaning and Effect.* Cambridge, Mass.: Cambridge University Press.

———. 1933. *Adventures of Ideas.* New York: Macmillan.

———. 1938. *Modes of Thought.* New York: Macmillan.

———. 1958. *The Function of Reason.* Boston: Beacon Press.

———. 1978. *Process and Reality: An Essay in Cosmology.* David Ray Griffin and Donald W. Sherburne, eds. Corrected ed. New York: Free Press.

———. 1996. *Religion in the Making.* New York: Fordham University Press.

Wiggins, James B. 1996. *In Praise of Religious Diversity.* New York: Routledge.

Wilcox, John R. 1991. "A Monistic Interpretation of Whitehead's Creativity." *Process Studies* 20 (3): 162–74.

Wilmot, Laurence F. 1979. *Whitehead and God: Prolegomena to Theological Reconstruction.* Waterloo, Ontario: Wilfred Laurier University Press.

Wilson, Thomas A. 1995. *Genealogy of the Way: The Construction and Uses of the Confucian Tradition in Late Imperial China.* Stanford, Calif.: Stanford University Press.

Wong, David. 1984. *Moral Relativity.* Berkeley: University of California Press.

Wu, Kuang-ming. 1990. *The Butterfly as Companion: Meditations on the First Three Chapters of the Chuang Tzu.* Albany: State University of New York Press.

Yang, Ru-pin, ed. 1993. *Chung-kuo ku-tai ssu-hsiang chung te ch'i lun nai shen-t'i kuan* [Ancient Chinese interpretations of matter-energy and the body]. Taipei, Taiwan: Chu-liu.

Yearley, Lee H. 1990. *Mencius and Aquinas: Theories of Virtue and Conceptions of Courage.* Albany: State University of New York Press.

————. 1994. "New Religious Virtues and the Study of Religion." Fifteenth Annual University Lecture in Religion at Arizona State University. Tempe: Arizona State University, Department of Religious Studies.

Yi T'oegye. 1988. *To Become a Sage: The Ten Diagrams of Sage Learning.* Translated and edited by Micheal C. Kalton. New York: Columbia University Press.

Young, John D. 1983. *Confucianism and Christianity: The First Encounter.* Hong Kong: Hong Kong University Press.

Young, Pamela Dickey. 1995. *Christ in a Post–Christian World: How Can We Believe in Jesus Christ When Those Around Us Believe Differently—Or Not At All?* Minneapolis, Minn.: Fortress Press.

Yu, David. 1959. "A Comparative Study of the Metaphysics of Chu Hsi and A. N. Whitehead." Ph.D. dissertation, University of Chicago.

Zaehner, R. C. 1970. *Concordant Discord: The Interdependence of Faiths.* Oxford: Clarendon Press.

Zagano, Phyllis. 1993. *Woman to Woman: An Anthology of Women's Spirituality.* Collegeville, Minn.: Liturgical Press.

Zhang Liwen. 1981. *Zhuxi sixiang yanjiu* [Investigations of Chu Hsi's Thought]. Beijing: Chinese Academy of Social Sciences.

Zhang Liwen et al. 1990. *Qi* [*Ch'i*]. Beijing: People's University Press.

————. 1991. *Li* [*Li*]. Beijing: People's University Press.

Zhang Longxi. 1992. *The Tao and Logos: Literary Hermeneutics, East and West* Durham, N.C.: Duke University Press.

Zheng Jiadong, and Xie Haiyan, eds. 1994. *Xinrujia pinglun* [A discussion of New Confucianism]. Beijing: Zhongguo guangbo dianshi chuban she.

INDEX

actual entities
  defined, 44
  divine creativity and, 49
  endurance of, 151
  God as, 48–50, and 78–79
  Hartshorne's view of, 49
  object-event and, 49
actuality, 119
actualization, process of
  interrelationship of principle and
    ch'i, 127
adventure, beauty and eros
  notion of, 193
American Pragmatic Tradition
  Peirce, C. S., and, 73
Analects, 101
Anaxagoras, 198
Anselm
  ontological proof of God's
    existence, 150
archic analysis of principle, 200
archic analysis, 132
  Chu Hsi, and, 215
  defined, 210
  dynamic trait and, 160
  method of, 132, 212
  Neville on, 64
  pluralistic philosophy and, 202
archic elements, 212
archic principles
  Aristotelian reading and, 217
archic profile
  of Chu Hsi, 164, 197, 216
  comparison of, 196
  of Whitehead, 164, 197, 217
archic variable,158, 200

and pluralism, 213
  of textual signification, 212
architectonic of meaning, 200
Aristotle
  Aristotelian forms, 157
  and Whitehead, 35
  and MacIntyre, 8
  Aristotle's *phronesis*, 26
ars contextualis qua creative synthe-
    sis, 204
ars contextualis, 31, 36
  Chinese notions of, 81
  Chu's thought as, 136, 165
  Confucian cosmology and, 154
  cross-cultural comparative thought
    and, 190
  process philosophy and, 86
  role of principle in, 177
  Whiteheadian understanding of
    creation and, 154
axiological *ars contextualis*, 153
axiological unity, 125

being and non-being
  Chinese view of, 103
Berger, Peter, 170
Birch, Charles, 180
Bloom, Irene, 32
Bol, Peter, 119, 216,
Booth, Wayne
  coduction, 26
  on pluralism, 29n13
Brightman, Edgar Sheffield, 92
Buchler, Justus, 59
  notion of parity, 191

241